Word and Soul

Word and Soul

A Psychological, Literary, and Cultural Reading of the Fourth Gospel

Michael Willett Newheart

A Michael Glazier Book

THE LITURGICAL PRESS
Collegeville, Minnesota

www.litpress.org

A Michael Glazier Book published by The Liturgical Press

Cover design by David Manahan, O.S.B. Illustration detail: *Mount Calvary* by William H. Johnson. Courtesy of the Smithsonian American Art Museum, gift of The Harmon Foundation.

1   2   3   4   5   6   7   8

Library of Congress Cataloging-in-Publication Data

Newheart, Michael Willett, 1955–
    Word and soul: a psychological, literary, and cultural reading of the
    Fourth Gospel / Michael Willett Newheart.
        p.   cm.
    Includes bibliographical references and index.
    ISBN 0-8146-5924-1 (alk. paper)
    1. Bible. N.T. John—Reader-response criticism.   I. Title.
BS2615-52.N49   2001
226.5'06—dc21

00-067167

To Joy,
who to me
is like her name.

Contents

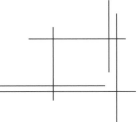

Acknowledgments

"State/meant" from the book *The LeRoi Jones Amiri Baraka Reader* by Amiri Baraka. © 2000 by Amiri Baraka. Appears by permission of the publisher, Thunder's Mouth Press.

"American Heartbreak," "The Black Man Speaks," "Me and My Songs," "Walkers with the Dawn," "Negro," "Song," "Helen Keller," "Un-American Investigators," and "Christ in Alabama" from *Collected Poems* by Langston Hughes. © 1994 by the Estate of Langston Hughes. Reprinted by permission of Alfred A. Knopf Inc.

"Monet's Waterlilies" by Frederick Glaysher, editor. © 1970 by Robert Hayden from *Collected Poems of Robert Hayden* by Robert Hayden, edited by Frederick Glaysher. Used by permission of Liveright Publishing Corporation.

"Man White, Brown Girl and All That Jazz" first appeared in *Poetry Northwest*. © 1973 by Gloria Oden. Reprinted by permission of the author.

"Primer for Blacks" first appeared in *Primer for Blacks* by Gwendolyn Brooks. Reprinted by permission of the author. © 1991 by Gwendolyn Brooks.

"Who Can Be Born Black?" first appeared in *Nightstar* by Mari Evans, published by CAAS, University of California at Los Angeles, 1981. Reprinted by permission of the author. © 1981 by Mari Evans.

"What Is Beautiful." From *Dimensions of History*, Kayak Books copyright © by Jay Wright. Reprinted in *Transfigurations: Collected Poems*, Louisiana State University Press. © 2000 by Jay Wright.

"Phenomenal Woman" and "Still I Rise." From *And Still I Rise* by Maya Angelou. © 1978 by Maya Angelou. Reprinted by permission of Random House, Inc. and Virago Press.

"My Father's Love Letters," *Pleasure Dome: New and Collected Poems, 1975–1999* by Yusef Komunyakaa. Reprinted by permission of the author.

"My Father's Ways." © 1997 by Leonard D. Moore. First published in *Father Songs* (Beacon Press, 1997). Permission to reprint granted by the author.

"The Invention of Comics." From *The Dead Lecturer* by Amiri Baraka. Reprinted by permission of Sterling Lord Literistic, Inc. © 1964 by Amiri Baraka.

"I, Too, Know What I Am Not." From the book *Solitudes Crowded with Loneliness* by Bob Kaufman. © 1965 by Bob Kaufman. Reprinted by permission of New Directions Publishing Corp.

"Exits and Entrances" first appeared in *Exits and Entrances* by Naomi Long Madgett. © 1987 by Naomi Long Madgett. Reprinted by permission of the author.

"Father, Son, and Wholly Ghost" first appeared in *Beyond the Frontier,* edited by E. Ethelbert Miller. Reprinted by permission of D. J. Renegade. © 2000 by D. J. Renegade.

"Bread" from *Whispers Secrets & Promises* by E. Ethelbert Miller. Reprinted by permission of the author. © 1998 by E. Ethelbert Miller.

"Love After Love" from *Sea Grapes* by Derek Walcott. © 1976 by Derek Walcott. Reprinted by permission of the author.

"I Know (I'm Losing You)" from *You Don't Miss Your Water: Poems* by Cornelius Eady. Reprinted by permission of the author. © 1995 by Cornelius Eady.

"Mingus Speaks: Found Poems" from *Gabriel* by George Barlow. (Detroit: Broadside, 1974). © 1974 by George Barlow. Reprinted by permission of the author.

Earlier versions of a portion of the following material from the book were (or will be) published in the following journals:

The Introduction as "The Soul in the New Testament," *The Bible Workbench* 5:4 (Easter 2–Trinity Sunday 1998) 116–25 and as "Soul in the New Testament: A Contemporary Psychological Perspective," *Journal of Religious Thought* 55.2–56.1 (1999) forthcoming.

Chapter 1 as "Christmas 1: John 1:1-18," *The Bible Workbench* 4:1 (Advent 1–Christmas 2 1996–97) 69–80.

Chapter 2 as "Trinity Sunday: John 3:1-17," *The Bible Workbench* 4:4 (Easter Season 1997) 109–25.

Chapter 3 as "Pentecost 12: John 6:35, 41-51," *The Bible Workbench* 4:6 (Pentecost 2 1997) 25–37.

Chapters 3 and 5 as "The Soul of the Father and the Son: A Psychological (yet Playful and Poetic) Approach to the Father-Son Language in the Fourth Gospel," *Semeia* 85 (1999) 155–75.

Chapter 4 as "Lent 4: John 9:1-41," *The Bible Workbench* 6:3 (Lent 1–Easter Sunday 1999) 53–68.

Chapter 5 as "Easter 6: John 14:23-29," *The Bible Workbench* 5:4 (Easter 2–Trinity Sunday 1998) 55–66.

I am grateful to the editors of these publications for permission to make available this material again in this format.

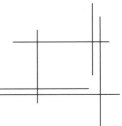

Preface

This book is probably different from any book you have read. It is a book of biblical interpretation, yet with a twist. I hope that it is interesting, insightful, informative, and entertaining, personal, pastoral, poetic, and playful. It describes a way to read biblical literature "soulfully" and applies it to the Gospel of John. I envision a rather broad readership for this book: scholars, pastors, students, and the general public. If you wish, you might skip the introduction and go right to chapter 1 in order to get a sampling of my "soul reading." As you feel the need you can go back to the introduction in order to learn more about the method of this madness. Come join the fun! Don't forget to bring your soul!

But before that, I must add a caution and a thank-you. First, the caution: Because of the experimental nature of this approach I do not deal with some of the more traditional aspects of critical scholarship, such as author, date, sources, and historical background. For these matters I would refer you to one of the many excellent critical commentaries on John. In my classes I use Frank Moloney's volume in the Sacra Pagina series published by The Liturgical Press (see the bibliography). I've also used Brown (a classic!) and Howard-Brook, as well as the monographs by Rensberger and Fehribach. Any of those would nicely supplement this book.

Now, thanks to those who have supported me in various ways on this project:

Howard University, which granted me a sabbatical leave in fall 1999 and awarded me a Faculty Research Grant for 1997–1998; Wabash Center for Teaching and Learning in Theology and Religion, which extended to me a grant for the summers of 1998 and 1999; students in my classes on the Gospel of John at Howard University School of Divinity, to whom I read much of the manuscript; the groups that have heard me read sections of the manuscript: the Johannine Literature Section of the annual meetings of the national and Mid-Atlantic regional Society of

Biblical Literature; the Psychology and Biblical Studies Group of the annual meeting of the Society of Biblical Literature, and the African-American Religious section of the annual meeting of the Mid-Atlantic regional American Academy of Religion.

Individuals who have read and commented on portions of the manuscript include Maya Angelou, Valerie Bridgeman Davis, Brian Blount, Thomas Moore, Fernando Segovia, Walter Wink, Diane Brenda Williams, Cain Hope Felder, Vincent Wimbush, and E. Ethelbert Miller, the last of whom gave permission to use his poetry and gave valuable aid in contacting other poets.

My research assistants at HUSD: Countess Clarke, Ethelbert Carter, Ostein Truitt, and especially Barbara Williams Skinner, all of whom worked long and hard, particularly with the poetry permissions.

The *Journal of Religious Thought* (editor Cain Hope Felder) and *Semeia: A Journal for Experimental Biblical Studies* (issue editor Adele Reinhartz) for publishing sections of the manuscript; The Liturgical Press and its academic editor Linda M. Maloney for recommending that the work be published.

My writing coach Mike Thomas, my writing/life buddy Mike Ashcraft, my psychologist Greg Grinc, the men's group at Adelphi Friends Meeting, and my daughters Anastasia and Miranda, who contributed to this book in ways visible and invisible, and to my wife Joy, who both loved and hated this book . . . yet continued to love me.

Introduction: Soul 2 Soul,
A Post-Modern Exegete in Search of
(Johannine) Soul

When I first began to work on this book I attended a "prayer night" at the Community of the Ark, the Washington, D.C. expression of l'Arche, the worldwide federation of religious communities for the developmentally disabled. My wife Joy was working there at the time. During the social time I met a couple visiting from California. We chit-chatted, and I told them that I was working on a book on the Gospel of John. The woman in that couple exclaimed, "Oh, John is so poetic!" My eyes brightened. "Yes," I said, "and in my book I approach the gospel as poetry and attempt to read it poetically." We then talked about the poetry of the gospel, including the "I am" sayings, the symbols, and the images.

A few years later my two-year-old daughter Anastasia came into the study at home early one morning while I was working on this book. She saw my Greek New Testament opened to John 14. She said, "Read me these poems." So I scooped her up into my lap and read, "Don't let your heart be stirred up. . . ." (John 14:1). Poems, yes they are. Poetry, yes it is. Not in the formal sense of conforming to the canons of first-century Greek poetry, though that case has often been made with the Johannine prologue.[1] No, the Gospel of John is poetic, full of poems and poetry, in that it is full of imagery and symbolism and irony and rhythm . . . and soul.[2] Yes, soul! The gospel contains, not concepts that speak to the mind, but poetry that speaks to the soul, the emotions, the

---

[1] See below, 1–3.

[2] The term "soul" often comes up in discussion of what poetry is. For example, in Bill Moyers, ed., *The Language of Life: A Festival of Poets* (New York: Doubleday, 1995) three different poets associate poetry with the soul. Carolyn Forche quotes Rainier Maria Rilke as saying that "poetry is the natural prayer of the human soul."

imagination.[3] The soul. In order to interpret the Gospel of John soul-fully, poetically, playfully, I have devised what I call a "soul hermeneu-tic."

A "Soul Hermeneutic"

This soul hermeneutic is psychological, literary, and cultural, for it brings together analytical and archetypal psychology, African-American cultural experience, and reader-response criticism. The psychological aspect comes from analytical and archetypal psychology, which at-tempts to bring soul back into psychology. Carl Jung, the founder of

---

She adds that it is "the voice of the soul," for it "allows the human soul to speak" (131). Similarly, Stanley Kunitz says that "poetry is ultimately mythological, the telling of the stories of the soul" (249). Cf. also the statement by Langston Hughes below, xviii.

Poets often use Johannine language in describing poetry. Victor Hernandez Cruz says that "poetry gives us revelations, which illumine those things which were mys-terious to us" (ibid. 108). Wallace Stevens writes that it is "a revelation in words by means of the words" (quoted in Xavier J. Kennedy and Dana Gioia, *An Introduction to Poetry*, 9th ed. [New York: Longman, 1997]). Dylan Thomas wrote that poetry is "the rhythmic, inevitably narrative, movement from an overclothed blindness to a naked vision" (quoted in William Packard, *The Poet's Dictionary: A Handbook of Prosody and Poetic Devices* [New York: HarperCollins, 1989] 146). Paul Valéry consid-ered poetry a separate language, or more specifically "a language within a lan-guage." Kenneth Koch quotes Valéry and develops his idea about poetry as a separate language in *Making Your Own Days: The Pleasures of Reading and Writing Poetry* (New York: Scribner, 1998). Such a conception is similar to that of the social-scientific biblical critics, who have characterized Johannine language as "anti-language," which is, in Bruce J. Malina's words, "a language deriving from and generated by an antisocietal group [which] is a social collectivity that is set up within a larger society as a conscious alternative to it." Cf. Bruce J. Malina, *The Gospel of John in Sociolinguistic Perspective*. Protocol of the 48th Colloquy, March 1984 (Berkeley: Center for Hermeneutical Studies, 1985); idem, "John's: The Maverick Christian Group: The Evidence of Sociolinguistics," *BTB* 24 (1994) 167–82; Richard L. Rohrbaugh, "The Gospel of John in the Twenty-First Century," in Fernando F. Segovia, ed., *What Is John? Readers and Readings of the Fourth Gospel*. SBL Symposium Series (Atlanta: Scholars, 1998); Bruce J. Malina and Richard L. Rohrbaugh, *Social-Science Commentary on the Gospel of John* (Minneapolis: Fortress, 1998) 7–11. Also cf. Norman R. Petersen, *The Gospel of John and the Sociology of Light: Language and Char-acterization in the Fourth Gospel* (Valley Forge, Pa.: Trinity Press International, 1993), 1–2, 89–91, who speaks about the gospel's "special language" as "anti-language."

[3] Cf. the discussion of the difference between poetry and prose in Kennedy and Gioia, *An Introduction to Poetry*. They write, "The reader expects the poet to make greater use, perhaps, of resources of meaning such as figurative language, allusion, symbol, and imagery." They quote Valéry: "Poetry is to prose as dancing is to walk-ing."

analytical psychology, wrote often of "soul."[4] He says, "The reality of the soul is the reality upon which I work."[5] He considers psychotherapy "the treatment of the soul," for "the soul is the birthplace of all action and everything that happens by the will of [hu]man[ity]."[6] Although "soul" is central for Jung, it does not always mean the same thing. At times he refers to it as "life-force"[7] and uses it interchangeably with "psyche."[8] At other times he distinguishes the two, defining the psyche as "the totality of psychic processes" and the soul as "the inner attitude toward the unconscious."[9] Jung also asserts the religious nature of the soul, maintaining that it contains within itself the faculty of relationship to God, which is, in psychological terms, the archetype of the God-image.[10] He points to the Bible as a "soul-book," for "the statements made in the Holy Scriptures are also utterances of the soul. . . . [T]hey always go over our heads because they point to realities that transcend consciousness."[11]

[4] In the index to his collected works the listings for "soul(s)," "soul(s) in alchemy," "soul and spirit," and "soul-images" take up over three pages. See the General Index to *The Collected Works of C. G. Jung* (hereafter Jung, *CW*) (Princeton, N.J.: Princeton University Press, 1966–1979) 20:624–27. (I refer to the volume and page number of the English translation of Jung, *CW*.) Jung wrote principally in German, and he used the word *Seele*, which, according to the editors of Jung's collected works, lacks an English equivalent because it combines both "psyche" and "soul." The editors, then, translate the word as "psyche" or "soul" depending on the context. See their explanation in C. G. Jung, *Psychology and Alchemy*, 2nd ed. (Jung, *CW* 12:8–9 n. 2).

[5] Quoted in Hans Schaer, *Religion and the Cure of Souls in Jung's Psychology*. Translated by R.F.C. Hull. Bollingen Series XXI (New York: Pantheon, 1950) 21.

[6] Carl Gustav Jung, "Psychotherapy Today," in idem, *The Practice of Psychotherapy: Essays on the Psychology of the Transference and Other Subjects*. 2nd ed. (Jung, *CW* 16:94).

[7] Carl Gustav Jung, "Basic Postulates of Analytical Psychology," in idem, *The Structure and Dynamics of the Psyche*. 2nd ed. (Jung, *CW* 8:344).

[8] Ibid. 167–68.

[9] Carl Gustav Jung, *Psychological Types* (Jung, *CW* 6:467–68). For this latter concept Jung preferred the term *anima* or *animus* because he felt that the term "soul" was too vague (cf. Carl Gustav Jung, *Aion: Researches into the Phenomenology of the Self*. 2nd ed. [Jung, *CW* 9.2:13]). The *anima* is the feminine soul in the man, and the *animus* is the masculine soul in the woman; cf. his *Two Essays on Analytical Psychology*. 2d ed. (Jung, *CW* 7:188–211); "Concerning the Archetypes, with Special Reference to the Anima Concept," in idem, *The Archetypes and the Collective Unconscious*. 2d ed. (Jung, *CW* 9.1:54–72); idem, *Aion: Researches into the Phenomenology of the Self*. 2d ed. (Jung, *CW* 9.2:11–22).

[10] Carl Gustav Jung, *Psychology and Alchemy*. 2d ed. (Jung, *CW* 12:10–11).

[11] Carl Gustav Jung, "Answer to Job," in idem, *Psychology and Religion: West and East*. 2d ed. (Jung, *CW* 11:362). The term "soul-book" is mine, not Jung's. For further (though still brief) discussion of the concept of soul in Jung's writings and a short

James Hillman takes Jung's emphasis on soul and twists it in his own brand of psychology, which he calls archetypal psychology. He defines soul as "a perspective rather than a substance, a viewpoint rather than a thing itself."[12] Early in his work Hillman suggests that soul makes meaning possible, turns events into experiences, is communicated in love, and has a religious concern.[13] In his foundational book *Re-Visioning Psychology* Hillman adds three necessary modifications: First, soul refers to the deepening of events into experiences; second, its significance derives from its special relation with death; third, it is the imaginative possibility within human nature, experienced through reflective speculation, dream, image, and especially fantasy, "which recognizes all realities as primarily symbolic or metaphorical."[14] Hillman continues by saying that fantasy images are the primary data of the soul and the privileged mode of access to knowledge of the soul. He then works toward what he calls "a psychology of soul that is based in a psychology of image" and, with a poetic basis of mind, starts in the processes of imagination.[15] Hillman also contends that in order to get to the soul of the image (or the image of soul) one must "love the image," that is, stick with it and twist it by doing wordplays, for the words are "soul mines."[16] He further maintains that one deepens the image by making analogies, or likenesses, for the images. What is this image like? Analogies, according to Hillman, "keep the image there, alive and well, returning to it each time for a fresh sense of it."[17]

Like Jung and Hillman I am searching for soul, for my soul, for the biblical soul. Analytical and archetypal psychology encourage me to find soul in the images, so I focus on the biblical images. And with what Hillman calls "a poetic basis of mind" I open up these images (and my own soul) by twisting them and doing wordplays with them.[18]

---

comparison with its appearance in the New Testament see Wayne G. Rollins, *Jung and the Bible* (Atlanta: John Knox, 1983) 42–55.

[12] James Hillman, *Re-Visioning Psychology* (New York: Harper & Row, 1975) x.

[13] James Hillman, *Suicide and the Soul* (New York: Harper & Row, 1964) 47; idem, *Insearch: Psychology and Religion* (New York: Charles Scribner's Sons, 1967) 42.

[14] Hillman, *Re-Visioning* x.

[15] Ibid. xi.

[16] James Hillman, "An Inquiry into Image," *Spring* 39 (1977) 81–82.

[17] Ibid. 86–87. Hillman develops his approach to image still more in "Further Notes on Images," *Spring* 40 (1978) 152–82, and "Image-Sense," *Spring* 41 (1979) 130–43.

[18] At this point my method is similar to that of French psychoanalyst Jacques Lacan, who in his literary method also uses wordplays, witticisms, and puns. See his *Écrits: A Selection,* translated by Alan Sheridan (New York: Norton, 1977). For the relevance of Lacan to biblical studies, see The Bible and Culture Collective, *The Postmodern Bible* (New Haven: Yale University Press, 1995) 196–211.

Furthermore, I also open up the images by finding contemporary analogies, or likenesses, for them.

My soul hermeneutic is shaped not only by analytical and archetypal psychology but also by the cultural experience of persons of African descent. African-American experience is often referred to as "soul," as African Americans have given us "soul music" and "soul food," and they refer to one another as "soul brother" and "soul sister." In the United States, then, persons of African descent have been the carriers of soul. African-American soul, however, has been described variously. In their book *Soul Theology* Nicholas Cooper-Lewter and Henry H. Mitchell list a number of definitions: the sum of all that is typically black, emotive spontaneity, and cultural compulsion to compassion.[19] In *Soul-Force* Leonard E. Barrett says that "soul" is the moral and emotional fiber that sustains blacks in their struggles.[20] In "The Soul of Black Religion" Peter J. Paris defines soul as the drive toward effective wholeness in the totality of life.[21] Lerone Bennett, in his book *The Negro Mood*, contends that it is the acceptance of the contradictions of life.[22] I have found the most satisfactory definition in *Roots of Soul: The Psychology of Black Expressiveness* by Alfred Pasteur and Ivory Toldson. They identify soul with black expressiveness, which is based in rhythm. They write, "Rhythm is the thread that runs through the fabric of black culture; it is therefore at the base of black expressive behavior."[23] As poet Guy Tirolier says:

> (. . . I want to proclaim out loud / / /
> that life is only rhythm / /
> and rhythm within a rhythm).[24]

Furthermore, Pasteur and Toldson identify five elements of soul, or black expressiveness: depth of feeling, naturalistic attitudes, stylistic

---

[19] Nicholas Cooper-Lewter and Henry H. Mitchell, *Soul Theology: The Heart of American Black Culture* (Nashville: Abingdon, 1986) iv.

[20] Leonard E. Barrett, *Soul-Force: African Heritage in Afro-American Religion.* C. Eric Lincoln Series on Black Religion (Garden City, N.Y.: Doubleday Anchor, 1974) 1–2.

[21] Peter J. Paris, "The Soul of Black Religion: A Lesson for the Academy (Basic African American Values)," unpublished paper presented at the annual meeting of the American Academy of Religion, November 1996.

[22] Lerone Bennett, *The Negro Mood* (New York: Ballantine, 1965) 89.

[23] Alfred B. Pasteur and Ivory L. Toldson, *Roots of Soul: The Psychology of Black Expressiveness* (Garden City, N.Y.: Doubleday, 1982) 4.

[24] E. A. Hurley, "Guy Tirolier: In Search of an Attitude," *Black Images* 3/1 (1974) 61, quoted in Pasteur and Toldson, *Roots of Soul,* 59.

renderings, poetic and prosaic vernacular, and expressive movement.[25] In their chapter on depth of feeling the authors say that soul is "the ability to feel and express feelings creatively, or through forms touched with artistic sensibilities."[26]

One such form of "artistic sensibility" is poetry, in which African-Americans have contributed significantly to world literature. Poetry has often been called the voice of the soul, so African-American poetry might be considered the "soul of soul." Langston Hughes writes that poetry "is the human soul entire, squeezed like a lemon or lime, drop by drop, into atomic words."[27] African-American poetry shapes my soul hermeneutic in two ways: my poetic readings of the biblical images reflect the rhythms of this poetry, and I find likenesses to these images in this body of literature. As Paul Lawrence Dunbar writes in his classic poem "The Poet":

> He sang of life, serenely sweet,
> With, now and then, a deeper note,
> From some high peak, nigh yet remote,
> He voiced the world's absorbing beat.[28]

A soul hermeneutic seeks that "deeper note" and that "absorbing beat" in the biblical text and in the contemporary world.

"Soul 2 Soul" in my title indicates not only my indebtedness to African-American culture but also the depth at which I want to engage the biblical images. I realize that my reading of the Bible is shaped by the longings of my own soul. Enter here reader-response criticism, a branch of literary criticism that has been increasingly employed in recent years by New Testament critics.[29] It focuses on the reader's role in shaping the meaning of a text.[30] Reader-response criticism has been practiced in two modes: the text-dominant mode, which focuses on the

---

[25] Ibid. 10.

[26] Ibid. 103.

[27] Langston Hughes, *The Collected Poems of Langston Hughes*, Arnold Rampersad, ed. (New York: Alfred A. Knopf, 1994) 5.

[28] Paul Lawrence Dunbar, "The Poet," *Crossing the Danger Water: Three Hundred Years of African-American Writing,* Deirdre Mullane, ed. (New York: Doubleday Anchor, 1993) 353; from *The Complete Poems of Paul Lawrence Dunbar* (New York: Dodd, Mead, 1905).

[29] For a survey of the use of reader-response criticism in New Testament studies see Stephen D. Moore, *Literary Criticism and the Gospels: The Theoretical Challenge* (New Haven: Yale University Press, 1989) 71–107; The Bible and Culture Collective, *The Postmodern Bible* (New Haven: Yale University Press, 1995) 38–67.

[30] Cf. Jane P. Tompkins, ed., *Reader-Response Criticism: From Formalism to Post-Structuralism* (Baltimore: Johns Hopkins Press, 1980).

"implied (or encoded) reader" embedded in the text, and the reader-dominant mode, which emphasizes the flesh-and-blood "real reader" who actually reads (or hears) the text. Biblical reader-response critics working in the reader-dominant mode have taken one of two tracks: autobiographical biblical criticism[31] or biblical cultural criticism.[32] Some critics, taking their lead from autobiographical literary criticism, reflect on how their own personal narrative impacts their biblical interpretations.[33] Other scholars, influenced by cultural studies, are more interested in "interpretative communities," and they examine a reader's "social location," including race, gender, class, sexual orientation, and religious affiliation.[34]

With my soul hermeneutic I am solidly in the camp of those reader-response critics working in the reader-dominant mode, for I am concerned about the soul of the real reader and not the soulless, textually bound "implied reader." I have, then, learned much from the biblical critics who are autobiographically or culturally inclined. From both I have learned that I must read myself as closely as I read the biblical text. From the cultural biblical critics I have learned that my soul is shaped by my social location as a European American, heterosexual, Christian intellectual male working in a predominantly African-American institution. Exploring one's social location is essential, then, but so is plumbing one's psychological situation. How does one's biblical interpretation address the emotional issues with which one is struggling, such as grief, anger, and anxiety? Writing from a psychological literary critical perspective, Ralph Maud says that one brings the "sufferings of the soul" to the reading of a book. "We sit down with a serious book prepared to give the author something of ourselves to work on: we move toward the reading experience with our sorrows, all our woe."[35]

---

[31] Cf. Jeffrey L. Staley, *Reading with a Passion: Rhetoric, Autobiography, and the American West in the Gospel of John* (New York: Continuum, 1995), and Janice Capel Anderson and Jeffrey L. Staley, eds., *Taking It Personally: Autobiographical Biblical Criticism. Semeia* 72 (1995).

[32] Cf. Fernando F. Segovia and Mary Ann Tolbert, eds., *Reading from this Place.* 2 vols. (Minneapolis: Fortress, 1995). The first volume deals with biblical interpretation in the United States and the second in "global perspective."

[33] See especially Stephen D. Moore, "True Confessions and Weird Obsessions: Autobiographical Interventions in Literary and Biblical Studies," *Sem* 72 (1995) 19–50.

[34] See especially Fernando F. Segovia, "'And They Began to Speak in Other Tongues': Competing Modes of Discourse in Contemporary Biblical Criticism," *Reading From This Place* 1:1–32.

[35] Ralph Maud, "Archetypal Depth Criticism and Melville," in Richard P. Sugg, ed., *Jungian Literary Criticism* (Evanston, Ill.: Northwestern University Press, 1992) 259.

How much more so is this true with the Bible, which is often said to be able to "heal the hurts" of the reader. Psychological situation, then, must be brought into consideration with social location. In another place I have referred to the "psycho-social location" of the reader.[36] Now, however, I call this phenomenon the reader's "soul-state," or "soul struggles," which include both psychological and social dynamics.

This concern for both "body and soul" seems to be present in the autobiographical biblical critics. For example, Jeffrey Staley, one of the leaders in this critical movement, calls for "an exegesis of souls that parallels our exegesis of texts."[37] As soul exegetes, he continues, we "unearth elements in our personal experience" that have influenced our biblical interpretations.[38] My soul hermeneutic, then, takes an autobiographical turn. I begin with a consideration of my own soul-state and I conclude with attention to the likenesses of the biblical images in my own soul. Two images seem to me to express the state of my soul. The first comes from the domestic scene. My two-year-old daughter Anastasia circles the living room, demanding that I put some music on and join her dancing: "I dance! . . . Daddy dance!" So she grabs my hand and invites—no, drags—me to the dance, the dance of life, of growth, of resurrection.[39] Usually I dance with her, but I wonder: Shouldn't I be working instead of playing? Shouldn't I be grading or writing or preparing classes instead of dancing?

The second image does come from my "work." I stand (or sit) before my students on the first day of class. The faces before me are all of a darker hue than mine. I ask myself: What can I say to them? My experience is so different from theirs. They want me to "teach them," to dole out the wisdom (defined as a collection of facts and aphorisms) that I as a white Ph.D. have accumulated. But I want them to teach *me*—teach me about reading the Bible "from the margins," teach me about using this book for social uplift. So the question vexes me: How can I share with them my "expertise" while still honoring their experience? How can I be accepted (liked *and* respected)?

---

[36] Michael Willett Newheart, "Toward a Psycho-Literary Reading of the Fourth Gospel," in Fernando F. Segovia, ed., *"What is John?" Readers and Readings of the Fourth Gospel.* SBL Symposium Series 3 (Atlanta: Scholars, 1995) 47–51, 55–57; cf. also my "Johannine Symbolism," in David L. Miller, ed., *Jung and the Interpretation of the Bible* (New York: Continuum, 1995) 89.

[37] Staley, *Reading with a Passion*, 115.

[38] Ibid.

[39] The name Anastasia is derived from the Greek *anastasis*, which means "resurrection."

As I consider these two images I see a certain amount of anxiety, a certain amount of "tornness" ("twoness"?[40]) in my soul, as I am torn between work and family, black and white. I long for acceptance from my daughter (now daughters), my wife, my students, my colleagues, yet I also want to be true to who I am. There, then, is my soul, my torn soul, the soul that investigates the Johannine soul. So(ul) it goes. My soul hermeneutic is one way in which I attempt to mend this rip in the fabric of my soul, for it is a way that I can both work and play, bring together (at least in my own experience) white and black.

Johannine Images in My Own Soul

I begin, then, with my own soul, and I try to read it "johanninely." What has been so enticing, so beckoning about this gospel for me for so many years? I have studied the gospel in an academic context for over twenty years, but I loved it long before that. I began my love affair with it on September 16, 1967 at Municipal Stadium in Kansas City, Missouri. There, on the same field where I watched the Kansas City Chiefs and Athletics play ball, I made my "public profession of faith in Jesus Christ as personal savior and lord" at a Billy Graham crusade (though I was prepared for that decision through growing up in a Southern Baptist church in suburban Kansas City). The counselor handed me a copy of Kenneth Taylor's "Living Translation" (what later became *The Living Bible*) of the Gospel of John. (I "die" when I read the "Living" John 1:1: "Before anything else existed, there was Christ." But "Christ" is not an accurate translation or paraphrase of the Greek *logos*. Christ is not the *logos en archē*, word in the beginning, but the *logos en sarkē*, the word enfleshed! At age eleven, though, I had not yet learned *koinē* Greek and thus did not know the problem.)

Fast forward almost eleven years to August 1978, when my love affair with John "went to school." As a good Southern Baptist preacher-boy-to-be I entered The Southern Baptist Theological Seminary in Louisville, Kentucky. My very first class, at 8:00 in the morning (when the darkness was being overcome by light), was the Gospel of John, taught by R. Alan Culpepper (at that time of *The Johannine School* fame,[41]

[40] I am alluding to a famous quotation in W.E.B. DuBois, *The Souls of Black Folks,* Penguin Classics (New York: Penguin Books, 1989) 5: "One ever feels his twoness—an American, a Negro; two souls, two thoughts, two unreconciled strivings, two warring ideals in one dark body, whose dogged strength alone keeps it from being torn asunder." The "twoness," though, I refer to here is somewhat different.

[41] R. Alan Culpepper, *The Johannine School: An Evaluation of the Johannine-School Hypothesis Based on an Investigation of the Nature of Ancient Schools.* SBLDS 26 (Missoula: Scholars, 1975).

only later, when I was in graduate school under his direction, of *Anatomy of the Fourth Gospel* fame).[42] The syllabus stated, "The intent of this course is simply to launch the student on . . . a lifelong love affair with the Fourth Gospel." (So Professor Culpepper lovingly "schooled me" in things Johannine.) As with many such college and seminary Gospel of John classes, we used Raymond E. Brown's two-volume Anchor Bible commentary. (That commentary certainly "anchored me" in the sea of biblical criticism, and Brown in many ways fathered me. He was one of the few to footnote my published dissertation.)[43]

Fast forward another six and a half years to May 1985, when I received my Ph.D., "partially fulfilled" by writing the dissertation *Wisdom Christology in the Fourth Gospel* (published in a "thoroughly revised" form in 1992).[44] The idea for the dissertation, as I said in my prospectus, was "born in the shadow of the great Norman cathedral" in Durham, England, where I studied with James D. G. Dunn in the fall of 1982. There I was following the lead of Dunn's essay "Let John Be John," which he had delivered as a lecture that semester.[45]

So here I am in 1999, still working on the Gospel according to John. For nearly thirty-three years of my life I have been fascinated with this book. Why? When someone asked me that question I would generally say something vague like "the portrait of Jesus" or "Johannine christology," depending upon whether I wanted to sound like an artist or a theologian. Let me be more specific: I realize that the "draw" of the gospel for me has been in three images that recur in Jesus' speech: father-son, "I am," and "not of this world."

First, father-son: Jesus, as well as the narrator, speaks frequently about God as "the father" and himself as "the son." The narrator trumpets this note twice early in the gospel, first in the prologue: As the enfleshed word, Jesus' glory is "glory as an only-born son from a father" and as the son he "is into the bosom of the father" (John 1:14, 18).[46] And

---

[42] R. Alan Culpepper, *Anatomy of the Fourth Gospel: A Study in Literary Design.* Foundations and Facets (Philadelphia: Fortress, 1983).

[43] Raymond E. Brown, *An Introduction to New Testament Christology* (New York: Paulist, 1994) 207, n. 312. Culpepper has also footnoted it in his "The Gospel of John as a Document of Faith," in *"What Is John?"* 123, n. 34. A book that has just come to my attention, *Wisdom's Friends* by Sharon H. Ringe (Louisville: Westminster/John Knox, 1999) footnotes my book extensively.

[44] Michael E. Willett, *Wisdom Christology in the Fourth Gospel* (San Francisco: Mellen Research University Press, 1992).

[45] James D. G. Dunn, "Let John Be John: A Gospel for Its Time," in Peter Stuhlmacher, ed., *Das Evangelium und die Evangelien: Vortrage vom Tubinger Symposium 1982* (Tübingen: J.C.B. Mohr [Paul Siebeck], 1983).

[46] All translations from the NT are are my own, while verses from the Jewish Scriptures (usually called OT in Christian circles) are slight modifications of the NRSV.

again, "the father loves the son and has placed all things in his hands," including eternal life (3:35-36). Then Jesus takes over, grounding his authority to perform signs, such as healing a paralytic, feeding a multitude, and giving sight to a man born blind, in his intimate relationship as son to his father: "The father loves the son and shows him everything he is doing" (5:20). "This is the will of my father, that everyone who sees the son and believes into him might have eternal life" (6:40). "I and the father are one" (10:30).

Furthermore, Jesus draws the disciples into this intimate familial relationship with God: "The one who has seen me has seen the father. . . . I am in the father and the father is in me" (14:8, 10). "That they might be one just as we are one. I in them and you in me, so that they might be completed as one, so that the world might know that you sent me, and you have loved them just as you loved me" (17:22-24). "But go to my brothers and say to them, 'I am ascending to my father and your father, to my God and your God'" (20:17). Thus Jesus' (and the narrator's) name for God is "father," and thus Jesus' name for himself in relationship to God is "son." Jesus' relationship to God as son to father is the key to the gospel. Out of this relationship Jesus reveals, "signs," and saves.[47]

This language resonates in my own soul. When I read the Gospel of John I long for the intimacy that Jesus had with his father. I am an only son of a father (full of grace and truth, 1:14?), and my father, Edward Efton Willett, known to me as "Dad," was, to use my wife Joy's phrase, my "parent of choice." In other words, I was a daddy's boy. We looked alike, enjoyed sports together, and had much the same sense of humor. During my teenage years, however, "Dad" became ill for an extended period of time, and he died two minutes after my sixteenth birthday had passed.[48] But I lost him long before that, even before his final illness. Lost him? Or did I ever have him in the first place? He was always an

---

[47] Cf. Willett, *Wisdom Christology,* 67–80, where I discuss the intimacy of Jesus and God under three rubrics: will, knowledge, and love. It is interesting to note that this subsection is the longest in the book. For a recent treatment of the father-son theme in the gospel, see *"God the Father" in the Gospel of John. Semeia* 85, Adele Reinhartz, ed. (Atlanta: Scholars Press, 1999).

[48] When my mother informed me that my father had died she said, "At least he didn't die on your birthday." Several years later my mother told me that he really did die on my birthday and that the attending physician had recorded the wrong date and time on the death certificate because he knew it was my birthday. Not long ago my mother denied that that was so. Did he die on my birthday or not? In his last moments was he attempting to make it past my birthday, which we had celebrated earlier with him at the nursing home? Or was it his last cruel joke on me? I don't know, but for me my birthday and his deathday are tied together.

enigma to me, a mystery. I wondered: What was going on for him? Was he happy? What did he think about, feel, believe in? I wanted to be close, and I was close to a certain extent, yet I still felt distant. I saw a contradiction: in pictures appeared this smiling, happy man who held his baby with such pride, but I knew a man who was uncomfortable with physical affection, one who, for example, shook off my handshake when he was to leave on a business trip. The father loved the son, yes, but not always in a way that the son wanted.

In reading the Gospel of John I found my father: Jesus' father, God. He became my loving and all-powerful father. He was "my father and your father," as the risen Jesus says (20:17). Jesus' language fathered me . . . as scholar, as believer, as "child of God." Jesus' father language allowed me a place to work out (on?) my grief over the loss of my own father. This sick, unloving, dead father was replaced by a loving, living, omnipotent father. But this father was fictive, a creation of language. He could not shake my hand any better than my late father. I am stuck with (in?) my grief, my anger. Through studying that language, though, I became a father myself, that is, a scholar, a professor. I beget sons and daughters in learning. And I also became a biological father of two girls. (I am a fatherless son and a sonless father!) Is my grief better worked out by being a father than by looking for a father, whether textual or physical? Nevertheless, the father-son imagery in the gospel has been powerful for me.[49]

The second aspect of Jesus' language that has attracted me in the gospel is his "I am" sayings. Jesus says "I am," usually "I am" plus a significant image from Hebrew tradition, such as "I am the bread of life" (6:35), "I am the light of the world" (8:12), "I am the good shepherd" (10:11), and "I am the true vine" (15:1). Sometimes Jesus simply says "I am," in such passages as "When you lift up the son of humanity you will know that I am" (8:28) and "Before Abraham came to be, I am" (8:51). Like the father-son sayings, the "I am" sayings authenticate Jesus' message and serve to draw disciples closer to him.[50]

"I am." Wow! I have always marveled over these sayings. In part I am attracted to the poetry. Jesus says, "I am the bread of life." I am intrigued and puzzled. This statement is not literally true. Jesus is not

---

[49] For more discussion of my personal reflections on the Johannine father-son language in my life see below, chapter 3, 50–51, and chapter 5, 101–02.

[50] For a brief discussion of the "I am" sayings and the images used with them see Willett, *Wisdom Christology*, 85–95. I list the various scholarly discussions of the "I am" sayings on 86 n. 107. More recently cf. D. M Ball, *"I Am" in John's Gospel: Literary Function, Background and Theological Implications.* JSNTSup 124 (Sheffield: Sheffield Academic Press, 1996). For a more playful approach to the "I am" sayings, see below, chapter 3, 56.

bread; he is a human. He is then speaking metaphorically, poetically, and this poetry cannot be put into prose without losing something significant.[51] The meaning must be teased out, plumbed, meditated upon, played with. And there is no final meaning, but layers upon layers upon layers as it is read anew.

But there is something more here for me. Jesus: "I am," or better, "I AM." I have always struggled with my own "I am," or sometimes better "i am." I have wrestled with identity, self-esteem, and self-confidence, in short, who or what "I am." In some ways my identity struggles have been revealed publicly in the names I have called myself. Most of my life I simply said, "I am Mike Willett." In graduate school, after coming back from study in England, wanting to express my newfound confidence as a scholar, I said, "I am Michael Willett."[52] Then when my wife and I married, both taking a new name, I said, "I am Michael Newheart."[53] I have been constantly reinventing myself, constantly transforming my "I am."

Many of my identity issues, I'm sure, are tied in with my relationship with my father. He was simply not there when I was developing my own identity as an adolescent male. I am also sure that these issues are tied in with the anxiety (and depression) that I have experienced all my life, though it was only diagnosed and treated in recent years. Part of my self-therapy (to complement my psychological and pharmacological therapy) is to complete "Daily Mood Logs" in which I (1) describe an upsetting event, (2) record my negative feelings, (3) identify my automatic thoughts, the cognitive distortions in those thoughts, and rational responses to those thoughts, and (4) check how I feel after the

[51] Cf. Edward Hirsch, *How to Read a Poem: And Fall in Love with Poetry* (New York: Harcourt Brace, 1999) 13–15, with a rich discussion of the use of metaphor in poetry. He writes, "Poetry is made of metaphor. It is a collision, a collusion, a compression of two unlike things: A is B" (p. 13). He also quotes philosopher Ted Cohen, who said that a main point of metaphor is "the achievement of intimacy," in which the poet and the reader relate more deeply to one another because the reader makes a special effort to accept and interpret the poet's metaphor. Such a "transaction constitutes the acknowledgement of a community" (ibid. 15, quoting Cohen, "Metaphor and the Cultivation of Intimacy," *Critical Inquiry,* 5 [1978] 1–13). Certainly this is the way Jesus' "I am" metaphors function, as they bring the reader into a deeper intimacy with Jesus, facilitated through a community of readers whether in late-first-century Ephesus (where the gospel was probably written) or in late-twentieth-century/ early twenty-first-century Washington, D.C. (where this book was definitely written).

[52] "Michael" is derived from the Hebrew, meaning "Who is like God?" The final syllable "el" represented "God," so calling me "Mike" left out God!

[53] The theme verse for our wedding was Ezek 36:26: "A new heart I will give you, and a new spirit I will put within you."

exercise.[54] My automatic thoughts often read, "I'm a loser," "I'm a failure," "I'm incompetent." I respond rationally by saying, "I am a winner and a success and competent," which is usually helpful—until another "upsetting event" comes along, when I again say, "I'm a loser," etc.

So in reading the gospel I hope to ground my "i am" in Jesus' I AM. His is so sure and mine so shaky. My I am in his I AM: It seems like such a safe place to dwell, to abide, to live in one of those many dwelling places in the father's house. So I dwell there, in the text, and also in the communities and institutions that serve as custodians of the text. Because I have dwelt a long time in those institutions and have been credentialed by them, I have status. So now I not only dwell in the father's house; I exercise power there. I am one of the fathers! So now I Am because of the I AM. How do I wield that power, to oppress or liberate, to empower or disempower? (I am not wholly comfortable with the term "empower" because it implies that I have power that I am putting into people. Often, instead, I simply lead folk to recognize the power they already have.) I AM/iam/I am//////you are.

I am . . . writing (and you are reading) about three aspects of Jesus' language that have attracted me over the years: father-son, I AM, and finally, "not of this world." That is what Jesus says in a number of different ways, that he is not of this world (explicitly in 8:23; 17:14, 16). He is an alien, from the world above (3:31; 8:23), also called heaven (6:33, 38, 41, 42, 50, 51), where God his father is (17:1) and whence his followers are born (3:3; 17:14, 16). In contrast to Jesus and his followers, however, Jesus' opponents, often called "Judeans,"[55] are of this world; they are from below (8:23). Such is one example of "Johannine dualism," which slices reality up into separate spheres, such as this world and the heavenly world, above and below, light and darkness, spirit and flesh.[56] These dualisms overlap in that the world above is the source of light and spirit while the world below is in darkness and of the flesh.

I have identified with this portrayal of Jesus as an alien or outsider because I have always felt much the same way. It seems that whatever world I find myself in, I am not of it. I am a European American teaching at Howard University, a predominantly African-American institution.

---

[54] Cf. David D. Burns, *The Feeling Good Handbook* (New York: William Morrow, 1989) 73–96.

[55] I translate *hoi Ioudaioi* as "Judeans." Cf. Wes Howard-Brook, *Becoming Children of God: John's Gospel and Radical Discipleship* (Maryknoll, N.Y.: Orbis, 1994) 41–43; Malina and Rohrbaugh, *Social-Science Commentary on the Gospel of John*, 44–46. Cf. also Tina Pippin, "'For Fear of the Jews': Lying and Truth-Telling in Translating the Gospel of John," *Sem* 76 (1996) 81–97.

[56] Cf. the list of scholarly discussions of Johannine dualism in Willett, *Wisdom Christology* 57, n. 23.

But my "alien-ness" (alienation), my not-of-this-world(li)ness, did not begin with my service at Howard. In my family of origin I was the sensitive intellectual in an unreflective, cold family. In an evangelical seminary preparing people to go out and "save souls" I was interested in peace, social justice, and contemplative prayer. On the mission field in Costa Rica I was the biblical critic among evangelical missionaries. In seminaries in Kansas City I was the Southern Baptist teaching Methodists (at Saint Paul School of Theology), Nazarenes (at Nazarene Theological Seminary), and even (God forbid!) American Baptists (at Central Baptist Theological Seminary). (Indeed, I am the only one who has taught at all four denominational seminaries in the Kansas City area: the institutions listed above, plus Midwestern Baptist Theological Seminary.)

There is a difference, though, between the group tolerating aliens and the group rejecting them. In July 1988, while I was in language school preparing to teach at the Venezuela Baptist Seminary, I was dismissed by the Foreign Mission Board for "doctrinal ambiguity" and thus became a casualty of the Southern Baptist "Holy War" raging at the time.[57] This experience gave me new appreciation for the man who was healed of his blindness and then tossed out of the synagogue (John 9) and for the Johannine Jesus, who was rejected by "his own" (1:11).

As I have read the gospel, Jesus' "not-of-this-world" language legitimates my own sense of alienation. (This is the "nation" I feel most a citizen of!) It soothes my wounds of loneliness, guilt, and grief. ("Yes, there is a balm in Gilead!") The Johannine Jesus says to me that it's okay to be different, okay even to be rejected because Jesus and his followers were. (Often in meditation during my missionary tribulation I imagined myself coming to Jesus bruised and bloody. He showed me his own wounds, and then he embraced me and assured me that he loved me.) I became convinced that God was on the side of the marginalized! (True, I am a white, male, heterosexual intellectual, but I have still been marginalized by "the powers" in my community!) God is, then, on my side, and against those who reject me, whether they be parents, administrators, missionaries, or church people.

Uh oh! I can sense the serpent of self-righteousness slithering up my leg! I am not just celebrating my difference but asserting my superiority! In the gospel when Jesus says that he and his followers are "not of this world," that they are "from above," he is saying that they are "over" those who are "of this world," better than those who are "from below." Do I really want to say that about myself? I certainly want to

---

[57] For a report on that event see the Associated Press article reprinted in Michael Willett Newheart, "Lent 4: John 9:1-41," *The Bible Workbench* 6:3 (Lent 1 to Easter Sunday 1999) 63–65.

celebrate my differences (my uniquenesses) and to heal my wounds incurred by those who rejected me for those differences, but do I also want to say that I am better than, or "above" those who have rejected me? Doing so would land me in the same dualistic chasm as those who reject me and further fracture community. Perhaps I am both of this world and not of this world, born from above and from below.

Agenda for My Soul Reading of the Gospel of John

With these general themes lined out, I turn my attention to the gospel narrative. I will attempt a soul reading of selected passages in the gospel in order to plumb the Johannine soul and my own soul. Those passages include the prologue (John 1:1-18), conversations with Nicodemus and the Samaritan (3:1-21; 4:4-42), disputes with the Judeans (5:19-47; 6:25-59; 8:12-59), the healing of the man born blind (9:1-41), the raising of Lazarus (11:1-44), the first farewell discourse (14:1-31), Jesus' prayer to the Father (17:1-26), the trial before Pilate (18:28–19:16a), and the resurrection appearances to Mary and to the disciples (20:1-31). With each passage I first translate a section from the gospel, then I poetically and playfully engage the key images and rhythms of that section; next I consider the likenesses in twentieth-century African-American poetry, and finally, I summarize the likenesses of the Johannine images and rhythms in my own soul.[58]

So soul, both mine and the reader's, "rise, let's go forward!" (14:31).

---

[58] My method is very much informed by that of *The Bible Workbench,* a lectionary study resource produced by The Educational Center of St. Louis, Missouri. (I am an associate editor for the *Workbench.*) In dealing with a particular text, the reader wrestles with ever-deepening questions organized in the following pattern: What is going on in this text? How is what is going on in this text also going on in the world around me? How is what is going on in this text also going on in my life? See William L. Dols, *Awakening the Fire Within: A Primer on Issue-Centered Education* (St. Louis: The Educational Center, 1994) 165–81. For further information about *The Bible Workbench,* call The Educational Center at 1-800-624-4644.

1

ForeWord:
The Johannine Prologue (John 1:1-18)

Forward we go. Forward. Into space, into time. Where shall we begin? Where the gospel begins: in the beginning, with the word, which was enfleshed. So we go forward and backward. But either way we go "word." Fore-word and back-word. So, let's go fore/back-word.

First the word itself:

> In the beginning was the word,[1]
> and the word was face to face with God,
> and the word was God.
> This one was in the beginning face to face with God.
> Everything came to be through him,
> and apart from him not one thing came to be.
> What has come to be in him was life,[2]

---

[1] Most translations capitalize "the Word" (cf. NRSV). "The word" (Greek *ho logos*), however, is not a proper name but a common noun and therefore should be placed in lower case.

[2] Some translators and commentators take "What came to be" with v. 3, so that it reads: "And without him not one thing came into being that has come into being. In him was life . . ." (NRSV margin; cf. C. K. Barrett, *The Gospel According to St. John: An Introduction with Commentary and Notes on the Greek Text* (2nd ed. Philadelphia: Westminster, 1978) 157; Rudolf Schnackenburg, *The Gospel According to St. John.* Translated by Kevin Smyth (New York: Crossroad, 1982) 1:240; Bruce Metzger, *A Textual Commentary on the Greek New Testament: A Comparison Volume to the United Bible Societies' Greek New Testament* (London: United Bible Societies, 1971) 196. It is better, however, to take the phrase with v. 4 because, among other reasons, the poetry of the prologue demands it; see n. 6 below. See the NRSV; Raymond E. Brown, *The Gospel According to John, I–XII.* AB 29, 29A (Garden City, N.Y.: Doubleday, 1966) 14; Bruce Vawter, "What Came to Be in Him Was Life, Jn 1,3b-4a," *CBQ* 25 (1963) 401–6; F. W. Schlatter, "The Problem of Jn 1:3b-4a" *CBQ* 34 (1972) 54–58; Kurt Aland, "Eine Untersuchung zu John 1.3-4: über die Bedeutung eines Punktes," *ZNW* 59

and this life was the light of people;
And the light shines in the darkness,
and the darkness did not overtake it.[3]

A person came to be,
sent from God,
named John;
This one came as a witness,
so that he might witness to the light,
so that all might believe through him.
He was not the light,
but he came to be
so that he might witness to the light.
The true light,
which enlightens every person,
was coming into the world.

He was in the world,
and the world came to be through him,
but the world did not know him.
He came into his own things,
and his own people did not receive him.
But to those who received him,
to those who believed into his name,
he gave power to come to be children of God,
who were born not of blood nor of the will of flesh
    nor of the will of man but of God.

And the word came to be flesh and tabernacled among us,
and we saw his glory,
glory as an only-born son from a father,[4]
full of grace and truth.

(1968) 174–209; Rudolf Bultmann, *The Gospel of John: A Commentary.* Translated by G. R. Beasley-Murray (Philadelphia: Westminster, 1971) 39; Ed L. Miller, "The Logic of the Logos Hymn," *NTS* 29 (1983) 552–61.

[3] The word translated "overtake" here *(katelaben)* can also mean "understand"; cf. Acts 4:13; 10:34; 25:25; Eph. 3:18. The verb appears again in the fourth gospel in 12:35, and it clearly means "overtake." Some commentators have translated the verb as "grasp" in order to take in both meanings; cf. BAGD 413. Thomas L. Brodie, *The Gospel According to John: A Literary and Theological Commentary* (New York: Oxford University Press, 1993) 138, argues for both, referring to H. K. Granskou, "Irony" (unpublished paper, 1985) 7–10, observing that "in the context of ancient writing practices, particularly the practices of constructing literary riddles and of using irony, it is a mistake to attempt to regard one meaning as right and the other as wrong."

[4] The word translated here as "only-born" *(monogenēs)* is often rendered in modern translations as "only son" (cf. RSV, NRSV; also cf. BAGD 527). For a recent argu-

John witnesses to him and has cried out saying,
> "This is the one about whom I said,
>> 'He who comes after me has come to be ahead of me,
>> because he was before me.'"

From his fullness we all have received grace upon grace;
For the law was given through Moses;
grace and truth came to be through Jesus Christ.
No one has ever seen God;
the only-born son, God,[5]
who is into the bosom of the father,
> has exegeted him.

Playing with the Images in the Prologue

John 1:1-18 is often called the gospel's "prologue"—the word before the word, or the fore-word. It is the word in all eternity before the word in history. The word, therefore, is not only before Jesus but before all things. The word is *the* fore-word. And in introducing the word the poet is quite forward, saying that the word is in the beginning, is face to face with God, and is God. And this word goes forward: into the world, where it meets rejection, but also forward into a believing community, where it meets acceptance, makes believers children of God, and reveals glory, grace, truth, and God. What a word!

Scholars often note the "poetic" or "hymnic" nature of the prologue.[6] Yet scholars read this poetic piece in a most prosaic way! They allow

ment for "only-begotten" see J. V. Dahms, "The Johannine Use of Monogenēs Reconsidered," *NTS* 27 (1983) 1–31.

[5] There are a number of textual variants for this line: the oldest and best manuscripts have "only-begotten God" *(monogenēs theos)*, some have "only-begotten son" *(monogenēs huios)*, and others simply have "only-begotten" *(monogenēs);* cf. Metzger, *Textual Commentary* 198, and the thorough discussion by Elizabeth Harris, *Prologue and Gospel: The Theology of the Fourth Evangelist.* JSNTS 107 (Sheffield: Sheffield Academic Press, 1994) 91–115.

[6] Cf. Brown, *John I–XII* 19–23; Schnackenburg, *John* 1:224–29; S. de Ausejo, "¿Es un himno a Christo el prólogo de San Juan?" *EstBíb* 15 (1956) 223–77, 381–427; Bultmann, *John* 14–18; John Painter, "Christology and the History of the Johannine Community in the Prologue of the Fourth Gospel," *NTS* (1984) 463–64; Francis J. Moloney, *Belief in the Word: Reading John 1–4* (Minneapolis: Fortress, 1993) 25–26; Ben Witherington III, *John's Wisdom* (Louisville: Westminster/John Knox, 1995) 49–52. C. K. Barrett, *Gospel* 151; idem, *The Prologue of St John's Gospel* (London: Athlone Press, 1971) 27, however, considers it a prose introduction to the gospel. Cf. also Walter Eltester, "Der Logos und sein Prophet," in *Apophoreta: Festschrift für Ernst Haenchen* (Berlin: Topelmann, 1964) 109–34; Peder Borgen, "Logos Was the True Light: Contributions to the Interpretation of the Prologue of John," *NovT* 14 (1972) 115–30; Brodie, *John* 134 notes the "interweaving of soaring poetry with simple prose." He goes on to say, "The interweaving is a way of expressing, through the very form of the language,

themselves to become entangled in the thicket of ego-concerns such as the background of the concept of the word,[7] the original form of the "hymn" that underlies the prologue,[8] and the structure of the final form of the text.[9] In other words, scholars generally keep their feet firmly planted on well-trod, dry, and dusty ground. Their souls do not soar with the Johannine eagle to the world above, nor do they swim in or even drink from the living water, nor do they munch on the bread of life. In my reading of the prologue, however, I will depart from the worn path; I will let my soul soar, swim, drink, munch, dance, and laugh. The best interpretation of a text is one that stays as close as possible to the form of the text. Poetry, then, is best interpreted by poetry.

---

one of the prologue's central ideas—the descent of the (soaring, poetic) Word into the (prosaic) reality of human life." Brodie seems to have fallen into the dualistic thinking of the gospel, associating poetry with the divine and prose with the human. But is there nothing prosaic about the divine or poetic about the human? And are not poetry and prose both human products?

Cf. also Harris, *Prologue and Gospel* 25, who maintains that the Johannine prologue functions in much the same way as a prologue in a Greek religious drama, "with the foreannouncing of the past events, the present situation and the final outcome as being with the preordained will of God, and with the introduction in advance of principal figures as chief characters." Cf. also Sharon H. Ringe, *Wisdom's Friends* (Louisville: Westminster/John Knox, 1999) 46–63. Cf. the discussion of the role of poetry in oral societies in Bruce J. Malina and and Richard L. Rohrbaugh, *Social-Science Commentary on the Gospel of John* (Minneapolis: Fortress, 1998) 34–35. They write: "In oral societies, in which the vast majority cannot read or write, poetic verse is a principal form in which the tradition is recalled. It is an especially honorific way of speaking and is a common feature of everyday speech for both mean and women" (34).

[7] Cf. Willett, *Wisdom* 31–47 for a brief discussion of the various proposals for the background of the word and a demonstration of the widely-held thesis that wisdom lies behind the word. For a more recent treatment of the wisdom background see Witherington, *John's Wisdom* 19–20, 47–59. Werner Kelber, "The Birth of a Beginning: John 1:1-18," *Sem* 52 (1990) 123 adds an important cautionary note: "To rely on Wisdom as the explanatory model is to content ourselves with surface answers, and to sustain our belief in the beginning of the Logos as a theological commonplace."

[8] For the various suggestions as to what constituted the original hymn see G. Rochais, "La formation du prologue Jn 1, 1-18," *Science et Esprit* 37 (1985) 5–44, 161–87. At minimum the lines concerning John the Baptist (vv. 6-8, 15) are considered prose additions.

[9] Growing in popularity in recent years have been the ideas of a spiral and a chiasm. For the spiral see Ignace de la Potterie, "Structure du Prologue de Saint Jean," *NTS* 30 (1984) 354–81; Charles H. Giblin, "Two Complementary Literary Structures in John 1:1-18," *JBL* 104 (1985) 87–103; Willett, *Wisdom* 34. For the chiasm see R. Alan Culpepper, "The Pivot of John's Prologue," *NTS* 27 (1980) 1–31; Giblin, "Literary Structures"; Jeffrey L. Staley, "The Structure of John's Prologue: Its Implications for the Gospel's Narrative Structure," *CBQ* 48 (1986) 241–64.

So poetic my reading will be . . . and imagistic, rhythmic, and playful, as much as the prologue itself. I will allow the Johannine prological poem to sweep me off my feet and carry me wherever it wants to go.[10]

So let's get to work! Let's play!

The poem begins "In the beginning." In the bebebebebeginning, the beginning of the be. In the beginning, the genesis time, the God-created-the-heaven-and-earth-time, the void-and-darkness time, the wind/spirit-hovering-over-the-deep time (cf. Gen 1:1-2). All this in the beginning (Greek *en archē*), in the "archaic" time, the ruling and unruly time,[11] the "arche"-typal time, the fundamental and original time. In this archaic time, this beginning of the be, the word be. (And God said, "Let there be . . ." cf. Gen 1:3, 6, 14.) Not words or a word but *the* word. The Word. WORD. Worddddddd. It is a beginning word, a worded beginning. An archaic Word, a ruling WORD. *Archē logos.* The poet goes on an "archeo-logical" dig. (You dig?) What "arty facts" will be uncovered?

The first uncovered fact is that this archaic word is a face-to-face-with-God *(pros ton theon)* word. The word is God-faced and God is word-faced. The word has not yet become flesh, but it does have a face, as does God. Can the word and God be faced? And is this God-faced word God's word? ("And the word of the Lord came to . . ." cf. Jer 1:4; Ezek 1:3; Hos 1:1, etc.) Or is it the word's God? The word is not only God-faced but God-loved and God-gloried (cf. John 17:24). And this God-faced word is God. The worddddd is Goddddd.[12] The word is godly, godded, or "goddy," and God is worded, or wordy.[13] The word not has only a God-face but a "God-bod." *Theos logos.* The poem is now explicitly "theo-logical."

Through this archaic, God-faced, goddy word everything *(panta)* comes to be. EverythingEVERYthingEVERYTHING![14] The word: "genesis," "creation." All things come to be through / by / through-the-agency-of

---

[10] Perhaps I should also say that I will sweep the prologue off its feet and carry it wherever I want to go. Sometimes it is difficult to determine who is leading this dance.

[11] *Archē* can also mean "rule," or "ruler," cf. Luke 12:11; Titus 3:1; Jude 6; cf. also BAGD 112.

[12] Norman R. Petersen, *The Gospel of John and the Sociology of Light: Language and Characterization in the Fourth Gospel* (Valley Forge, Pa.: Trinity Press International, 1993) 9, notes that this statement "violates everyday language (and logic) because the nouns no longer serve to differentiate either meanings or entities." He goes on to say that the poet's language here and elsewhere in the prologue is "a special language, one that is used to speak about a world (i.e., of referents) that is different from the everyday world that everyday language enables us to speak about" (10).

[13] The Judeans in 5:18; 10:33 are wrong in saying that Jesus makes himself equal to God because as the word he is God from the beginning.

[14] Cf. 3:35: The father loves the son and has placed everything *(panta)* in his hands.

word, *dia logou*. Creation is "dia-logical." ("By the word of the lord the heavens were made, and all their host by the breath of his mouth," Ps 33:6.) Everything, all things, all the things through word; nothing, no thing, not one thing apart from word. Every-thing speaks; no-thing is mute. The word "everythings."

What comes to be in (as well as through) this archaic, God-faced, godly, everything-ing word is life, *zoē* not *bios*, so that the subject is "zoo-logy" not "bio-logy." This life is eternal, never-seeing-death life (cf. John 3:15-16; 10:28; 11:26); resurrected, coming-out-of-the-grave life (cf. 5:28-29; 11:25); abundant, "pasturized" life (10:9-10); watered and breaded life (4:10, 14; 6:35, 51; 7:38). The word is a living word, a lively word, an enlivening word, and life is worded.[15]

This worded life is the light of people (". . . and there was light," Gen 1:3), the light of the world, the light of life (cf. John 8:12; 9:5; 12:46), illumined life, living light, lively light, worded living light. And this light is a shining-in-darkness light, a not-overtaken-by-darkness light (cf. also 8:12b; 12:35, 46b). The darkness is illuminated, but the darkness doesn't over-take (or under-stand) this invincible (incomprehensible) light. Darkness cannot grasp light with its arms (or with its mind).[16] (After all, its deeds are evil, 3:19.) Light and darkness stand together on the same footing. ("And God separated the light from the darkness," Gen 1:4.)[17]

Of the all-things that come to be, a sent-from-God person comes to be: John.[18] He is the first man, a new Adam. He is sent-from-God as a witness (cf. John 5:33, 35) ("Do you solemnly swear to tell the truth, the whole truth, and nothing but the truth, so help you God?" "I do."), light-witnessing, so that all people might word-believe through him (cf. 3:26; 10:41-42). All things come to *be* through the God-faced light; all people come to *be*-lieve through the light-faced witness. This light-witnessing person is *not* the light. John agrees: "I am not the messiah, not Elijah, not the prophet" (1:20-21). Not, not, not! What a not-ty boy that John is![19] He is a light, witless witness.[20]

---

[15] Cf. 5:21, 25-26, where the father gives the son life-giving power.

[16] Cf. 3:1-9, where Nicodemus comes by night and fails to understand Jesus' words.

[17] For a provocative study of light and darkness in the prologue and its ancient milieu see Craig R. Koester, *Symbolism in the Fourth Gospel: Meaning, Mystery, Community* (Minneapolis: Fortress, 1995) 124–33.

[18] For a discussion of the role of John in the prologue and gospel, see Harris, *Prologue and Gospel*, 26–62.

[19] Simon Peter is a naughty "not-ty" boy because he says three times "I am not" in denying that he is Jesus' disciple; cf. 18:17, 25-27.

[20] John, however, is not the only one who witnesses to the light; Jesus' father-assigned works, his sending father, the truthful spirit, and the beloved disciple also witness, cf. 5:36-37; 8:18; 10:25; 15:26-27; 19:35; 20:24.

The TRUE light[21]—the word—in contrast to the NOT-light—John—is coming (down from heaven above, 6:33) into the world (cf. 3:19; 11:27), sent by God (cf. 3:17; 5:36, etc.) to speak openly to the world (18:20).[22] The wordy light now becomes worldly, and the world becomes worded and enlightened. It is a world-word, *kosmos logos.* The poem now turns "cosmo-logical." This true light, or illuminated truth, an every-person-enlightening light, is now an in-the-world (but not of-the-world, cf. 17:16) light. In archaic time the enlightened word is with God; now in John-witnessing time the worded light is in the world. The world, as part of the all-things, comes to be through the wordy light, but this enlightened world does not know him.[23] It does not know where he comes from or where he is going (cf. 8:14); it prefers darkness to light because it does not want its evil deeds exposed (cf. 3:19-20); it hates the light (and his followers) and seeks to kill him (and them) (cf. 5:18; 7:7; 8:37; 15:18, 23-24; 16:2; 19:15). The world is enlightened yet unknowing, much as the darkness is illumined but uncomprehending. This worded, all-creating yet unknown light comes into his own things, but his own illumined people, the Judeans (cf. 5:16 etc.) and even his brothers (cf. 7:5), are not light-receivers (cf. also 8:43; 12:48). Darkness is a non-comprehender, the world a not-knower, his own people non-receivers. Enlightened yet darkened world, enlightened yet darkened his-own.

But those who are not the world (cf. 17:16) and not his-own *are* light-receivers; they are fully enlightened. Their blind eyes are opened (cf. 9:1-41), and they into-the-light's-name believe, just as they in-his-name pray (cf. 14:13-14; 15:16; 16:23-24, 26) and have life (cf. 20:31). These light-namers are the new his-own, to-the-end loved (13:10), shepherd-known and name-called (cf. 10:3, 14, 27), lively-water drinkers (4:14), breaded-life eaters (6:35), and non-death-seers (cf. 8:51). These light friends (cf. 15:15) are empowered to come to be children of God, godly children, gathered together into one (cf. 11:52). Through the enlightened word all things come to be; now through the wordy light godly children come to be. (The world and the word's own, which reject the word, come to be devilish children; cf. 8:44. The word infantilizes all persons, making them either godly or devilish children, *tekna;* the word

---

[21] Cf. 6:55, where Jesus refers to the "true bread from heaven" and his flesh as "true bread" (also v. 32) and his blood as "true blood." Also the one who sent Jesus is true (7:28; 8:26; 17:3).

[22] How "in the world" is the light? Scholars have often debated whether this section (vv. 9-12) refers to the period of the Hebrew Scriptures or to the Incarnation. Brodie, *John* 140 sees it as ambiguous, referring first to the Hebrew Scriptures and then, as it advances, to the Incarnation.

[23] Cf. 7:28, where Jesus, perhaps ironically, tells the people of Jerusalem that they know him. Then in the next chapter he says that they do not know him or his father, 8:19. While persons may not know the Jesus-word, he knows them; cf. 2:24-25.

"techno-logizes" them.) As godly children, light-receivers become light-dwellings in which God and the light are home-makers (14:20, 23), cleaning with the word (15:3). Godly children are born/gotten/begotten not bloodily or fleshly or willfully or manly. Flesh (and blood and will and man) is useless (cf. 6:63)! (Useless?! Then what do believers live in if not flesh and blood and body?) Birth as godly children is not a bio-logical process but zoo-logical; it comes from above (cf. 3:3), from the spirit (cf. 3:5-8; 6:63), from God, who through the godly, wordy light becomes a father (cf. also 20:17) (but who is the mother?) to those not of this world.

All things come to be, the world comes to be, children of God come to be. Now the word comes to be . . . FLESH! The enlightened, empowered word is now enfleshed.[24] It is worded, wordy flesh; breaded, enlivening, edible, munchable (and bloody, dying!) flesh (cf. 6:51). Fleshly will does not birth godly children, but fleshly word lives gloriously (though briefly, cf. 7:33). The enfleshed word is a living/dwelling/tabernacling/pitching-a-tent-of-meeting-in-the-wilderness-where-God-is-met-face-to-face (cf. Exod 33:7-11) word.[25] The wordy flesh among-us resides, and we, enlightened godly children, the "we(e)"-ones, are glorious light-seers. Come and see, Jesus says (cf. John 1:39); come and see glo-glow-glory; come and see the glory word, *doxa logos*. The "we(e)-ones" see, and they sing doxo-logy! (Music: "Glory be to the fleshy word . . .!") Wordy fleshly glory is not a sea-parting, manna-giving, fire-burning, or cloud-appearing glory (cf. Exod 14:17-18; 16:7, 10; 24:16-17), but a sign-working, water-wining, dead-raising, and (especially) cross-dying glory (cf. John 2:11; 11:4, 40; 12:16, 23, 28, 33; 13:31-32, etc.). Archaic-word-face-to-face-with-God time is genesis; fleshly-word-among-we(e)-godly-children time is exodus.

Enlightened God-born children recognize the worded flesh's glory, Isaiah-like (12:41), not as the glory of persons (cf. 5:41, 44; 6:18; 12:43), but as the glory of a fathered, or fatherly, only-born son (cf. 8:54; 17:24); it is male-fleshly glory, privileging father over mother and son over daughter in the godly family. This gloriously fathered, fleshly word is

[24] Bultmann, *John* 63 maintains that the paradox of the prologue—indeed, the entire gospel—is that the glory is seen in the flesh. But Ernst Käsemann, "The Structure and Purpose of the Prologue to John's Gospel," in idem, *New Testament Questions of Today* (London: SCM, 1969) 159–61 argues that the paradox was not in the word becoming flesh but in the presence of God on earth. His view of Johannine christology is further developed in his *The Testament of Jesus*, translated by Gerhard Krodel (Philadelphia: Fortress, 1968), in which he labeled it "naïve docetism" (26). Cf. Kelber, "Birth," 133–35 for a brief discussion of their positions.

[25] The word translated "lived" here is *eskenosen*, which is etymologically related to the word translated "tent" or "tabernacle," *hē skēnē*, in Exod 33:7-11 LXX.

full of grace and truth, truly graceful, gracefully true, gracious and truthful. He is full of truth, inspirited truth (cf. 4:23-24; 14:17; 15:26; 17:17) and liberating truth (cf. 8:31), to which the enfleshed word testifies (cf. 18:37). (But can the enfleshed word be truly graceful and liberating if woman as mother and daughter is left out?)

John comes back on stage; he is Johnny-on-the-spot. Again he witnesses, but this time he speaks. The fleshy, glorious, truthfully gracious word gives words to John's flesh. He CRIES OUT (You've got our attention, John!) that the wordy flesh is the one he spoke about: the fleshy word, who as godly lamb, godly son, and inspirited one, outranks John because, despite the wordy flesh's post-John coming, he as the beginning word has a pre-John "is-ing" (cf. 1:29, 30, 33, 34). John is a good soldier, and he salutes his ranking officer, the archaic, God-faced, fleshy word. John is only a voice (cf. 1:23); he has no body. He is not light but witness *(martus)*, martyr. And as martyr John eventually "dies" to the word with the words "He must increase and I must decrease" (3:30). Thus John leaves the gloriously illuminated stage.[26]

From the fully graciously true fleshly word we(e) ones are all receivers of grace after grace, grace upon grace, grace against grace, everflowing grace, gracegracegrace. (So much grace; how a-Paul-ing![27]) Law is given, graced, gifted through Moses (cf. also 7:19-23), that serpent-lifting, Judean-accusing, Jesus-writing Moses (cf. 3:14; 5:45-47).[28] While law is given through Moses, gracious truth comes to be through Jesus Christ. As all things, the world, and children of God come to be through the word, so true grace comes to be through the fleshly word, Jesus Christ. ("I don't condemn you either; go, and don't sin from now on," 8:11). Graciously truthful Jesus Christ, Jesus Messiah, Jesus Anointed (cf. 1:41).[29] Jesus is messianically/anointedly, gracefully true. He is true

---

[26] Harris, *Prologue and Gospel* 62, writes, "Thus John's seminal witness in 1:15-18, it may be maintained, functions as a prologue to prepare for the rest of chs. 1–3 of the Gospel, which themselves form a historical prologue, moving Jesus into the centre of the picture, to remain there throughout the remainder of the Gospel."

[27] Grace *(charis)* is a key Pauline term; cf. his customary greetings ("Grace to you . . ." Rom 1:7; 1 Cor 1:3 etc.) and benedictions ("The grace of the Lord Jesus be with you," 1 Cor 16:23; 2 Cor 13:13 etc.), as well as the body of his letters, where grace is a frequent theme; cf. Rom 5:2; 1 Cor 1:4 etc. Indeed, Painter, "Christology," 466 argued, based on the threefold appearance of grace in the prologue (and nowhere else in the gospel), that the hymn was edited by a "'Hellenist' Christian community where the Pauline Law/Grace antithesis was known and accepted."

[28] Cf. Harris, *Prologue and Gospel* 63–90 for a discussion of the role of Moses in the prologue and gospel. Cf. also Marie-Emile Boismard, *Moses or Jesus: An Essay in Johannine Christology,* translated by Benedict T. Viviano (Minneapolis: Fortress, 1993).

[29] "Christ" *(christos)* literally means "anointed," which is the way the NRSV translates it in 1:41 but nowhere else it appears in the gospel, e.g., 1:20, 25; 4:25.

light (1:9), true heavenly bread (6:32), true living way (cf. 14:6). Thus, gloriously, graciously, and truthfully the name of the fleshly, son-like word appears: Jesus Christ. This is the name into which light-receivers believe.

Truly and gracefully, no one has seen God—ever (cf. 6:46). Not even lawful (legal eagle) Moses has seen God.[30] God is an invisible God, the subject of no verbs in this poem. We(e) ones do not see God their (absent) father, but they do see the glorious, fleshly word (cf. 14:9) who is only-born *(monogenēs)*. Godly children are godly born, but the enfleshed word is only-born, God. (Does he have siblings or not?) The archaic word is God, and the fleshly only-born is God, indeed, masterly God (cf. 20:28). And this only-born God is into the father's bosom. They recline together at the banqueting table, feasting upon the flesh of one another's presence. The word is God-faced, and the only-born is father-bosomed, an intimate and beloved position.[31] Father and son are bosom buddies, enjoying oneness (cf. 10:30; 17:11, 20). The father is in the son and the son in the father (cf. 10:38; 14:10-11; 17:20). ("I don't know where I end and you begin."[32]) The son is begotten from the father's loins and goes into the father's bosom. There the father shows the son what he is doing (cf. 5:20). (Where is the son's mother in this love feast? Is she serving? Maybe she is tapping her son on the shoulder, saying, "They have no wine," cf. 2:3.) While reclining on the father's bosom, the wordy only-born son holds a symposium. For the wee godly children (and for the world, cf. 8:26) he exegetes *(exegesato)* God (cf. also 16:25). He is an exegetical and enfleshed word, a bosomed and born God, the only God that godly children have seen. The only-born's pri-

---

[30] Cf. Exod 33:11, 18-23, where the narrator says that Moses speaks with God "face to face," but when Moses asks to see God's glory he is told that he can see God's back but not face because no one can see God and live.

[31] Cf. 13:23, where at the Last Supper the Beloved Disciple reclines in the bosom of Jesus *(en to kolpon tou Iesou)*. Luise Schottroff, "The Samaritan Woman and the Notion of Sexuality in the Fourth Gospel," in Fernando F. Segovia, ed., *"What Is John?" Vol. II. Literary and Social Readings of the Fourth Gospel*, SBL Symposium Series (Atlanta: Scholars, 1998) 177 writes, "The expression 'to lie on the breast *(kolpos)'* of someone describes the most intimate physical communion: nursing infants lie on their mothers' breasts (Num 11:12; 1 Kgs 17:19; Ruth 4:16; Plutarch, *Pericles* 1). In the same way, the intimate physical communion of fathers and children and of a man and his wife is described as 'lying on the breast' or 'in the lap' of the other (Deut 13:7; 28:54)."

[32] To the best of my memory this line is spoken by a woman reclining on her lover in a television commercial a few years back for the Calvin Klein fragrance "Obsession." But cf. George Barlow's poem "Nook," which says, "Now it's hard to tell / where I end / and you begin" in Clarence Major, ed., *The Garden Thrives: Twentieth-Century African-American Poetry* (San Francisco: Harper Perennial, 1996) 312, from Barlow, *Gumbo* (New York: Doubleday, 1981).

mary mode of exegesis is "word-study." The word comes to be flesh; the flesh comes to be words, enspirited and enlivening words (cf. 6:63; 16:13-14), words from the father (cf. 8:38; 12:49-50; 15:15; 17:8). In the beginning is the word; in the end are the words, the exegesis.

Exploring Likenesses to the Prologue in African-American Poetry

I have played in, with, and on the word; it is now time to play in, with, and on the world. I play the role of John, light-witnessing in the world. The world I have chosen to play in is twentieth-century African-American poetry. Where do we find in that poetic world the likenesses of the images and rhythms of the Johannine prological poem? Amiri Baraka writes in his "State/meant": "The Black Artist must draw out of his soul the correct image of the world. He must use this image to band his brothers and sisters together in common understanding of the nature of the world (and the nature of America) and the nature of the human soul."[33] The Johannine poet is such an artist, drawing (and painting and singing and dancing) out of the soul—the world of images—the correct image of the world. It is a dark world that not-knows and non-receives the word. Yet out of the world the poetic word bands together brothers and sisters as god-children, glory-seers, and grace-receivers.

Sterling D. Plumpp writes in a like vein in his "Poem":

> Poems are bridges, neon
> reaches across worlds
> where language seeks
> a voice for itself. Where words
> are steps up towers
> of perception. I exist
> in language I invent
> out of ruins.
> Out of the nameless sand wind
> scatters as my soul.[34]

The Johannine prologue is a poetic, neon, light-filled bridge between this world and the world above. Like John, the poem seeks a voice, a crying-out, witnessing voice, which twists, ruins, and invents words in order to perceive the word.

[33] Amiri Baraka, "State/meant," in William J. Harris, ed., *The LeRoi Jones/Amiri Baraka Reader* (New York: Thunder's Mouth, 1991) 169, from Baraka's *Home: Social Essays* (New York: William Morrow and Co., 1966). The full text of this poem appears in the Appendix, 146.

[34] Sterling D. Plumpp, "Poem," in Major, ed., *The Garden Thrives*, 216–17, from Plumpp's *Johannesburg & Other Poems* (Chicago: Another Chicago Press, 1991).

A word that receives such a twist is "flesh": Willful, manly flesh cannot (be)get godly children, but worded flesh is gloriously and gracefully true. It is no surprise that "flesh" or "skin" is also prominent in twentieth-century African-American poetry. Black flesh, in the world of white America, is evil-worded, not-known and not-received. Sekou Sundiata writes in his poem "Blink Your Eyes" about an instance of being stopped for "DWB," driving while black.

> Up to the window comes the Law
> with his hand on his gun
> what's up? what's happening?
> I said I guess
> that's when I really broke the law.
> He said a *routine, step out the car*
> a routine, *assume the position.*
> *Put your hands up in the air*
> *you know the routine, like you just don't care.*
> *License and registration.*
> Deep was the night and the light
> from the North Star on the car door, deja vu
> we've been through this before,
> why did you stop me?
> Somebody had to stop you.
> *I watch the news, you always lose.*
> *You're unreliable, that's undeniable.*
> *This is serious, you could be dangerous.*
>
> I could wake up in the morning
> without a warning
> and my world could change:
> blink your eyes.
> All depends, all depends on the skin
> all depends on the skin you're living in.[35]

Yes, it all depends on that skin, that flesh. The world, represented by "the Law," words this flesh as "unreliable" and "dangerous." The flesh is not known. As June Jordan writes in "Poem About My Rights: Do You Follow Me": "We are the wrong people of / the wrong skin on the wrong continent and what / in the hell is everybody being reasonable about . . ."[36]

[35] Sekou Sundiata, "Blink Your Eyes," in Bill Moyers, ed., *The Language of Life: A Festival of Poets* (New York: Doubleday, 1995) 398.

[36] June Jordan, "Poem About My Rights: Do You Follow Me," in E. Ethelbert Miller, ed., *In Search of Color Everywhere: a Collection of African American Poetry* (New York: Stewart, Tabori & Chang, 1994) 42, from Jordan, *Passion: New Poems, 1977–1980* (Boston: Beacon, 1980).

Langston Hughes' poetry often sounds a contradictory note concerning America as "home of the free" for whites but home of the non-free for African-Americans. In "American Heartbreak" he writes: "I am the American heartbreak / Rock on which Freedom / Stumps its toe . . ."[37] And then "The Black Man Speaks":

> I swear to my soul
> I can't understand
> Why Freedom don't apply
> To the black man.
>
> . . .
>
> Down South you make me ride
> In a Jim Crow car.
> From Los Angeles to London
> You spread your color bar.
>
> Jim Crow Army,
> And Navy, too—
> Is Jim Crow Freedom the best
> I can expect from you?[38]

For blacks, America is their own land, and Americans their own people, but like the enfleshed word among his own, black-fleshed people are rejected among their own.

African-American poets often look at their role as that of witnesses to the rejection their flesh experiences. In "Blink Your Eyes" quoted above, Sundiata refers to the "deep night" of injustice and the "light from the North Star" shining "on the car door." In commenting on this poem, Sundiata says,

> If we just go back to the days of slavery when it was illegal for the slave to bear witness against the slave master, then you can see that in this case I wanted to make that kind of testimony too. I wanted to call out against the injustice of that kind of treatment. I wanted to bring testimony, to bear witness to the importance of injustice.[39]

Similarly, Victor Hernandez Cruz says, "The purpose of the poet [is] to throw light on his or her individual [and community?] situation within

---

[37] Langston Hughes, "American Heartbreak," in idem., *The Collected Poems of Langston Hughes* (New York: Alfred A. Knopf, 1994) 348. The full text of this poem appears in the Appendix, 148.

[38] Langston Hughes, "The Black Man Speaks," in Hughes, *The Collected Poems* 288–89. The full text of this poem appears in the Appendix, 149.

[39] In Moyers, ed., *The Language of Life*, 398.

a human society."[40] Cruz and Sundiata, then, join John as witnesses to light in/on darkness.

Another poetic light-in/on-darkness witness is Lucille Clifton, who writes "at the cemetery, / walnut grove plantation, south carolina, / 1989":

> nobody mentioned slaves
> but somebody did this work
> who had no guide, no stone,
> who moulders under rock.
> tell me your names,
> tell me your bashful names
> and I will testify.
> . . .
> tell me your names
> foremothers, brothers,
> tell me your dishonored names.
> here lies
> here lies
> here lies
> here lies
> hear.[41]

Clifton testifies, witnesses. She tells their names, so people can believe in their names, and she says: "here lies . . . hear," so that people will no longer hear the lies but the truth, the full gracious truth.

Poetic light not only shines on darkness but also on persons who walk in darkness. Hughes echoes Johannine imagery in his "Walkers with the Dawn":

> Being walkers with the dawn and morning,
> Walkers with the sun and morning,
> We are not afraid of night,
> Nor days of gloom,
> Nor darkness—
> Being walkers with the sun and morning.[42]

Robert Hayden also speaks about the light emanating from "Monet's 'Waterlilies,'" which for him counters the dark events of the 1960s:

---

[40] Ibid. 107.

[41] Lucille Clifton, "at the cemetery, walnut grove plantation, 1989," in Moyers, ed., *The Language of Life* 85–86; from Clifton's *Quilting: Poems 1987–1990* (Brockport, N.Y.: BOA Editions, 1991).

[42] Langston Hughes, "Walkers with the Dawn," in idem., *The Collected Poems*, 45.

Today as the news from Selma and Saigon
poisons the air like fallout,
I come again to see
the serene great picture that I love.
Here space and time exist in light
the eye like the eye of faith believes.
        The seen, the known
dissolve in iridescence, become
illusive flesh of light
        that was not, was, forever is.

O light beheld as through refracting tears.
Here is the aura of that world
        each of us has lost.
Here is the shadow of its joy[43]

Hayden, like the godly children in the prologue, sees the light with "the eye of faith" and believes, and thus eternal "was" and "forever-is" light becomes flesh, giving a glimpse of that lost world, the world above.

This world, however, is dark, and one can merely glimpse the light through a painting, as Hayden says, or through an intimate relationship, according to Gloria C. Oden in her poem "Man White, Brown Girl and All That Jazz":

We were a happy consequence
to paths of darkness
in a world
no less terrible or strange
for all our years of toiling
through it.

I valued you for what I took.
That burning in you bright
illumined our collision;
your phosphorence still
must be reckoned with
when night
heretic with your memory
trespasses.[44]

---

[43] Robert Hayden, "Monet's Waterlilies," in Major, ed., *The Garden Thrives*, 49, from Frederick Glaysher, ed., *Collected Poems of Robert Hayden* (New York: Liveright, 1985).

[44] Gloria C. Oden, "Man White, Brown Girl and All That Jazz," in Major, ed., *The Garden Thrives*, 76, orginally appearing in *Poetry Northwest* (1973).

The heretical, trespassing night cannot overtake the light burning in the lovers.

Darkness, however, is also the color of African-American flesh, and another way to experience the light is by celebrating one's own dark flesh, as Hughes sings in his "Song":

> Lovely, dark, and lonely one,
> Bare your bosom to the sun.
> Do not be afraid of light,
> You who are a child of night.
>
> Open wide your arms to life,
> Whirl in the wind of pain and strife,
> Face the wall with the dark closed gate,
> Beat with bare, brown fists—
> And wait.[45]

This dark one is a lovely night-child, who must embrace light and life even in the midst of pain and darkness. Similarly, Gwendolyn Brooks writes in "Primer for Blacks":

> Blackness
> is a title,
> is a preoccupation
> is a commitment Blacks
> are to comprehend—
> and in which you are
> to perceive your glory. . . .[46]
> . . .
>
> The huge, the pungent object of our prime out-ride
> is to Comprehend,
> to salute and to Love the fact that we are Black.
> Which *is* our "ultimate Reality,"
> which is the lone ground
> from which our meaningful metamorphosis,
> from which our prosperous staccato,
> group or individual, can rise.[47]

---

[45] Langston Hughes, "Song," in idem., *The Collected Poems*, 45.

[46] Gwendolyn Brooks, "Primer for Blacks," in E. Ethelbert Miller, ed., *In Search of Color Everywhere: A Collection of African-American Poetry* (New York: Stewart, Tabori & Chang, 1994) 85–86; from Brooks, *Primer for Blacks* (Chicago: Third World Press, 1991). The full text of this poem appears in the Appendix, 147–48.

[47] Perhaps the "you" is both singular and plural, because the last line of the second stanza I have quoted speaks of "group or individual."

The God-faced word, the "ultimate Reality," is blackness, BLACKNESS, which must be comprehended, received as glorious. Doxology, then, is sung to black flesh. In this doxological poem the first stanza uses the second-person pronoun (singular or plural?): "*you* are to perceive *your* glory.*"* The poem's fourth stanza (the second one quoted above), however, uses the first-person plural: "*we* are Black . . . *our* 'ultimate Reality' . . . *our* meaningful metamorphosis . . . *our* prosperous staccato." Indeed, the Johannine prological poem has a similar pronomial progression: third-person plural "he gave *them* power" to first-person plural "the word . . . lived among *us,* and *we* saw his glory . . . *we* all have received grace upon grace." In both instances the poet joins in the celebration of the enfleshed word.

Another poet, Mari Evans, calls for celebration of black flesh in "Who Can Be Born Black?"

> Who
> can be born black
> and not
> sing
> the wonder of it
> the joy the
> challenge
>
> And/to come together
> in a coming togetherness
> vibrating with the fires of pure knowing
> reeling with power
> ringing with the sound above sound above sound
> to explode/in the majesty of our oneness
> our comingtogether
> in a comingtogetherness
>
> Who
> can be born
> black
> and not exult![48]

The poet summons the "we-ones" of black-worded flesh to come together, to become one, just as we(e) Johannine godly children are empowered and gathered into one by worded flesh.

---

[48] Mari Evans, "Who Can Be Born Black?" in Miller, ed., *In Search of Color Everywhere* 62, from Evans, *Nightstar* (Los Angeles: CAAS: University of California at Los Angeles, 1981).

This world does not accept dark flesh, but the enlightened are graciously transformed and see the flesh as glorious as they affirm themselves, participate in an intimate relationship, or celebrate with others in group solidarity. A poem that "embodies" many of the images and rhythms of the Johannine prological poem and their likenesses in African-American poetry is Jay Wright's "What Is Beautiful":

> Now I invest the world
> with the song of your flesh,
> song of your bones, your blood, your heart.
> I pitch all dark things still
> to the scale of my voice.
> I name what I distinguish.
> I discern what rises without a name.
> Here, there is no form untuned by eye, or voice;
> there is no body waiting for its metaphor.
> My canon gathers all the turnings
> of your light, all the offices
> and arguments of your soul's intent.
> Your body has a province in my two worlds,
> begins its own exchange in my eye.
> So as my music is exampled only
> in the movement, so is your body simplified,
> made absolute and able to bear
> the God's chill piping in your bones,
> his red eye scanning your skin.
> But I do not shape you two-in-one,
> or call you from the darkness,
> a scruffy thing, enhanced and visible
> only when the light leaves you.
> I turn you to the tuning fork of solid
> walls, my rolled corn, my tiled squares,
> the rose windows of my altars.
> I turn your ear, now transformed,
> to the imperfection of sacred things,
> your body's distant vibrations.
> And so each element of my song moves,
> and my voice takes back its absence,
> my eye searches a new light, another exchange.
> This is the gift of being transformed,
> the emptiness that calls compassion down.
> I pitch my eye to my uneven form,

my voice to the depths of your grace.
I reason with the sound and movement
of your body to the vision
    that my body bears."[49]

Exploring Likenesses to the Prologue in My Own Soul

The Johannine prological images and rhythms find many likenesses in African-American poetic images and rhythms. The soul of the prologue emerges in the soul of African-American poetry. But in what ways does it emerge in my own soul? Only a word—an enfleshed word—must suffice. In a word, I am a man of the word; I am a minister, teacher, and scholar: I preach, teach, read, and write words. Occasionally I, as well as my hearers and readers, succumb to the fantasy that my words come from above, either through divine revelation or scholarly research. My word, though, rises up from my flesh—my white, male, heterosexual, middle-aged, Midwestern, well-fed, well-clothed, highly educated flesh, which has been shaped by the white, patriarchal, religiously affiliated, wealthy communities of flesh of which I have been part. Though I am flesh from their flesh, these fleshly communities have not always received my fleshly word. I think of my parents, who often did not know how to receive my intellectually curious and emotion-laden words, and Southern Baptist Foreign Mission Board executives, who did not accept my historical-critical words. Though such words had brought me much light, others perceived them as darkness. My own people did not accept me and my fleshly word.

Now my wordy white flesh is found among black flesh, as I live, work, and worship among African-Americans. While my word (and thus flesh) has often been rejected by my world, their flesh (and thus word) has been rejected by the larger white world (flesh of my flesh). How does my participation in this community of world-rejected flesh (and word) shape my world-rejected word (and flesh)? How does my white-among-black fleshly word reject and/or accept their black-in-the-presence-of-white wordy flesh? How does my flesh become word?

I close this chapter with—what else?—a poem:

---

[49] Jay Wright, "What Is Beautiful," in Major, ed., *The Garden Thrives* 140, from Wright, *Selected Poems of Jay Wright*, ed. Robert B. Stepto (Princeton, N.J.: Princeton University Press, 1987).

In the beginning   and the end
is the flesh
   bony   bloody   sinewy sweaty
   smelly   shaky snotty

                             teary

flesh
What is the word? the word?
There is no word   no
word
Only
  flesh
mine
        and yours
  ours
gracious truth
God[50]

---

[50] My perspective in this poem and concluding word is much influenced by Naomi R. Goldenberg, *Returning Words to Flesh: Feminism, Psychoanalysis, and the Resurrection of the Body* (Boston: Beacon, 1990). See p. 6 for her discussion of the title.

    Unfortunately the provocative book by Alison Jasper, *The Shining Garment of the Text: Gendered Readings of John's Prologue* (Sheffield: Sheffield Academic Press, 1998), came to my attention as I was finishing this book. She offers a feminist analysis of five interpreters of the prologue: Augustine, Hildegard of Bingen, Martin Luther, Rudolf Bultmann, and Adrienne von Speyr. She then sets forth her own insights on the prologue, using the work of Julia Kristeva.

2

Word for Word:
Jesus' Conversations (John 2–4)

The word is now completely fleshed out. He has been John-the-Baptist-introduced (as lamb of God and son of God, 1:19-34) and has disciple-called ("Come and see!" 1:35-51). In this next section of the gospel (chs. 2–4) Jesus goes Cana-to-Cana (2:1; 4:46),[1] signing all the way (water-wining first, distance-healing second). He not only signs but also "words," conversing with Nicodemus first (3:1-21) and then the Samaritan (4:1-41).

Let's "fly by night" with Nicodemus so that we can be with the light of the world.

Nick at Night (John 3:1-21)

Now there was a person of the Pharisees
named Nicodemus,
a ruler of the Judeans.
He came to him at night and said to him,
"Rabbi,
we know that you are a teacher who has come from God,
for no one can do these signs that you do,
unless God is with you."
Jesus answered him,
"Amen amen I say to you,
unless one is born from above/anew,[2]
one cannot see the reign of God."

---

[1] Raymond E. Brown, *The Gospel According to John, I–XII*, AB 29 (Garden City, N.Y.: Doubleday, 1966) 95 calls this section of the gospel, which for him is Part Two of the Book of Signs, "From Cana to Cana."

[2] The Greek word used here, *anothen*, can be translated either "from above" or "anew." Here it probably has both meanings. Cf. Francis J. Moloney, *Belief in the*

Nicodemus says to him,[3]
"How can a person who is old be born?
One cannot enter into the mother's womb a second time
        and be born, can one?
Jesus answered,
"Amen amen I say to you,
unless one is born of water and spirit,
        one cannot enter into the reign of God.
What is born of the flesh is flesh,
and what is born of the spirit is spirit.
Do not marvel that I said to you,
        'You[4] must be born from above/anew.'
The wind-spirit[5] blows where it wants
and you hear its sound,
but you do not know where it is coming from or where it is going;
so it is with everyone who is born of the spirit."

Nicodemus answered and said to him,
"How can these things come to be?"
Jesus answered and said to him,
"You are a teacher of Israel,
and you do not know these things?
Amen amen I say to you
that what we know we speak
and what we see we bear witness,
and you[6] do not receive our witness.
If I said earthly things to you
and you do not believe,
how will you believe if I say heavenly things to you?[7]

Word: Reading John 1–4 (Minneapolis: Fortress, 1993) 110, who talks about the "temporal (again) and spatial (from above) meaning."

[3] The gospel often alternates past and present tense verbs in narration. I have preserved that in translation.

[4] The Greek word here, *humas,* is plural, while in the previous line it is singular, *se.*

[5] Like *anothen* mentioned above, the Greek word used here, *pneuma,* has a double meaning: it can mean either "wind" or "spirit." Cf. Moloney, *Belief,* 114.

[6] This "you" also renders the plural *humas,* as do the rest of the "yous" in the passage.

[7] It is difficult to know where Jesus' words end and the narrator's begin since no quotation marks appear in the original. Some interpreters hold that Jesus' speech ends here because this is the last appearance of "you." Cf. Rudolf Schnackenburg, *The Gospel According to John,* trans. Kevin Smyth, et al. (New York: Crossroad, 1968–82) 1:361, who contends that vv. 13-21 is a "kerygmatic exposition of the evangelist." It is more likely, however, that Jesus' speech continues through v. 21 because issues of belief, life, and judgment continue to be addressed. As Moloney, *Belief* 107, notes, the dialogue becomes a discourse.

No one has ascended into heaven
except the one who has descended from heaven,
the son of humanity.
Just as Moses lifted up the serpent in the wilderness,
so the son of humanity must be lifted up,
so that everyone who believes in him might have eternal life.
For God so loved the world,
that he gave his only-born son,
so that everyone who believes into him might not die
    but have eternal life.
For God did not send the son into the world
so that he might judge the world,
but so that the world might be saved through him.
The one who believes into him is not judged,
but the one who does not believe has already been judged,
because one has not believed into the name of the only-born
    son of God.
Now this is the judgment,
that the light has come into the world
and people loved the darkness more than the light;
for their works were evil.
For everyone who practices wickedness hates the light
and does not come to the light,
so that one's works might not be exposed;
but the one doing the truth comes to the light,
so that it might be revealed that one's works are worked in God."

Playing with the Images in the Conversation/Discourse

After gloriously Cana-signing-and-believing, Jesusanddisciples join Jesusmotherandbrothers in Capernaum (2:12). From there Jesus passes-over, passovers in Jerusalem (2:13), where he does some spring cleaning, some spring father's-housecleaning (2:14-16). The Judeans, passover-owners (2:13), demand that Jesus present his credentials—a sign—for doing this (2:18). (These are Judeans, not Galileans, and they have not seen the water-wining sign in Cana and believed into him, 2:11.) Jesus says that his credentialing sign is his raising up the destroyed temple, but the Judeans don't understand—these darkened ones don't comprehend the light (cf. 1:5)[8]—because they are thinking of the Herod stone-temple and not the Jesus body-temple (2:19-21). While these Jerusalemite Judeans do not believe, many others do into-his-name believe (and become godly children, 1:12?) because they sign-see (and

---

[8] Ugh! I wince each time I read John's vilification of the Judeans (usually rendered "Jews"), esp. as it has fed Christian anti-Judaism. But see below chapter 3 and the conclusion.

glory-see too, 2:11?). (What signs does Jesus do? More water-wining, distance-healing, paralytic-raising?) Though many believe into Jesus, he does not believe them because he knows all people (2:24). No need for a John-witness to testify, to shine the light on dark humanity, on the dark *anthrōpos* (cf. 1:6-8), for Jesus knows what is in the *anthrōpos* (2:25).

The spotlight shines on one particular darkened, Jesus-known *anthrōpos*, this one from the Pharisees. (The Pharisees sent interrogators to John, 1:24; now this Pharisee goes to interrogate Jesus.) He is named Nicodemus, Nico-Nico-Nicodemus. He is a ruler of the passover-owning, sign-demanding, misunderstanding Judeans (who are also Jesus-kill-seekers and devilchildren, 5:18; 8:44). He comes to Jesus at night. Nick at night. Night, the Judas-going-out-to-betray night (13:30). But Nick does not go out into the night; he comes out of the darkness into the light, for he is a truth-doer (cf. 3:21), or so it seems. So Nick the dark *anthrōpos* says to Jesus the light, "Rabbi, we sign-seeing, into-your-name believing Jerusalemite Judeans, of whom I am a ruler, know that you are a come-from-God teacher. (I am a teacher too, 3:10, and it takes one to know one.) No one does those undescribed and indescribable signs that you do unless God is with one" (and God, Jesus' father, is always with him, 8:16, 29; 16:32).

Jesus then says, "Amenamen Yesyes Trulytruly Verilyverily I say to you, come-by-night Nicodemus, unless one has been born from above/anew, from the spirit, from God (not from manly, willful, bloody flesh, 1:13), one cannot see God's kingly rule," in which Jesus reigns with God as king (cf. 12:12; 18:36). Jesus from-above comes (3:31), and a follower from-above is born. It is so even for a Judean ruler to see God's rule. No from-above birth, no reign-of-God seeing—no truly graceful, only-born glory-seeing (1:14). "Come and see," Jesus says (1:39). See, enter into the godly reign, the reigning God, eternal life, living eternal, the living reign of the eternal God. But only if one is from-above/newly born.

Nick, however, is still in the dark; he only sees the literal shadows of the night and not the metaphorical light of day. "How can an old *anthrōpos* enter into his mother's womb a second time and be born?" Nick speaks of a second birth, a birth anew but from below and not from above. Jesus is into his father's bosom (1:18) and comes from above; Nicodemus wants to be into his mother's womb and be born. But being born from above/anew is not from the earthly mother but from the heavenly father.

Jesus again amens and amens and says to the old born-from-below *anthrōpos*, "Unless one is born from water and spirit, spirited water, inspired water, watery spirit, watered spirit, flowing spirit, one cannot enter into God's reign." Not enter into a mother's womb but enter into the father's bosom, where Jesus is. Flesh begets flesh. (Does wordy flesh beget wordy flesh, 1:14?) And spirit begets spirit. And never the two shall meet!? Again the Johannine dualism dueling. (Is there such a thing as fleshly spirit, spirited flesh, enfleshed spirit, inspired flesh, indeed wordy flesh, enfleshed word?) Jesus says to Nick, "You fleshly, unspirited *anthrōpos*, don't marvel, or be a-mazed (in a maze), that I tell you that you sign-believing, untrustworthy *anthrōpoi* must be born from above/anew." Jesus then uses a from-below example to illustrate his from-above point: "The wind(spirit?) blowblowbloooows where it wants (a willful wind), and you fleshly *anthrōpoi* hear its sound, or its voice (crying in the wilderness through John, 1:23, now speaking at night through Jesus). But you do not know where it comes from (from above, from God) or where it goes (back to the world above, back to God, 16:28). That is the way it is with the one who is born from the spirit(wind?)."

Nicodemus, still in the dark, says, "How can these windy, spirited, birthing things come to be?" He is blown away by a stiff wind from above! Although he hears Jesus' voice, he does not know where the discussion has come from or where it is going. Jesus himself then marvels that Nicodemus is the Israelite teacher, yet he does not know these things. He is not a come-from-God teacher (like Jesus, 3:2), and therefore he is not a knower of these come-from-God things. (Teacher, teach thyself!) Indeed, Nick is from-below and worldly, who does not know the wordy light (cf. 1:10).

Jesus for a third time amensamens and says that the "we"-ones, the godly children who believe into the name of the light (cf. 1:12) speak what they know (the windy, spirited, birthing things) and witness (that is, light-witness, like John, 1:7-8) what they have seen (the glorious enfleshed word, 1:14); however, the worldly, fleshly *anthrōpoi*, whom Nick represents, do not receive their witness (cf. 1:11; 3:32: 5:43). Jesus says that he has spoken to them things earthly or earthy (about the wind?), which the *anthrōpoi* do not believe (they believe the signs, 2:23, but not the words), so it is doubtful that they will believe if Jesus talks about things heavenly. (But what has Jesus been talking about if not "things heavenly," like being born from above, from the spirit?) Jesus is from heaven, but Nick and his ilk are from earth (cf. 3:31). ("Heaven to earth. Do you read me?")

This earthy *anthrōpos* cannot believe things heavenly by ascending heavenward, for no one has done that (cf. also Deut 30:12; Prov 30:4), except the one who has descended earthward, the son of humanity *(huios tou anthrōpou),* and he ascends heavenward too (John 6:62). Upon him godly messengers ascend/descend (1:51). How de(s)cent of that son of humanity! Moses the lawgiver (1:17) in the wilderness uplifted (on a pole) the (poisonous) serpent (cf. Num 21:8-9), and in the world-wilderness the serpentine son of *anthrōpos* (poisonous to the world) must be lifted up (on a pole, i.e., a cross), so that all people, being drawn to him (12:32), might know the heavenly thing "I AM" (8:28) and believe and eternally live.

Through son-belief be life eternal . . . for the world. Jesus continues: The world is so God-loved (even though the world hates Jesus and his followers, 7:7; 15:18) that the only-born (born from above?) son (son of humanity? son of God?) is God-given (given to die!), so that into-him (that is, into-his-name, 1:12) believers might not be diers but be eternal livers. The son is not God-sent to world-judge but to world-save, that is, the world is God-saved through the only-born son. The world comes to be through the word (1:3); the world is saved through the son, who is the world-sav(i)or (cf. 4:42). Into-him believers are not judged; they experience no crisis.[9] But non-believers are already judged because they have not into-the-name-of-the-only-born-son believed (and thus have not become godly children, 1:13).

Jesus then defines the judgment, THE CRISIS: the light into-the-world comes, and the *anthrōpoi* are darkness-lovers rather than light-lovers (they don't even know the light, 1:10, much less love it). They love darkness because they are evil deed-doers. Every wickedness practitioner is a light-hater and a light-stay-awayer, so that the light might not expose their evil deeds and wicked practices. (That would be an inde(s)cent exposure!) Truth-doers are light-comers, and the light reveals that their deeds are deedeedeeded in God. LIGHTS! CAMERA! ACTION . . . in God!

Jesus finishes his speech, now a monologue rather than dialogue. But where is Nicodemus? Nick, oh, Nick, Ni-co-de-mus. He has certainly not ascended into heaven, nor has he reentered his mother's womb. Apparently the wind from above has blown him back into the night. Is Nick after all a darkness-lover? As a truth-doer he came to the light, but now in the light have his evil deeds been exposed? Light Jesus, the only-born son of *anthrōpos,* shines in the midst of dark Nick, the born-from-below *anthrōpos,* and the darkness has not comprehended the light (cf. 1:5).[10]

---

[9] The Greek word usually translated "judgment" is *krisis,* from which is derived the English word "crisis."

[10] Nicodemus comes to light again in 7:50 among the chief priests and Pharisees, and in 19:39 when he brings a hundred pounds of spices to Jesus' tomb. David Rensberger, *Johannine Faith and Liberating Community* (Philadelphia: Westminster, 1988) 39–40, briefly discusses these passages and concludes that Nicodemus is "a man of inadequate faith and inadequate courage" (40). Jouette M. Bassler, "Mixed Signals: Nicodemus in the Fourth Gospel," *JBL* 108 (1989) 646, says that Nicodemus is a "marginal" figure, who from the standpoint of the Johannine community is still an outsider.

*Exploring Likenesses to the Conversation/Discourse
in African-American Poetry*

Light/darkness, birth from above/birth again, spirit/flesh, descent/
ascent: The primary images in Jesus' poetic discourse are oppositional;
one image is affirmed, the other denied. Dueling dualisms! In twentieth-
century African-American poetry, however, these dualisms are decon-
structed: light is seen in darkness, spirit is experienced in flesh. For
example, darkness and night are affirmed as a way to affirm the black
flesh. Langston Hughes has a number of poems in this vein. He writes
in "The Negro": "I am a Negro: / Black as the night is black, / Black
like the depths of Africa. / . . ."[11] and in "Me and My Song": "Black /
As the gentle night / Black / As the kind and quiet night / . . . / Kind
/ As the black night / . . . / Beautiful / As the black night / . . . ."[12]
(Cf. also his "Song," quoted in the previous chapter.)[13]

The night, however, stands over against the day, just as black stands
over against white. Amiri Baraka writes:

> We are unfair, and unfair.
> We are black magicians, black art
> s we make in black labs of the heart.
>
> The fair are
> fair, and death
> ly white.
>
> The day will not save them
> and we own
> the night.[14]

Like light and darkness, spirit and flesh are also presented as polar
opposites by Jesus. Yet spirit also is experienced through the flesh, as
shown in a poem by Countee Cullen. He takes the title, "The Wind
Bloweth Where It Listeth," from John 3:8 in the King James Version.

---

[11] Langston Hughes, "The Negro," in idem., *The Collected Poems of Langston Hughes* (New York: Arnold A. Knopf, 1994) 72. The full text of this poem appears in the Appendix, 150–51.

[12] Langston Hughes, "Me and My Song," in idem., *Collected Poems* 296–97. The full text of this poem appears in the Appendix.

[13] See above, chapter 1, 149–50.

[14] Amiri Baraka, "State/meant," in William J. Harris, ed., *The LeRoi Jones/Amiri Baraka Reader* (New York: Thunder's Mouth, 1991) 170, from Baraka, *Home: Social Essays* (New York: William Morrow and Co., 1966). The full text of this poem appears in the Appendix, 146.

"Live like the wind," he said, "unfettered,
   And love me while you can;
And when you will, and can be bettered,
   Go to the better man.

"For you'll grow weary, maybe, sleeping
   So long a time with me;
Like this there'll be no cause for weeping;
   The wind is always free.

"Go when you please," he would be saying,
   His mouth hard on her own;
That's why she stayed and loved the staying,
   Contented to the bone.

And now he's dust, and he but twenty,—
   Frost that was like a flame;
Her kisses on the head death bent, he
   Gave answer to his name.
. . .

Her grief is crowned with his child sucking
   The milk of her distress,
As if his father's hands were plucking
   Her buds of bitterness.
. . .

He may be cursed and be concerned
   With thoughts of right and wrong,
And brand with "Shame" these two that burned
   Without the legal thong.
. . .

Still, she's this minted gold to pour her,
   This from her man for a mark:
It was no law that held him for her,
   And moved his feet in the dark.[15]

The wind does blow where it wills, and here it has fanned the flame of passion between these two lovers. The windy spirit, more so than the stagnant law, has burned these two together and brought about birth, rebirth, and death.

   Spirit sparks a love relationship with another, but it also sets one free to be one's true self, as Keorapetse Kgositsile writes in his "Spirits Un-

[15] Countee Cullen, "The Wind Bloweth Where It Listeth," in Clarence Major, ed., *The Garden Thrives: Twentieth-Century African-American Poetry* (San Francisco: Harper Perennial, 1996) 44–45, from Cullen, *Copper Sun* (New York: Harper & Brothers, 1927).

chained." The author writes that he and others walk against evil, oppressive Spirit-killers to the "rhythm of guts / blood black, granite hard / and flowing like the river or the mountains." This rhythm to which they walk, he concludes, "is the rhythm of unchained Spirit / will put fire in our hands / to blaze our way / to clarity to power / to the rebirth of real men."[16] The spirit here is expressed in "guts, blood, and fire." In flesh. As in Jesus' poetic conversation with Nick, it leads to rebirth, rebirth of authentic humanity. This is a birth from above. A birth from the spirit and the flesh. Light from darkness.

Exploring Likenesses to the Conversation/Discourse in My Own Soul

And my own rebirth/birth from above, my own light in darkness? While I was writing this book, two daughters were born from their mother's womb. The first was named Anastasia, our own "resurrection," our own rebirth, birth from above, and the second Miranda, our wonderful, wondrous one. ("How can these things come to be?") Furthermore, in the last several years I have been enlightened through being plunged into darkness through my participation in a black community, black university, and black church. My own dark presuppositions, privileges, and prejudices have come to light. I am judged; it is a crisis. Sometimes I cannot breathe, but breathe I must . . . deeply and then feel in my flesh the wind of the spirit.

Breathe.

Living Watery Woman (John 4:4-42)

> Now he had to go through Samaria.
> So he comes into a Samaritan city called Sychar,
> near the field that Jacob gave to his son Joseph.
> Jacob's well was there.
> Then Jesus, tired from the journey, sat down at the well.
> It was about the sixth hour.
> A woman from Samaria comes to draw water.
> Jesus says to her,
>   "Give me a drink."
> His disciples had gone away into the city to buy food.
> The Samaritan woman says to him,
>   "How can you, a Judean, ask a drink from me, a Samaritan
>   woman?"

[16] Keorapetse Kgositsile, "Spirits Unchained," in idem, *My Name Is Afrika* (New York: Doubleday, 1971) 85.

For Judeans did not associate with Samaritans.
Jesus said to her,
  "If you knew the gift of God and who is the one saying to you,
      'Give me a drink,'
  you would have asked him,
  and he would have given you living water."
The woman says to him,
  "Master, you do not have a bucket
  and the well is deep;
  where then do you get this living water?
  Are you greater than our father Jacob,
  who gave us the well and drank from it along with his sons
      and his cattle?"
Jesus answered and said to her,
  "Everyone who drinks from this water will be thirsty again;
  but those who drink from the water that I give them
      will never ever be thirsty,
  and the water that I give will become in them a well of water
      springing up into eternal life."
The woman says to him,
  "Master, give me this water,
  so that I might not be thirsty or come here to draw."

He says to her,
  "Go call your husband and come here."
The woman said to him,
  "I don't have a husband."
Jesus says to her,
  "You answered well when you said,
      'I don't have a husband';
  for you have had five husbands,
  and the one you have now isn't your husband;
  you have spoken truly."
The woman says to him,
  "Master, I perceive that you're a prophet.
  Our ancestors worshiped on this mountain;
  but you say that the place where people must worship is in
      Jerusalem."
Jesus says to her,
  "Believe me, woman:
  the hour is coming when you will worship the father neither on this
      mountain nor in Jerusalem.
  You worship what you don't know;
  we worship what we know,
  because salvation is from the Judeans.
  But the hour is coming and now is,
  when the true worshipers will worship the father in spirit and

    truth,
for the father seeks such people who worship him.
God is spirit,
and the ones who worship must worship in spirit and truth."
The woman says to him,
    "I know that Messiah, who is called the Christ, is coming;
    when he comes, he will tell us all things."
Jesus says to her,
    "I am, the one who is speaking to you."
At this his disciples came and were amazed that he was speaking
    with a woman,
though no one said,
    "What are you looking for?" or
    "Why are you speaking with her?"
Then the woman left her water jar and went away into the city and says
    to the people,
    "Come see a person who told me everything I have done.
    This isn't the Christ, is it?"
They went out of the city and were coming to him.

Meanwhile the disciples were asking him,
    "Rabbi, eat."
He said to them,
    "I have food to eat that you don't know anything about."
The disciples said to one another,
    "Nobody has brought him anything to eat, have they?"
Jesus says to them,
    "My food is to do the will of him who sent me and to complete his
      work.
    You say, don't you,
      'Four months more, and then the harvest comes'?
    Look, I say to you,
    Lift up your eyes and see the fields, for they are white for harvest.
    Now the harvester has a reward and gathers fruit for eternal life,
    so that the sower and the harvester might rejoice together.
    In this way the word is true:
      'One is the sower, and the other is the harvester.'
    I sent you to harvest what you didn't work for.
    Others have worked, and you have entered into their work."

Many Samaritans from that city believed into him because of the word
    of the woman who witnessed:
    "He told me everything that I had done."
So when the Samaritans came to him, they asked him to stay with them.
And he stayed there two days.
And many more believed because of his word.
They said to the woman,

"We believe now not because of what you said,
for we have heard and seen for ourselves that
this man is truly the savior of the world."

Playing with the Images of the Conversation

Jesus leaves Nick (though apparently Nick has already left him) and goes baptizing in the Judean countryside, where John also is and johndisciples come to the master to master this problem (3:22-26). Non-messianic John is also nonbridegroom but the voice-rejoicing bride-groomfriend, who decreases at the increasing Jesus, the from-abover, the fatherloved God-word witness, the unmeasured-spirit-and-eternal-life-giver (3:27-36). This Jesus hears that the Pharisees hear that he is a bigger baptizer than John (though surprise! Jesus really wasn't the baptizer but his disciples) and Judea-leaves in order to Galilee-go. But gotta-go through Samaria. ("Gotta?" Why? Don't gotta. Could go around Samaria, through Perea. Is this a God-gotta? Let's luke.[17])

After being in the Judean country for awhile, Jesus is now Samaritan citified, near the Jacob-gift-to-Joseph field (a portion more than his brothers, taken by sword and bow from the Amorites, Gen 48:22, or bought from the sons of Hamor for a hundred moneypieces, where he had tent-pitched, Gen 33:18-19; Josh 24:32) and where the Jacobwell is. (What well is that? Only one associated with Jacob in the Jewish Scripture is the well at which he met his future wife Rachel, Gen 29:1-20.[18] But that well is not in Samaria. We'll have to dig for this one!) So we are in Jacob (true Israelite, John 1:51?) territory. Perhaps a ladder-from-heaven-to-earth-for-angelic-descending/ascending should be constructed here? (Gen 2:12).

Jesus, journeytired, sits down at the well at the hour six (either Jewish noon or Roman dusk). A woman from Samaria comes to draw water. This Samaritan water-drawing woman has no name; let us call

---

[17] In Luke Jesus often says that it is necessary *(dei)* for him to do something (2:49; 4:43, etc.), but in John such a statement only appears one other time (3:14).

[18] The connections between betrothal scenes and John 4 have long been noted. For representative works see Craig R. Koester, *Symbolism in the Fourth Gospel: Meaning, Mystery, Community* (Minneapolis: Fortress, 1995) 48, n. 30. More recently see Adeline Fehribach, *The Women in the Life of the Bridegroom: A Feminist Historical-Literary Analysis of the Female Characters in the Fourth Gospel* (Collegeville: The Liturgical Press, 1998), who argues that the Samaritan woman is depicted "as a fictive betrothed and bride of the messianic bridegroom on behalf of the Samaritan people, as a symbolic wife to Jesus who produces abundant offspring after Jesus plants the seeds of faith in her" (47). Teresa Okure, *The Johannine Approach to Mission: A Contextual Study of John 4:1-42* (Tübingen: J.C.B. Mohr, 1988) 87–88 doubts this, however, as does Moloney, *Belief* 138–39, n. 29.

her "Sam." "Sam-I-am," she says (though Jesus also says, "I am"). Sam comes to water-draw (and husband-meet?) from the Jacob-well. (Well?!) Jesus says to her (since he is the Abrahamic servant at the well, Gen 24:17), "Gimmedrink (from the father's cup, John 18:11; I'm thirsty; I hope you're not going to give me vinegary water, 19:28-29)." Why doesn't he ask his disciples? Oh, they are citified for a grocery-run (which seems to be their job, John 6:5). Sam say (not Rebecca-like, "Drink, master," Gen 24:18, but) "How can YOOOOOOOU a JUUUU-UUDEEEAN ask MEEEE a SA-MAR-ITAN woman for a drink?" Waddya expect me to say, "Hi, I'm Sam, and I'll be your server. What would you like to drink?" No, Judeans don't have NOTHIN' to do with Samaritans, nononohuhuhnoway. (The Judeans' Godsoul detests the Shechem fools, Sir 50:25-26.) Jesus says, "If you knew the Godgift (not the Jacobgift (the field) but the Godgift—the godson, given to die! John 3:14-16) and who it is that's saying to you, 'Gimmedrink' (the fleshy word, the come-from-above one, 1:14; 3:31), you woulda asked him, who woulda given you living water—lively water, alive water, flowing water, watery life, flowing life," unmeasured spirited water (3:34; 7:39), belly-flowing river water (7:38).[19] Fountains that God's people have rejected, digging out cracked, non-water-holding cisterns (Jer 2:13). Flowing living waters from Jerusalem (Zech 14:8).

Jesus asked Sam for a drink—of well-water (well!?); she should have asked him for a drink—of living water. Instead, Sam says, "Master/sir, you got no bucket, and the well's deepdeepdeep. How you gonna get this livinglivelyaliveflowing water? Are ya greaterGreaterGREATER than our Jacob-father (and Abraham-father, John 8:53), the well-giver (Well?!) and well-drinker, along with his cattlesons?" Jesus: "Every this-well-water-drinker will be an again-thirster. (Pantpantpant! My tongue is dry.) But the water-I-will-give-drinker will be a neverever thirster; the I-will-give-water will become a well gugugushshshing upupup toward eternallife (WELL!?)." (This eternally living water is breaded, fleshly, and bloody, raising believers up and not letting them die, 6:27, 35, 50-51, 53-58.)

Sam smacks her lips and says, "Sir/master, now *you* gimmedrink / gimmeTHISwater." (She now asks Jesus to be her server, for she is a deer longing for flowing streams, Ps 42:1. At least Judeans associate with Samaritans on this point: they both ask Jesus to give them this life-giving bread and water, John 6:34.) Sam says that she doesn't want to be a thirster (Sam's got it; she understands about the living water) or a

---

[19] For a detailed discussion of water in the gospel see Koester, *Symbolism*, 155–84. See also Larry Paul Jones, *The Symbol of Water in the Gospel of John*, JSNTS 145 (Sheffield: Sheffield Academic Press, 1997).

here-to-draw-comer (Oh-oh! No, she doesn't got it; she still MISunderstands—<u>ms</u>understands). She still wants that flofloflowing Jacob-well-
water, not the alively Jesus-spirit-water. Her cistern is cracked and
doesn't hold the living water (Jer 2:13). There she is, Sam the Samaritan
woman in the dark with Nick the Judean teacher-ruler. Samaritans also
associate with Judeans in misunderstanding.

Jesus tells her to go husband-call, but Sam says that she ain't got no
husband, and Jesus says, "That's right. Have had five husbands (one
for each book of the Pentateuch? five foreign nations settled in Samaria,
2 Kgs 17:24?) and current man not your husband." Sam obviously does
not come to the well in order to find a husband, because she's had
plenty of them. (After all, Jesus is a what's-in-everyone knower, John
2:24-25. Unlike many commentators, however, Jesus does not condemn
the woman.[20]) Sam's impressed with Jesus' knowledge and says, "Hey,
I think that you, Judean, are a prophet (maybe even the prophet-to-
come, 6:14)." Her congenitally blind eyes have been opened (9:17).
(There's something about living water that flows right into saying
Jesus is the prophet, 7:40.)

"Because you know these things, I have a theological question to ask
you," Sam says. (Hmm, she is as astute as Nick in discussing theology.)
"It's a mountain of a question. Our Samaritan ancestors mounted up and
worshiped here at Mount Gerizim (where Moses set the blessing, Deut
11:29; 27:12), but you Judeans say that Jerusalem is the gotta-worship
place, to which the Judean tribes go up (Ps 122:1-5)." Jesus tells Sam to
believe him and says that the coming hour will be a father-worshiping
(and dead-raising, John 5:25-29) hour, neither this-mountained nor
jerusalemed. Place is not important! You Sams don't-know-worship.
They're all agnostics! (But don't the Samaritans father-worship the God
of Jacob, Joseph, and Jesus? Maybe they don't really know whom they
worship because they don't know Jesus. Sounds awfully parochial,
though.) We know worship (because we speak what we know and you
don't accept it, 3:11, but who are we? who are you?) because salvation
is Judean.

---

[20] See Gail R. O'Day, *Revelation in the Fourth Gospel: Narrative Mode and Theological
Claim* (Philadelphia: Fortress, 1986) 67–68, and Luise Schottroff, "The Samaritan
Woman and the Notion of Sexuality in the Fourth Gospel," in Fernando F. Segovia,
ed., *"What Is John?"* Vol. II. *Literary and Social Readings of the Fourth Gospel*, SBL
Symposium Series 7 (Atlanta: Scholars, 1998) 158–59 for a discussion of the misogy-
nistic interpretation of this verse. Schottroff goes on to discuss the "real life" of the
Samaritan woman. She writes, "We must conclude that the Samaritan woman had
to marry repeatedly for economic and social reasons. . . . In what Jesus says about
the woman's successive marriages, we can discover no hint of condemnation of her
actions" (163–64).

Judean?! JUDEAN!!!??? Is this a joke? The Judeans do not receive Jesus' and his followers' witness! Indeed, they seek to kill Jesus! (5:18) Salvation is not from the Judeans any more than it is from the Samaritans. Rather, salvation is from the God-sent-into-the-world son (3:17), the Godgift. And that saving, father-worshiping, (resurrecting) coming hour is NOW (the Jesus-sitting-by-the-well noon now, 4:1, 6), when worshipers will not only worship truly but truth-fully and spiritually. The father is seeking such worshipers. (What do you seek? 1:38.) God's spirit, and Godworshipers gotta worship in spirit (which Jesus gives immeasurably like water, 3:34; 7:37-39) and in truth (which Jesus is, 14:6). Sam says that she knows that Messiah-Christ (the Lord's anointed judge-king, 1 Sam 2:10; Ps 2:2) is coming (and Andrew says that he's found him, John 1:41). This Messiah will not only be a comer but an all-thing teller. Jesus, the Messiah-Christ who has come and has been all-things-telling her, says, "I am." I AM. IIIIIIIIIIIIII AM. The Messiah-Christ, who will come as the true spiritual father-worshiper, is the I AM speaking to her.

The disciples return from their grocery run, amazed that I AM speaking with a woman. ("We thought that he was too tired and hungry to talk to anyone.")[21] But they don't say anything. They don't ask him what he's seeking (the father's will, always, 5:30) or why he's speaking with her (because he's gotta, in order to give her living water). When the disciples come, Sam leaves. (Maybe she doesn't want to amaze them anymore.) She leaves her water jar there. (Is she coming back? Or maybe she's just so amazed herself that she's forgotten it. Hey, maybe she still thinks that lively-water-giving means no more well-water-drawing.[22]) Both unjarred and jarred, she goes to the city, saying, "Comesee comesee comesee (Philip-like, 1:46) this all-things-I've-done sayer. (All things you've done? All he did was tell you that you've had five husbands and you're with a non-husband now. Indeed, now you're with Jesus, who's offered you living water. Have you drunk it?) This can't be the Messiah-Christ, the coming all-things teller, can it can

---

[21] Schottroff, "Samaritan Woman," discusses the oft-repeated statement that the disciples are surprised because in first-century Palestine Jewish men did not speak to women in public, based on a rabbinic statement (*m. Aboth* 1.5). She writes, "Contrasting Jesus with the rabbis who would not speak with women is one of the older topoi of Christian anti-Judaism" (166). She contends that the disciples are surprised at the simple fact that he was speaking to anyone, because he was so exhausted (167).

[22] Ibid. 169, contends that her leaving the water jar indicates that she is leaving the relationship in which "she continues to live as a prisoner dependent upon a man who exploits her and will not even marry her."

it canit?" (Martha: Heck yes, it is, the Messiah-son-of-God, the coming into-the-worlder! 11:27.[23]) So now the cityfolk become uncitified to come see Jesus.

But first it's the disciples' turn to talk with Jesus. They rabbi him (not messiah) to eat the cityfood they've brought. ("Hi, I'm Peter, and I'll be your server/servant. Would you like a footwashing with that?") But Jesus asked for a drink not food. This wait-staff is no better than the Samaritan. Jesus tells them that he has food they don't know anything about. (They may worship what they know, but their rabbi eats what they don't know. They're gastronomical agnostics!) The disciples wonder if anyone has slipped him some food on the side. (The disciples, like the early Sam, also misunderstand about food/water.) Does Jesus have a "secret server"? In a way he does: God. And the food that God supplies Jesus is to senderswill-do (which, after all, is the reason that he's heaven-come-down as living bread, 6:35, 38, and that he justly judges, 5:30) and to work-complete (which Jesus does on the cross, 19:28, 30, thus Godglorifying, 17:4, and father-sent-him witnessing, 5:36).

The disciples have a saying about four months 'til harvest, but Jesus says that they ought to lift their eyes (to heaven? 11:41; 17:1) and see the white (the light has shone on them), harvest-ready fields. (See the Sams coming from the city?) The hour has come: the seed has fallen into the earth and died, therefore bearing much fruit (12:24). So the harvester goes out in the field and is rewarded through gathering together (into one, through the cross, 11:51-52) eternally living fruit. This fruit can be plucked from the tree of the garden so that one can live forever (Gen 2:16-17; 3:22). The seed-planter and the fruit-harvester whoop it up together, so that they can prove another saying about one being planter and another harvester. Sam is the planter, sowing seeds of proclamation in the city, and the disciples are the harvesters, reaping eternal-life fruit among the cityfolk. (The disciples apparently didn't witness while they were in the city; they just went to grocery-shop.) The sent Jesus sends the disciples (into the world, John 17:18, breathing on them the spirit, 20:22) to gather the fruits that they didn't work for; others have worked, like Sam, whose food (and water) is to complete Jesus' work, and the disciples enter into their/her work.

The result of Sam's work is that many Sams believe into Jesus because of her womanly witness, which, like John's witless witness, leads people to believe (1:7). The Samaritan cityfolk ask Jesus the coming Christ to remain/stay/dwell/abide with them (so that the descending

[23] Cf. Ingrid Rosa Kitzberger, "'How Can This Be?' (John 3:9): A Feminist-Theological Re-Reading of the Gospel of John," in Segovia, ed., *"What Is John?"* 2:24–25, on how the character of the Samaritan woman is developed further in Martha.

dove-like spirit might abide with them, 1:32, and they might abide in the true vine and much-fruit-bear, 15:1-4), and he does, for two days. And manymany more believe, this time not because of Sam's word but because of Jesus' word, and they say to Sam, "We're now believers not because of what you said but because of what we've heard and seen from him. We have come and seen! We know (and we worship what we know) that this one, this Judean prophetic Christ is the world's savior (and savor)."[24] Through this God-sent one the world is saved (3:17); salvation is from him and not the Judeans. Andrew stays with Jesus and then says that he's messiah (1:39-41); the Samaritans stay with Jesus and call him savior. For them the hour—the coming spiritual, truthful father-worshiping hour—now is.

How does Sam respond? Maybe she says, "This can't be the savior of the world, can it?" Like Nick, she faded into the darkness from which she came. But what's happened to Sam? She has become dispensable, "deprived of her missionary achievement by her townsfolk."[25] Does she join this group of saved Sams? Does she remain on the outside, still the "other"? Oh, I think I see her over there, at another well, trying to engage someone in theological discussion. What is that she's saying? "Gimmedrink."[26]

Exploring Likenesses of the Conversation in African-American Poetry

Water, water everywhere, not just in this story but throughout the gospel: water changed into wine, living water, supposed troubled healing water, and bloody water flowing from Jesus' side. "There was much water there" (3:23). Yes, there is also much water in African-American poetry. I immediately think of the spiritual "Wade in the Water" ("Wade in the water, children / God's gonna trouble the water.") This spiritual, like many others, alludes to a number of different Scripture

---

[24] For an extensive treatment see Craig R. Koester, "'Savior of the World' (John 4:42)" *JBL* 109 (1990) 665–80.

[25] Kitzberger, "'How Can This Be?'" 34.

[26] Gary A. Phillips, "The Ethics of Reading Deconstructively, or Speaking Face-to-face: The Samaritan Woman Meets Derrida at the Well," in Edgar V. McKnight and Elizabeth Struthers Malbon, eds., *The New Literary Criticism and the New Testament* (Valley Forge, Penn.: Trinity Press International, 1994) 312, writes, "The text presents the feisty Samaritan woman's refusal to engage Jesus in an exchange relationship (in contrast to the normative Rebecca and Hagar)—as a sign of *another way* to engage the otherness of the gift of life and the otherness of the text itself that the text narrates theoallegorically [and] *another way* to be a responsive disciple and a responsible reader whose resistance and non-compliance reaffirms the alterity of the gift of God that lies outside of all theological categories."

references: the Hebrews' crossing the Red Sea, Jesus' baptism, and the man at the pool of Bethzatha. In the story of the Samaritan woman, God (in Jesus) does trouble the water that Sam has come to draw, and Jesus encourages her to wade into the living water that he gives.

Another spiritual: "Deep River": "Deep river, my home is over Jordan, / Deep river; I want to cross over into camp ground."[27] Langston Hughes perhaps echoes this spiritual in his classic poem "The Negro Speaks of Rivers."[28] He says that through ancient, old, dusky river-knowledge his soul "has grown deep like the rivers." He has obtained this knowledge through Euphrates-bathing, Congo hut and Nile-pyramid building, and Mississippi muddy bosom singing. Similarly, Sterling D. Plumpp says that the "Mississippi griot," who emits dark seeds of prophecy, "had the river inside him." From this inner flowing river he takes civil rights activist Emmet Till's decomposing body and those of other nameless black victims who have been interred in the river. This river runs down through Plumpp's eyes and pen, leading him to confess, "The river is my history."[29] Jesus' living water too, tells Sam of her history, and that water flows into her mind, soul, and jar.

Carolyn Rodgers, in "how i got ovah," says that she has "shaken rivers / out of my eyes." In crossing these rivers "her ancestors' dark root fingers" have grabbed, pulled, rocked, cupped, and carried her.[30] ("Are you greater than our ancestor Jacob?" "Our ancestors worshiped on this mountain.") Sam's ancestors carry her too, from the well and over the mountain to the spiritually true worshiping water of Jesus. Both Rodgers and Sam have been baptized in these rivers.

Water flows in African-American poetry not only in rivers but also in seas and oceans. Kiarri T.-H. Cheatwood, in her "Visions of the Sea," writes of a shore wedding: "From him came the Sea / and / from her came the Ocean."[31] She continues, "To these waters came the shores . . . to know the healing salts of tired and hungry souls." Also the anointer came ("This can't be the messiah, can he?") She writes, "In their running together, the Ocean and the Sea / procreated the Anointer and with him visions beyond // the transient realm of peace." Also, "In this time, words were not dead things / useless and without resonance of meaning they too / knew the / purity of the waters and lived

---

[27] Anonymous, "Deep River," in Dudley Randall, ed., *The Black Poets* (New York: Bantam, 1971) 26.

[28] Langston Hughes, "The Negro Speaks of Rivers," in Jerry W. Ward, Jr., ed., *Trouble the Water: 250 Years of African-American Poetry* (New York: Mentor, 1997) 121, from Hughes, *The Collected Poems.*

[29] Sterling D. Plumpp, "Mississippi Griot," in Ward, ed., *Trouble the Water,* 387–90.

[30] Carolyn Rodgers, "how i got ovah," ibid. 437.

[31] Kiarri T.-H. Cheatwood, "Visions of the Sea," ibid. 504.

. . . and lived." This water, sea from Jesus Anointer, ocean from Sam, enlivens words and gives peace.

Primus St. John often plunges into the sea in his poetry. In "Sunday" he writes, "The sea has its own religion," and he thinks of swimming out in prayer and never struggling back in doubt.[32] In another place he says that in deciding to marry a woman he has come to believe in "the ocean of our streams of story / That has made us join our hearts . . ."[33] and in "Song" he sings, "Fishermen / Pursue the sea / As if it were / A naked woman." He continues, "The fishermen / Are able to find / In the essential qualities / Of the plain deep water itself / That source / For the silence in themselves, / For their ecstatic gasps of joy / And their pruned, unwilling / Sighs of loss."[34]

River water, sea water, also well water (Well!). Joseph Seamon Cotter, Sr. says that a "fancy" brought him to "The Way-Side Well."[35] He did not come to drink, tryst, rest, or muse. (Sam came to her way-wide well to drink: to draw water for drinking, to be precise. And Jesus came to rest. He asks Sam for a drink, presumably from the well. Thus they begin their tryst, a prophetic, messianic tryst. In the context of this well tryst, they begin to muse—about water and about worship.) Cotter drops a pebble in the well and questions it for his "secret." What secret does he have? He keeps it secret even from the reader. Perhaps it has to do with "the heart at the mile's end," which is "food for his being" (just as Jesus' food is to do his sending fatherswill). "Ah," Cotter says, the well is dry. He continues on his journey, concluding that "hearts are like wells. You may not know that they are dry 'til you question their depths." Yes, yes. Jesus questions not the well, which is deep, but the heart of Sam, which is also quite deep. And Sam questions Jesus, who has a deep heart too, and from his heart flow livingwater streams. Cotter concludes that "saints miss their crown," but this saintly Sam, deep-hearted as she is, did not miss her crown, for she drinks the wateroflife and father-worships truly and spiritually.

Each time I read this story, I am impressed with the character of (the) Sam(aritan woman). She is a strong woman, who is not afraid to go toe

---

[32] Primus St. John, "Sunday," in E. Ethelbert Miller, ed., *In Search of Color Everywhere: A Collection of African-American Poetry* (New York: Stewart, Tabori & Chang, 1994) 122.

[33] Primus St. John, "Ocean of the Streams of Story," in Major, ed., *The Garden Thrives*, 198, from St. John, *Love is not a Consolation; It is a Light* (Pittsburgh: Carnegie Mellon University Press, 1982).

[34] Primus St. John, "Song," in Major, ed., *The Garden Thrives*, 201–2, from St. John, *Dreamer* (Pittsburgh: Carnegie Mellon University Press, 1990).

[35] Joseph Seamon Cotter, Sr., "The Way-Side Well," in Ward, ed., *Trouble the Water*, 59.

to toe with this prophet-messiah. She could sing Maya Angelou's refrain: "I'm a woman / Phenomenally. / Phenomenal woman." Angelou goes on to say, "Men can't touch / My inner mystery."[36] Sam is a phenomenal woman, and no man, not even her five husbands, have apparently touched her inner mystery. But at the well Jesus plumbs her depths.

African-American women have had to affirm themselves over against the double whammy of racism and sexism. Mari Evans proclaims, "I / am a black woman / tall as a cypress / strong / beyond all definition still / defying place / and time / and circumstance / assailed / impervious / indestructible / Look / on me and be / renewed."[37] Sonia Sanchez traces her own conversion in "Young Womanhood," in which she says, "I lost myself / down roads / I had never walked." She then saw a vision in which she was confronted by three faces. "i moved away from reconciling to / murderers / and gave myself up to / the temper of the times." Sanchez "woke up alone / to the middle sixties / full of the rising wind of history // alive in a country of echoes."[38] She also says in "Towhomitmayconcern," "watch out for the full moon of sonia / shinin down on ya. / get yo / self fattened up man / you gon be doing battle with me."[39]

Exploring Likenesses of the Conversation in My Own Soul

Water water everywhere, and not a drop to drink. Water water, water woman, what-a woman is Sam. Drinking the living water. My living water? Sometimes I feel so dry, so dry, especially now as I write this, coming out of a chemical depression. I have searched for the living water; sometimes I find it in writing (poetry, journaling, this book), sometimes in family time with Miranda, Ana and Joy. For example, I find it in a family swim, where I swim laps, bob with my family, and finish off in the spa. Living water. Living. Springing up around me and within me.

Also: women women everywhere and not . . . not what? What not? Women everywhere in my life. Here at home I am outnumbered. Three females and only one lonely male. My own family of origin survives with me and my mother. My wife's family of origin: father died when

[36] Maya Angelou, "Phenomenal Woman," in Miller, ed., *In Search of Color Everywhere* 84, from Angelou, *And Still I Rise* (New York: Random House, 1978).

[37] Mari Evans, "I am a black woman," in Miller, ed., *In Search of Color Everywhere* 81, from Evans, *I Am a Black Woman* (New York: William Morrow, 1979).

[38] Sonia Sanchez, "young womanhood," in Ward, *Trouble the Water*, 287–90, from Sanchez, *A Blues Book for Blue Black Magical Women* (Detroit: Broadside Press, 1974).

[39] Sonia Sanchez, "towhomitmayconcern," in Ward, ed., *Trouble the Water*, 293, from Sanchez, *Under A Soprano Sky* (Lawrenceville, N.J.: Africa World Press, 1987).

she was a teenager, three sisters and one brother. Women, women. I feel caught in an eddy, in which a strong current propels me toward women, and another pushes me away. Witness only one serious romantic relationship with a woman prior to meeting my wife, whom I married when I was thirty-seven after dating for three years. Witness also my many female friends throughout my life. Witness finally my article favoring women ministers, which contributed in some measure to my firing as a Southern Baptist foreign missionary.[40] Witness. Witness. Women water. Female flood. Sometimes I feel cleansed, other times drowned.

[40] See the Introduction above, xxvi–xxvii. Initially my supervisor asked for my resignation based on the article, "Opposition to Women Ministers Is Unforgivable Sin" [not my title!], *SBC Today* (April 1988), but as the process went on the charges shifted to "doctrinal ambiguity."

3

My Word against Your Word: Jesus' Disputes with the Judeans (John 5–8)

The word is now fully worlded. Some have received him (believed into this glorious sign-er, confessing him as messianic world-saver) and become childrenofGod (been from-above-born, drunk lively water). Most of the world, however, did not know or accept him. These are the Judeans (hiss-boo), who have already reared their ugly heads in sending priestly Levites to interrogate John and in challenging Jesus' father'shousecleaning. In this, the largest section of the gospel (chs. 5–12), Jesus continues signing (paralytic-healing, bread-making, sight-giving, and dead-raising), but while earlier disciples believed, now Judeans misunderstand and try to kill him. Judeans get riled up not only because he's sabbath-working but also because he's fatherGod-talking, equalizing himself with God, and IAMtalking. All of this happens during festival (unidentified, passover, tabernacles, dedication), (party hardy! party hardly!) and most of it happens in or near Jerusalem. (Exception: Galilean breadmaking.) Not much of a city of peace for Jesus and the Judeans!

This chapter and the next look at five sections in which Jesus is locked in bitter debate with the Judeans. In this chapter are three sections: first, discourse about Father and Son working, which follows the healing of the paralytic at Bethzatha pool; second, bread of life discourse, which follows the loafmultiplication; third, light of the world discourse.

We pick up the action at a festival in Jerusalem, where Jesus heals a paralytic on the sabbath, provoking Judean persecuting/seeking to kill Jesus.

Like Father, Like Son (John 5:19-47)

Then Jesus answered them,
  "Amen, amen I say to you,
  the son cannot do anything on his own except what he sees the
    father doing,
  for whatever the father does, the son does likewise.
  The father loves the son and shows him everything that he is doing,
  and he will show him greater works than these,
  so that you will be amazed.
  Just as the father raises the dead and gives life,
  so also the son gives life to whomever he wants.
  For the father judges no one,
  but he has given all judgment to the son,
  so that all will honor the son as they honor the father.
  The one who does not honor the son does not honor the father who
    sent him.

  Amen, amen I say to you,
  the one who hears my words and believes in the one who sent me
    has eternal life
  and does not come into judgment,
  but that one has gone from death into life.

  Amen amen I say to you,
  the hour is coming and now is
  when the dead will hear the voice of the son of God,
  and those who hear it will live.
  For just as the father has life in himself,
  so also he has given to the son to have life in himself.
  And he has given him authority to execute judgment,
  because he is the son of humanity.
  Do not be amazed at this,
  because the hour is coming
  when all who are in the tombs will hear his voice and come out.
  Those who have done good will come out into the
    resurrection of life,
  and those who have practiced wickedness will come out into the
    resurrection of judgment.

  I can do nothing on my own.
  Just as I hear I judge,
  and my judgment is just,
  because I do not seek my own will but the will of the one
    who sent me.

  If I witness to myself, my witness is not true.
  There is another who witnesses to me,

and I know that his witness to me is true.
You sent messengers to John,
and he has witnessed to the truth.
But I do not accept a human witness,
though I say these things so that you might be saved.
John was a lamp that burned and shone,
and you wanted to rejoice for a time in his light.

But I have a witness greater than John's,
for the works that the father gave me to complete,
which are the very works that I am doing,
witness to me that the father sent me.
And the father who sent me has witnessed to me.
You have never heard his voice or seen his form,
and you do not have his word abiding in you,
because you do not believe in the one who sent me.
You search the scriptures,
because you think that you have eternal life in them,
but they witness to me.
Yet you do not want to come to me so that you might have life.

I do not accept glory from humans,
but I know that you do not have the love of God in you.
I have come in the name of my father,
and you do not accept me.
If another comes in his own name, you will accept him.
How can you believe when you accept glory from one another,
and you do not seek the glory that comes from the only God?

Do not think that I will accuse you to the father;
there is one who accuses you: Moses, in whom you have hoped.
If you believed Moses, you would believe me,
for he wrote about me.
But if you do not believe his writings,
how will you believe my words?"

Exploring the Images of the Discourse

It was festival time (yippee!): what festival we don't know, but a Judean festival, and after all, salvation is from the Judeans (4:22). (Right!) This is the first of several significant festivals in this section of the narrative, in which Jesus signs and discourses. Next come Passover (6:4), Booths (7:2), and Dedication (10:22). So for this unidentified festival Jesus leaves Galilee to goes up (upUpUP) to Jerusalem (though actually Jesus has already come DOWNDowndown from above, 3:13, 31). In Jerusalem Jesus has already passed-over, fathers-house-cleaned, and signed (2:13-23). This time the good shepherd (10:11, 14) goes to the Sheep Gate (in search of his own sheep?) and by the pool gives living water (4:10) to a thirty-eight-year paralytic. But it's a non-mat-carrying sabbath, and the Judeans decide to feast on this healed man and on Jesus. Thus begins the Judeans' persecuting, kill-seeking of the sabbath-working Jesus, who says that his father is a still worker (a steelworker? No, a still worker. Making moonshine? No, making son-shine—gloriously!), and he's a still worker too (though the water which Jesus gives is flowing not still). It's "still" the sixth day of crea-tion for Jesus and his father. No sabbath rest for them. Like father, like son. (But what about the son's mother? Is she not a "working mother"? Is she a "stay-at-home mom," and does Jesus not consider that work? Or maybe at the Cana wedding Jesus has divorced his mother: "Woman, what's it to me and to you?" [2:4]. With this divorce the father gets custody and thus becomes a single parent.) When Jesus says "my father," he's not talking about Joseph (1:45; 6:42) or Jacob (4:12) or Abraham (8:39) but God. (Jesus establishes a "fictive kinship" with the source of all that is. He is attempting to ground—or better, "sky"—his authority for sabbath-working. Jesus has a father complex, or at least a complex father! Now that Joseph is no longer on the scene, has Jesus projected his "ideal father" onto the heavens?) Jesus, then, is not just a sabbath-breaker but a godfather-caller and thus a God-equalizer (though the Judeans themselves call God their father, even though Jesus says that it's really the devil, 8:41-44). He must die!

Thus begins Jesus' capital offense trial in the Judean capital.[1] Jesus of course defends himself (he is the first paraclete, 14:16). He first amena-mens (as he did to Nicodemus, 3:3, 5, 11) that the son can't do anything (no way, hunh-unh) but what he sees (and hears, 5:30) the father doing. (No more "my father/I" but "the father/the son.") He is the apprentice learning from the master's "sign" shop.[2] (He has a ringside seat be-cause he is in the father's bosom, 1:18.) The father does it, the son does it. (Indeed, it is the son-abiding father doing his fatherly works, 14:10.) The father is a son-lover and thus a son-everything-shower (and son-everything-giver, 3:35). And this son-loving father gonna show the son greaterworks than these paralytic-healing (5:2-9), distance-fevered-

---

[1] Cf. A. E. Harvey, *Jesus on Trial: A Study in the Fourth Gospel* (London: SCM, 1972); Jerome H. Neyrey, *An Ideology of Revolt: John's Christology in Social Science Per-spective* (Philadelphia: Fortress, 1988). Also cf. Craig R. Koester, *Symbolism in the Fourth Gospel: Meaning, Mystery, Community* (Minneapolis: Fortress, 1995) 88–89 for a brief discussion of how this speech follows established patterns of Greco-Roman judicial rhetoric.

[2] Cf. C. H. Dodd,"A Hidden Parable in the Fourth Gospel," in idem, *More New Testament Studies* (Grand Rapids: Eerdmans, 1967) 30–40.

son-healing (4:46-54), and water-wining (2:1-11) works, and you (the Judeans and the reader) will be a-mazed (in a maze). ("How can these things come to be?" the a-mazed Judean ruler Nicodemus said, 3:9.) This amazing, greater-working father is a dead-raiser and a give-lifer (not the make-deader and give-lifer of the Jewish scripture, Deut 32:39; 1 Sam 2:6; 2 Kgs 5:7) and the son is a dead-lifer and a give-raiser too. (So hold on, Lazarus, the son gonna raise you, John 11:43-44! Indeed he gonna raise himself, 10:17-18!) This dead-raising father is not a judger, but he's given all judging to the son (who says that he judges no one, 8:15), so that the son will be all-honored (all people drawn to him, 12:32) as the father is all-honored. (All rise, the honor-able son of the father now presiding as judge!) Those non-honoring the son (i.e., the Judeans who want to kill/stone/crucify Jesus) non-honor the father too. Hate son, hate father (15:23).

Jesus amenamens againagain and says that the Jesusword-hearer/ Jesussender-believer is a non-judged death-to-life goer. (They to-the-light come and are from-above born as children of God, 1:12; 3:3, 21.) Amenamen say: Coming hour (the hour of truthful, spiritual father-worshiping, 4:23) IS, when dead (sheep) hear the (goodshepherding) godson-voice and come out into (the green pastures of) life (10:3). The father is a life-in-himself (living light, light living, 1:4; 8:12) father, and he's son-given that life, as well as POWER to judge, because the father-son is also the humanson, the descending-ascending, lifted-up, glorified, dying lifegiver (3:13; 6:27, 53, 62; 8:28; 12:23; 13:31). Jesus tells them (and us) not to be (from-below) amazed at this (from-above word). (Be amazed at the coming greater works, not the present living word.) The coming hour will be also the in-the-tombs coming-out hour (Ya listenin', Lazarus?), do-gooders coming out into resurrected (eternal) life, do-badders coming out into resurrected judgment. (The Hebrew prophetic vision resurrected! Day of the Lord Isaiah: "Your dead will live, their corpses will rise," 26:19. Valley of dry bones Ezekiel: "I am going to open your graves, and bring you up from the graves," 37:12. Day of Deliverance Daniel: "Many of those who sleep in the dust of the earth shall awake, some to everlasting life and some to shame and everlasting contempt," 12:2.)

Jesus the son can't do nothin' on his own (Nothing, nada, just like Godsent Moses, Num 16:28). He's now back to where he started, with the "do-nothing" son (cf. John 5:19). But this time it's "I" again instead of "son" (cf. 5:17). Jesus hears (and sees); he just judges (as son-of-humanity, 5:27). He's not his own will-seeker but his sender's will-seeker. (That's the food that nourishes him, 4:34. That's the reason he's heaven-come-down, 6:38.) Now Jesus/God not father/son but I/ sender. (Music: "Darling, yoooooooooooou send me.")

But Jesus can't be his own witness, for his self-witness is not true. (The Pharisees' witness at this point is true for once, 8:13.) Hey, he needs at least two non-self witnesses (Deut 17:6; 19:15). The first one that he calls is John, who gives true witness. ("Do you swear to tell the whole truth and nothing but the truth, so help you God?" "So help me God? I was sent from God!" John 1:9.) The Judeans sent messengers (Jerusalem priests and Levites, 1:19) to him, and he truly truthfully witnesses (I AM NOT Messiah, Elijah, or prophet, 1:19-21; Jesus I AM the lambofGod/son-of-God! 1:29, 34). Jesus doesn't need a human witness (he's got a divine one), but he wants his listeners to be saved (for which he into-the-world came, 3:17; 12:30). He says therefore that the human witness-ing John was a burning, shining lamp (but not the true light of the world, 1:8), in whose light the Judeans wanted temporarily to whoop it up. But Jesus' second non-self-witness is even better than John: his healing, wining works, which are the son's homework from the father, done in the father's name (10:25). They witness that Jesus is fathersent (and that he is in the father as the father is in him, 10:38; 14:11). And this sending father is also a witnessing father. Jesus therefore has a third non-self-witness (he does the law one better), which is even better than his own works: his father (Do they swear him in? ". . . so help you (gulp) God!?"). The Judeans haven't fathersvoice heard (though they will later and think that it's angelic thunder, 12:28-29), and they haven't fathersform seen (though Jesus the son has, 1:18). And they don't have fathersword dwelling in them (though Jesus is the fathersfleshedword dwelling among us, 1:14), because they're Jesussender non-believers, who scripturesearch (searching for life, even though Jesus I AM the life, 14:6), but the scriptures—like the father, like John, like Jesus' works—are witnesses to Jesus. (Philip had it right: Jesus is the one about whom Moses and the prophets lawfully wrote, 1:45.) The Judeans (who are dead) don't come (out of their tombs) to Jesus to be life-havers.

Jesus is a human-glory-nonaccepter (he accepts glory only from God) because they don't have Godlove in them (and Jesus knows what's in them, 2:24-25). Jesus the son in the fathersname comes, but they don't accept him (even though they are his own, 1:11) any more than he accepts their glory. They accept an own-name-comer and one another's glory, but they don't God's glory seek (instead they Jesus kill seek, 5:18; 7:19).

Jesus will not fatheraccuse them; he's only his own defense counsel. Their accuser, their prosecutor, will be Moses the law-giver (1:17, but not bread-giver, 6:32) and serpent-lifter (3:14), even though he is their hoper. (The Mosaic law then serves as a witness against them, Deut 31:26.) But they neither really hope nor believe in Moses, because if they did they would believe in Jesus because Moses wrote about him.

(How so? When Moses said that the lord God would raise up a prophet like him, Deut 18:15?). They don't believe Moseswritings, they don't then believe Jesuswords.

Exploring Likenesses to the Discourse in African-American Poetry

Father son. Father-son. Fatherson. Robert Hayden remembers "Those Winter Sundays" of his boyhood when his father would rise early to warm up the rooms and polish his shoes. Hayden says that he spoke indifferently to his father. He concludes, "What did I know, what did I know / of love's austere and lonely offices?"[3] The father loves the son and gives him all things (John 3:35), at least warmth and shine, love and glory.

E. Ethelbert Miller stands next to the sink as "My Father Is Washing His Face." He admires his father's young face and says, "I am happy when someone says / I look like my father or when my / father reminds me to wash my face / and I reach for the soap in his hand."[4] Similarly, Jesus says, "The one who has seen me has seen the father" (John 14:9). He takes the soap from his father's hand and washes the believer's face and feet so that one can see and be clean.

Lenard D. Moore remembers "My Father's Ways":

> I.
> You perch me on a stool
> like a blackbird on a branch,
> teach me time tables
> that multiply like rabbits.
>
> II.
> You take me to football games,
> coach me, draw plays
> in symbols
> on metal bleachers.
>
> III.
> You walk through your garden,
> farmer, harvesting crops;
> you name plants, show me
> how to harvest.

---

[3] Robert Hayden, "Those Winter Sundays," in E. Ethelbert Miller, ed., *In Search of Color Everywhere: A Collection of African-American Poetry* (New York: Stewart, Tabori & Chang, 1994) 130, from Frederick Glaysher, ed., *Collected Poems of Robert Hayden* (New York: Liveright, 1985).

[4] E. Ethelbert Miller, "My Father Is Washing His Face," in idem, *Whispers Secrets & Promises* (Baltimore: Black Classic Press, 1998) 37.

IV.
You mold me into
a potter spinning clay
in circles,
shaping bowls and vases.

V.
Now, full-grown,
like a tree rooted deep,
I bend forward into the light
of your voice in prayer."[5]

The father teaches the son "time tables" (the hour is coming and now is) and coaches him in playing with the symbols (light and darkness?). The father goes into the garden (tomb?) to witness, to name the vine I AM, and to show the son how to harvest, for "the fields are ripe for harvesting" (4:35). The father molds the son into a clayspinner, anointing people's eyes to give them sight. The vine is now full-grown, deeply rooted in the farming father, and prays for glorious light.

In another poem Moore celebrates "Black Father Man," whom he calls "the supreme earth dweller" and "the word-music messenger." He continues, "We are his ripe black crop / at the-beginning-of-the-harvest. . . . We are his grace black note / at the four-beating-of-the-song."[6] Here the role of the father takes on the role of the Johannine son, who, as the word (incarnate) messenger, is the earth dweller. Believers are harvested crop and experience in the son grace and truth, grace upon grace.

In a poem in the same volume Javaka Steptoe, who illustrates the book, writes of "Seeds" his father planted. Steptoe says that he not only listened but also ate his father's words so that he grew, "branches, leaves, flowers, and then the fruit." Steptoe says that he "became" his father's words, concluding that "the apple doesn't fall far from the tree."[7] (It certainly doesn't, for Steptoe is the son of children's book artist John Steptoe.) Again, the words the son takes from the father are not only heard but also eaten, and the son becomes the devoured words. He grows like a tree (the true vine?) and abiding in the father produces branches and fruit. (Must they be cleansed and pruned?)

The father lives on in the son not only in fullness but also in emptiness, as E. Ethelbert Miller inhales "The Gray Smoke of Clubs." He

[5] Lenard D. Moore, "My Father's Ways," in Gloria Wade-Gayles, ed., *Father Songs: Testimonies by African-American Sons and Daughters* (Boston: Beacon, 1997) 201.

[6] Lenard D. Moore, "Black Father Man," in *In Daddy's Arms I Am Tall: African Americans Celebrating Fathers,* illust. by Javaka Steptoe (New York: Lee & Low, 1997) 8.

[7] Javaka Steptoe, "Seeds," in *In Daddy's Arms I Am Tall,* 23.

writes, "I live my father's life / the absence of joy in the / center of responsibilities / the dark streets of early mornings / when he finds his way home / to a life already lost."[8] The son here is doing only what he sees the father doing, but his joy is not completed but absent, not light but darkness, lost life (not abundant life) in the father's house.

In the father's house words strengthen, weaken, hurt, and heal. Yusef Komunyakaa served as scribe for "My Father's Love Letters" to his mother, in which his father "promised never to beat her / Again." As he dictated, he "would stand there / With eyes closed & fists balled, / Laboring over a simple word, almost / Redeemed by what he tried to say."[9] Almost, almost. Can he be redeemed through the word? The flesh has been weak. And the spirit? Can his word become enfleshed?

Exploring Likenesses in My Own Soul

Johannine fatherson. African-American poetic fathersons. Now my own experience of fatherson. I have long longed for the kind of father that Jesus had. This father loved the son, was one with him, and showed him what he was doing. My own father and I were very much two, for much of the time I did not know what in the world he was doing. He worked in a large agribusiness firm "in the city," which I rarely visited. He was an avocational carpenter, building cabinets, shelves, and desks, but he did not take me to his workshop to apprentice me. And then he became ill and died. Who would then be my father? I have been looking for him the rest of my life. At times I think that I have found him, in a pastor, teacher, administrator, or senior colleague, but ultimately these fathers have failed me, some more dramatically than others, probably because they were not my father and could not make up for my lack.

Early in my graduate education the Gospel of John became my father. (Good news!) In reading Jesus' words, I could vicariously experience his relationship with his father. I was the son, all-loved and all-shown and all-given by my all-powerful father. He illumined the darkness of my ignorance (through biblical criticism!) and put me in a community (professional society) of beloved disciples, whose eyes had also been healed of from-birth blindness. What a father (whose power was mediated through the fathers)!

---

[8] E. Ethelbert Miller, "The Gray Smoke of Clubs," in idem, *Whispers Secrets & Promises*, 39.

[9] Yusef Komunyakaa, "My Father's Love Letters," in Miller, ed., *In Search of Color Everywhere*, 168.

But this father failed me too. As I became sensitive to feminist concerns I was uncomfortable with the gospel's exclusive male language for God (always "father-son" never "mother-daughter"). As I became interested in the religious experience of believers outside of Christianity I found that this text seemed to negate anything outside of Christ ("No one comes to the father except through me," 14:6b). As I became aware of the church's role in anti-Semitism, pogroms, and the holocaust I saw how this gospel had contributed ("You are from your father the devil," Jesus tells the "Jews," as it is usually translated, 8:44). The gospel too had become a failed father.

Now I am a father. I attempt to show my daughters "all that I am doing." I do much of my work at home (on the same computer where Anastasia plays "Reader Rabbit"), and the girls frequently come to school. I take Anastasia to art class (my avocation). I realize, however, that I will fail these girls; indeed, I already have—in small ways, I hope. ("I'm sorry, honey; I don't think I can fix that toy.") But a father who sometimes fails does not a failed father make! James Hillman reminds me that "failing belongs to fathering."[10] The "all-things" that I give my children include my failures.

Knowing that I too will fatherly fail, can I then relate in a healthier, more forgiving, more egalitarian way to my failed fathers? Can I accept my failed fathers, whether teacher, colleague, or even text? Can I see them as friends and brothers, even fathers to a certain extent, without expecting them to be my "ideal father"? Can I enter into a dia-logue with them, going "through the word" of the father, analyzing, critiquing, and appreciating it while speaking to them my own word, which is different from their word?[11] Can I?

If so, then I think my father would be proud.

Breaded Life, Lively Bread (John 6:22-59)

The next day the crowd that had stood across the sea saw
that only one boat was there
and that Jesus had not gotten into the boat with his disciples
but only his disciples had gone away.

---

[10] James Hillman, "Oedipus Revisited," *Eranos Jahrbuch* 56 (1987) 280, quoted in Thomas Moore, ed., *Blue Fire: Selected Writings by James Hillman* (New York: Harper-Collins, 1989) 221.

[11] A provocative example of dialoguing with the gospel is Fernando F. Segovia, "Inclusion and Exclusion in John 17: An Intercultural Reading," in idem, ed., *"What Is John?" Vol. II, Literary and Social Readings of the Fourth Gospel,* SBL Symposium Series (Atlanta: Scholars, 1998) 183–211.

Now boats from Tiberias came near the place
where they had eaten the bread after the master had given thanks.
When the crowd saw that neither Jesus nor his disciples were there,
they themselves got into the boats
and went into Capernaum to look for Jesus.
When they found him across the sea,
they said to him,
> "Rabbi, when did you come here?"

Jesus answered,
> "Amen amen I say to you,
> You're looking for me not because you saw signs,
> but because you ate from the loaves and were satisfied.
> Don't work for the food that perishes, but for the food that remains
> into eternal life,
> which the son of humanity will give you.
> For upon him God the father has placed his seal."

Then they said to him,
> "What should we do so that we might be working the works of
> God?"

Jesus answered them,
> "This is the work of God,
> that you believe into the one whom he sent."

Then they said to him,
> "Then what sign do you do,
> so that we might see and believe you?
> What do you work?
> Our fathers ate the manna in the wilderness,
> as it is written,
> > 'He gave them bread from heaven to eat.'"

Jesus then said to them,
> "Amen amen I say to you,
> Moses did not give you the bread from heaven,
> but my father gives you the true bread from heaven.
> For the bread of God is that which descends from heaven and gives
> life to the world."

Then they said to him,
> "Master, give us this bread always."

Jesus said to them,
> "I am the bread of life;
> the one who comes to me will never be hungry,
> and the one who believes into me will never ever be thirsty.
> But I said to you that you have seen me
> and you do not believe.
> Everything that the father gives me will come to me,
> and the one who comes to me I will never cast out,
> because I have descended from heaven

so that I might not do my will but the will of the one who sent me.
This is the will of the one who sent me,
　that I might lose nothing of all that he has given to me,
　but I will resurrect it on the last day.
　This is the will of my father,
　that everyone who sees the son and believes into him might have
　　eternal life,
　and I will resurrect that one on the last day."

Then the Judeans began to grumble about him
because he said,
　"I am the bread that descends from heaven,"
and they were saying,
　"Isn't this Jesus the son of Joseph,
　whose father and mother we know?
　How can he now say,
　　'I have descended from heaven'?"
Jesus answered them,
　"Do not grumble among yourselves.
　No one can come to me unless the father who sent me draws one.
　And I will resurrect that one on the last day.
　It is written in the prophets,
　　'And they will all be taught by God.'
　Everyone who has heard and learned from the father comes to me.
　Not that anyone has seen the father except the one who is from God;
　he has seen the father.
　Amen amen I say to you,
　The one who believes has eternal life.
　I am the bread of life.
　Your ancestors ate the manna in the wilderness and died.
　This is the bread that descends from heaven,
　so that one might eat of it and not die.
　I am the living bread that descends from heaven.
　Whoever eats of this bread will live forever,
　and the bread that I give for the life of the world is my flesh."

Then the Judeans quarreled with one another, saying,
　"How can this one give us his flesh to eat?"
Jesus then said to them:
　"Amen amen I say to you,
　unless you eat the flesh of the son of humanity and drink his blood
　you do not have life in yourselves.
　The one who munches on my flesh and drinks my blood has eternal
　　life,
　and I will resurrect that one on the last day.
　For my flesh is true food,
　and my blood is true drink.

> Just as the living father sent me and I live because of the father,
> then that one who munches on me will also live because of me.
> This is the bread that descended from heaven,
> not as the fathers ate and died;
> the one who munches on this bread will live forever."
> He said these things while teaching in the synagogue in Capernaum.

Playing with the Images of the Discourse

Jesus is now passovering by the Galilean (that is, Tiberian) sea. (Jesus must have secretly "passed-over" from Jerusalem to Galilee because he was just there disputing with the Judeans, 5:19-47. The previous year he had in fact passed-over in Jerusalem and people into-him believed because they saw him signing, 2:13, 23). By the sea he is followed by a great 5000-crowd that has seen his healing signs. From a little lad's lunch Jesus loaves-and-fishes them, and again sign-seeing, the crowd wants to crown him, but he mountains up instead. That evening he water-walks to the boating disciples, and suddenly they land on land.

The next day THENEXTDAY the standing-on-the-other-side-of-the-sea crowd sees that while disciples were boated, Jesus was unboated. So they boat from near the crowd-ate-and-master-thanked-bread place (6:11) to Capernaum—that Jesus-and-family-and-disciples-abiding place/royal-official-sick-son-place (2:12; 4:46), on a Jesus-search (searching to kill him, 5:18?). They track him down on the sea-other-side. (But do they "sea" the other side of the miracle?) He's synagogue-teaching (6:59). They say, in their best misunderstanding-disciple- and-Nicodemus voice, "Rabbi/teacher (1:38, 49; 3:2; 4:31; 9:2), when did you get here to Capernaum, to the other-side? (We know that you didn't boat with the disciples. You didn't WALK-ON-WATER, did you!? HaHaHaHa!)"

This crowd is made up of darkened, born-from-below Judeans (cf. 1:5; 6:41; 8:23), who do not comprehend the enlightening, born-from-above Jesus. Jesus answers them in typically evasive, amenamen style (cf. 3:3). He doesn't ask them what they're looking for (1:38), because he knows what's in a person (2:24-25), and he knows (AMENAMEN) that they're not looking for him because they saw glory-revealing signs (cf. 2:11). (But the crowd did in fact see sick-healing and bread-multiplying signs, 6:2, 14, and they wanted to king Jesus-prophet. That's not the way to sign-see, for it must lead to into-Jesus-godson believing, cf. 2:11.) They are look-look-looking, all right, but only because they filled up on the lad's lunch loaves. Stomach FILLED . . . spirit empty! Jesus tells them not to loaf but to work—for the non-perishable food (i.e., needs no refrigeration, because Jesus has it and works for it, 4:32, 34) that abi-bi-bides (in the spirit, as a disciple, with Jesus the true vine, 1:33, 39; 15:1-11) into eternallife. This eternally abiding food (as well as springing-up-to-eternallife water, 4:14) is given by the descending-ascending, lifted-up, judging humanson (cf. 1:51; 3:14-15; 5:27; 8:28), who bears the godfather seal of approval (much better than Good Housekeeping™).

The crowd then asks what God-works they must work. Jesus says: Only work one God-work: believe into the God-sent one, the God-sealed godson/humanson, abiding-food giver. Believe into his name and become godchildren (1:12). The crowd then, in typical temple-Judean fashion (2:18), asks Jesus for a seeing-and-believing SIGN. After all, the Jerusalemites sign-saw and believed (2:23; 7:31), so unless this crowd sees signs and wonders they won't believe (cf. 4:48). A sign? Sigh! Waddatheywant? Saw sick-signs and followed (6:2); saw loaffish-sign and attempted to crowd-crown him (6:15). Another sign—to see and believe him!? They sign-see but do not glory-see and into-Jesus believe. These folk don't understand Jesus' sign-language!

The crowd then talks about their wilderness-manna-eating fathers. (The Samaritan fathered in her Jesus-conversation too, 4:12, 20.) After all, it is passover-time, and Jesus has just come down from a mountain and given bread to the crowd, leading them to proclaim him the coming prophet. Passover/exodus/wilderness/complaining/bread-fromheaven/"waddizit?"/MANNA! (cf. Exod 16). The crowd scripture-quotes: "he" gave them heavenbread (Ps 78:24). "He?" This crowd misunderstands not only Jesus but also the scripture: they think that the bread-giving "he" is Moses and that Jesus the Moses-like prophet (John 6:14; cf. also Deut 34:10-12) must in the same way sign so that they can see-and-believe. (But haven't they already seen such a sign in Jesus' loafing-and-fishing?) Jesus says that it wasn't Moses the law-giver, serpent-lifter, and Judean-accuser (John 1:17; 3:14; 5:45) who gave (past tense) them heavenbread, but it is Jesus' father, who, as true God/true vinedresser (cf. 15:1; 17:3), gives (present tense, keeping it *tense* between Jesus and the crowd) them the TRUE heavenbread. This heaven-bread/God-bread heavendescends (spirit-, angel-, and humanson-like, 1:32, 51; 3:14) and lifeworldgives (like the God-sent son, 3:16-17). This bread is truly WONDERbread!

The crowd, again taking the desiring-water-Samaritan voice (cf. 4:15), says, "Master (has Jesus now mastered and not just rabbi-ed them?), give us givegiveGIVE us give us always/all-ways/all the way this true/heavenly/godly/heavendescending/worldlifegiving BREADDDD!" They're hun-gry, hun-ge-ring for it. Bread-giving humanson Jesus says, "I am the bread of life." I am. I am. Always, everywhere, to everyone, Jesus says I AM. Sometimes just "I AM": Worship-discussing Samaritan says: "Coming Messiah"; living-water-giving Jesus says: "I AM, to-you speaking" (4:25-26). Boating disciples terrified; water-walking Jesus says: "I AM; no fear" (6:20). Believing devilchildren Judeans say: "Seen Abraham?" Judean-accusing Jesus says: "Before Abraham, I AM" (8:57-58). Other times, "I AM . . . (often significant image from Hebrew tradition): I AM the bread-of-life/light-of-the-world/gate/good-shepherd/resurrection-and-life/way-truth-and-life/vine (6:35, 48; 8:12; 9:5; 10:7, 11, 14; 11:25; 14:6; 15:1, 5). Usually life-ly images, *eternal*life-ly images. Jesus eternally saying I AM; in Greek *egō eimi*. Jesus is ego-centric, preaching his "I." (The synoptic Jesus is *basileia*-centric, preaching the reign, *basileia*, of God.) I AM. Moses' burningbushGod says: "I AM" (Exod 3:14); Isaiah's choosingcreatingGod says: "I AM" (Isa 43:10; 45:18). Now the heaven-descending, life-givingJesus says: "I AM . . . .

I AM the bread of life—living bread, lively bread, enlivening bread, unleavened bread—that rises up and raises up! Waddizit? Manna-man in the world-wilderness. A long-lasting manna of bread, which forever satisfies the to-Jesus comer's hunger. A watery manna of bread, which forever slakes the into-Jesus believer's thirst (cf. John 4:14; 7:37-38). The proverbial table-setting wisdom calls: "Come, eat my bread, drink my wine" (Prov 9:5; cf. also Sir 24:21). The everlasting-covenant-making God calls: "Ho (hohoho!), all thirsty ones come to the waters; and you no-money ones, come, buy, eat!" (Isa 55:1). Comers-to/believers-into-Jesus are heavenbread-hungerers no more, lively-water-thirsters no more. Hungrrrr no more, thirstrrrr no more. No more/nomore/ NOMORE.

The crowd, however, is still hungry/thirsty because they are seers yet still non-believers, even though they say that they want to be seers-*and*-believers (cf. John 6:30). Every God-to-Jesus-given thing (such as the disciples, 17:2, 6-9, 12, 24; 18:9) to-Jesus comes (cf. 6:44, 65), and no comer will be thrown out of this heavenbread/livelywater feast, because as heavendescender, Jesus is not a his-will-doer but a senders-will-doer (cf. 5:30); that is his food (4:34). The sender's will: lose no God-given thing (cf. 10:28; 17:12; 18:9), every son-seer-and-believer an eternallifer, and RESURRECT, raise up, stand up the God-given, seeing-and-believing thing ON THE LAST DAY, the resurrection-of-righteous/judgment-of-evildoers day (11:24; 12:48). The breaded Jesus from heaven comes down; the Jesus-comer from earth rises up. down and UP. downdown-down, UPUPUP! Jesus RAISES UP; he tomb-shouts, "Come out!" and the dead live (cf. 5:25-29; 11:43-44). (Martha, standing in the crowd: Hey, that includes my bro Laz, who after dying will be last-day raised up, 11:23-24.[12]) The resurrection and/of life. In the last day. Last *(eschatē)*

---

[12] Cf. Ingrid Rosa Kitzberger, "'How Can This Be?' (John 3:9): A Feminist-Theological Re-Reading of the Gospel of John," in Fernando F. Segovia, ed., *"What Is John?"* 2:28–29, in which she argues that Martha was part of the crowd that heard the "bread of life" discourse.

day. The eschaton. The hour is coming, and now is (5:25). The last day—today?

Jesus the heavendescending/resurrecting bread? The crowd goes back into their fathers' wilderness and grumblegrumbleGRUMBLES (cf. Exod 15:24; 16:2, 7-8; also John 7:32). (Their mouths and stomachs grumbling?) They know this guy as Jesus Josephson, from Galilee (cf. 7:27). (No, he is not; he is Jesus godson, from above, 1:14, 18; 8:23) And they claim to be knowers of his father and mother, but if they were really his-father knowers, they would also be Jesus-knowers (7:28; 8:19, 54-55). And if they were his-mother knowers, she would have undoubtedly told them to do whatever he says (2:5). But they are worldly, from below, and they don't know dontknow dunno that Jesus is the bread from above.

Jesus tells them not to wilderness-bread grumble. He adds that a to-him comer must be father-drawn as well as father-given (cf. 6:37), and this father (not Joseph but God) is a Jesus-sender (in order to be a world-savior, 3:17). Jesus last-day-resurrects the father-drawn Jesus-comer, as well as the father-given Jesus-believer (cf. 6:39-40). Jesus then resurrects the prophet Isaiah, who wrote: "And they all will be taught by God" (54:13; cf. Jer 31:33-34). Jesus-raised, God-taught. In returning from the Babylonian exile all the children will be taught, Isaiah says. Tots taught. God-taught tots. God-tots, born from above, from the spirit (John 1:12-13; 3:3-8). The God-tots are father-hearers, father-learners, and Jesus-comers. Come and see (1:39)! But they are not father-seers (or heaven ascenders, 3:13; 5:37); only the from-God one, the father's bosom buddy (1:18), the heaven-descending humanson (3:13) is a father-seer.

Jesus amenamens and says that the (into-him) believer is an eternal lifer (not an eternal dier, 3:15-16, 36; 11:25-26), for Jesus is breaded life. The Judeans' fathers were wilderness-manna-eaters and diers (cf. 6:30). (The Judeans haven't seen these fathers either.) But the heavendescending-bread-eater is not a dier! (Whoa, Jesus! You said that the Jesus-comer will be a raised-upper. In order to be a raised-upper, one has to be a dier first! So, is the lively-bread-eater a dier or not? Raise up our understanding—and not at the last day, but now!)

Jesus says againagainagain that he is the bread, the lively-heavenly-descending bread (cf. 6:33, 35, 38, 41). This bread-eater will be a forever liver (a never-dier or a dier-and-raised-upper?). A forever liver, a never-hungerer, never-thirster. Forever-ever-never. And the heaven-descending-enlivening bread that Jesus is and that Jesus gives for the lively world is his fleshfleshFLESH—flesh that is not useless (6:63), for it is Jesus' own wordy, only-father-born glorious, truly graceful, *dying*, lifted-up-on-a-pole flesh (1:14; 3:14; 12:32). Jesus' gift to the world: breaded flesh, fleshy bread. (A meat sandwich!?)

Jesus' breaded-fleshy word turns the Judean crowd not only against him but also against one another. "How can he give us giveus his flesh HISFLESH to eat?!?!?!?" They have asked that Jesus humanson give them lifegiving heavenbread (6:34), but when they hear that this bread is his flesh, they recoil. "How can these things come to be?" Nicodemus the Judean representative said (3:9). Through the humanson heaven-descending and being uplifted through death (3:13-14); this is how he draws allpeople to himself (12:32). Yet EATING his FLESH?! Eternal-lifers must be CARNIVORES?! CANNIBALS!? How can they stomach this? Jesus amenamens againagain and says that a life-haver must be a humansonflesh-eater and blood-drinker. (YUCK!) Is this the eucharist, communion, Lord's supper? If so, how can one givethanks . . . commune . . . Lord! sup? Not just eat Jesusflesh, but GNAW (gnaw? Naw!) . . . MUNCH?! Muncha buncha Jesusflesh! (UGH!) Jesusfleshgnawers/blooddrinkers are eternallifehavers, lastday-raiseduppers (cf. 6:39-40). (Throwuppers too!?) Jesusflesh true food, true bread (cf. 6:27); Jesus-blood (mixed with water, 19:34) true drink from the true vine, in which Jesus and his fleshgnawers/blooddrinkers abide (cf. 14:20; 15:1-11). (But who can abide this stuff?) Jesus is the living-father-sent-one (on the father's s(c)ent), and the Jesusgnawer lives because of him (cf. 5:26) —if one can stand the s(c)ent! Jesusflesh is the heavendescended bread, different from the fatherly-manna-eaters who were diers, and the heav-enly-fleshly-bread-gnawers will be forever-livers (cf. 6:49-50)! (One can hardly hear Jesusword because of the munching sound Jesusflesh-eaters are making: munchmunchmunchmunch.)

Jesus said all this while Capernaum-synagogue-teaching. He said it in a religious gathering?! But Jesus didn't gather them long but rather scattered them because they couldn't stomach his flesh-eating words (6:60, 66). (Music: "Gnaw-gnaw-gnaw-gnaw, naw-naw-naw-naw, hey-hey, goodbye!") But his death would gather them together again (11:52; 12:32), where they would feast on Jesusfleshandblood.

Exploring Likenesses to the Discourse in African-American Poetry

Jesus puts out quite a spread, and African-American poets have shared in its bounty. First, Jesus says I AM. This is not the first time that Jesus has I AMed (cf. 4:26; 6:20), but it is the first time that I AM becomes the thesis of a discourse. African-Americans too say I Am. In the midst of a society that would deny the identity of African-Americans, their poets have asserted I Am. Perhaps this is nowhere better expressed than by eleven-year-old Chela Robinson in her "I Am," which was placarded in Washington Metrorail stations as part of the "Metro Muses" project:

> I am a heart that is broken but
>   glued together by my
>   heart-brokers.
> I am a snake crawling and
>   searching through my soul.
> I am the river connecting with the
>   ocean.
> I am brown becoming a new
>   member of the rainbow
> I am the key to my answers which
>   unlock my door.
> I am words joining paper to poetry.[13]

Jesus I AM peaces-together stirred-up hearts (John 14:1, 27), and the crucified, serpentine one (3:14) snakes through the soul, saying, "What are you searching for?" (1:38) The I AM gives rivers of living water (4:14; 7:38), which open the door to the sheepfold (10:7, 9), and speaks words joining paper to poetry to proclamation (20:30-31).

Amiri Baraka speaks his I Am words and echoes Johannine language in his "The Invention of Comics":

> I am a soul in the world: in
> the world of my soul the whirled
> light / from the day
> the sacked land
> of my father.[14]

As long as Jesus' soul is in the world, I AM is light of the world (8:12; 9:5), whirled light, which comes from his father's land, the world above.

Before one can affirm I Am one must first affirm I Am Not. For example, Calvin Hernton writes: "I am not a metaphor or symbol. / This you hear is not the wind in the trees. / Nor a cat being maimed in the street. / I am being maimed in the street." The words that his mouth speaks are his words. Hernton concludes: "I am a poet. / It is my fist you hear beating / Against your ear."[15] So also Jesus is not a metaphor / symbol but a sign, the word. And what we hear is not the wind but the spirit (3:8) from the tree, where Jesus is being maimed (19:30). He

---

[13] Marcia Davis, "The Poetry Shop: Metro Gives Young D.C. Writers a Platform for Their Work," *The Washington Post* (January 30, 1997) D.C. 1.

[14] Amiri Baraka, "The Invention of Comics," in Clarence Major, ed., *The Garden Thrives: Twentieth-Century African-American Poetry* (San Francisco: Harper Perennial, 1996) 133, from Baraka, *The Dead Lecturer* (New York: Sterling Lord Literistic, 1964).

[15] Calvin Hernton, "The Distant Drum," in Major, ed., *The Garden Thrives*, 121, from Hernton, *MEDICINE MAN* (New York: Reed, Cannon & Johnson, 1976).

speaks the word because he is I AM. His voice, like John's, cries out in the wilderness (1:23). His mouth speaks his words, which are not only his but his father's too, and his nailprinted hand (20:20, 25, 27) writes them (on the ground, 8:6, 8). As I AM the poet, Jesus raises his hand up from the dust, balls it into a fist, beats it against the Judeans' ears.

Similarly, Bob Kaufman says in "I, Too, Know What I Am Not": "No, I am not death wishes of sacred rapists, swinging on candy gallows. / No, I am not spoor of Creole murderers hiding in crepe-paper bayous. / No, I am not yells of some assassinated inventor, locked in his burning machine." He concludes, "No, I am not anything that is anything I am not."[16] John the Baptist says "I am not" (1:20), so as to point toward the I AM.

The I AM is part of the here-and-now, but it also goes back in time, as Nikki Giovanni writes in "Ego Tripping (There May Be a Reason Why)":

> I was born in the congo
> I walked to the fertile crescent and built
>   the sphinx
> I designed a pyramid so tough that a star
>   that only glows every one hundred years falls
>   into the center giving divine perfect light
> I am bad[17]

Through Jesus the word, the I AM, all things came into being (1:3). And I AM baaaaaaaaad, telling people to his-flesh eat and his-blood drink. E. Ethelbert Miller talks about eating his father's flesh in "Bread":

> your father's skin
> was soft like butter
> my mother tells me
> after grace
>
> the two of us sit
> at the kitchen table
> where he once sat
>
> our food cools
> and we count
> our blessings

[16] Bob Kaufman, "I, Too, Know What I Am Not," in Major, ed., *The Garden Thrives,* 79, from Kaufman, *Solitudes Crowded with Loneliness* (New York: New Directions, 1965). The full text of the poem appears in the Appendix, 151–52.

[17] Nikki Giovanni, "Ego Tripping (There May Be a Reason Why)," in Major, ed., *The Garden Thrives,* 246, from her *The Women and the Men* (New York: William Morrow and Company, 1975).

share the bread
between us[18]

His father's skin, like Jesus' skin, was full of grace and truth (John 1:14). His mother ("Woman, here is your son." . . . "Here is your mother," 19:26-27) and he share the blessed bread, the breaded blessing ("Blessed are those who have not seen yet believe," 20:29). Their father, like Jesus', gives them true bread that comes down from heaven and gives life to the world (6:32-33).

In "Breaded Meat, Breaded Hands," Michael S. Harper describes the foods that his wife is preparing in the kitchen: peanut paste for the chicken, rock salt and snow for the homemade ice cream. Finally, he writes,

At the hearth of this house,
my woman, cutting the bits of guile,
the herbs of warmth she has butchered
into the pots,
the pans of grease
that feed this room, and our children,
condensed in the opaque room—
the hearth of this house
is this woman, the strength of the bread
in her hands, the meat in her marrow
and of her blood.[19]

Not through death but through life, "this woman" not only prepares food but becomes food for her family. They eat her flesh and drink her blood. Every meal then becomes a thanksgiving feast!

Eucharist, then, happens when one eats with loved ones, especially when a loved one is oneself, as Derek Walcott writes in "Love After Love":

The time will come
when, with elation,
you will greet yourself arriving
at your own door, in your own mirror,
and each will smile at the other's welcome,

and say, sit here. Eat.
You will love again the stranger who was yourself.

[18] E. Ethelbert Miller, "Bread," in idem, *Whispers Secrets & Promises*, 38.
[19] Michael S. Harper, "Breaded Meat, Breaded Hands," in E. Ethelbert Miller, ed., *In Search of Color Everywhere*, 132, from Harper, *Images of Kin* (Urbana: University of Illinois Press, 1977).

Give wine. Give bread. Give back your heart
to itself, to the stranger who has loved you

all your life, whom you ignored
for another, who knows you by heart.
Take down the love letters from the bookshelf,

the photographs, the desperate notes,
peel your own image from the mirror.
Sit. Feast on your life.[20]

Life, yes, the bread of life. It comes down from heaven . . . and from
another . . . and from within. It is the heart given and known by itself,
the peaceful, untroubled, fearless heart (John 14:1, 27). The hour is
coming (4:21, 23; 5:25, 28), that elated, joyful hour (16:20-24), and now
is. Sit. Eat. Feast! Life!

Exploring Likenesses to the Discourse in My Own Soul

This is the feast that I have longed to eat, the bread of self-acceptance,
the wine (not whine) of self-confidence. I am the bread of life, Jesus
says. Something both attractive and repulsive about that saying. I AM.
I am. I Am. Jesus, this man who lived, died, ate, drank, eliminated, says
I AM, not i . . . am but I AM. I marvel at, long for, yearn for such confidence, such sense of self, such, such such, such self-possession, grasp of
who he is. My own ego, lack of self-confidence, know who i am but
don't love who i am. Anxiety about who I am. What do I fear? There is
no fear in I AM. I want that. I want it.

Or do i? Jesus takes the divine name I AM. He is a human, yet he is
claiming participation in creation, preexistence, omniscience, omnipo-
tence. Confidence or arrogance? Can a man (and not a woman) be
God? Is it a fantasy we all have but now projected onto Jesus? I can't be
God but i know someone who is. I find both quietude and disquietude
in that. Is this dependency? co-dependency? lack of independence?

I want to find my own iam. There is no I AM. Or better, the only I AM
is found in my (our) iam(s). I AM only legitimates authority of those in
power. The hierarchy shares in the I AM but I do not. Can my iam be the
I AM? How? By believing in myself, loving myself, being productive,
feeling good about who I am and what I have done, being in meaningful relationships with others, participating in community.

[20] Derek Walcott, "Love After Love," in idem, *Sea Grapes* (Farrar, Strauss & Giroux,
Inc., 1976), quoted in David Whyte, *The Heart Aroused: Poetry and Preservation of the
Soul in Corporate America* (New York: Doubleday, 1994) 206.

IAM . . . the bread of life (!?). This man Jesus of Nazareth says that he is both God and bread. Bread? Foodstuff that is made, eaten, and then eliminated? Necessary, now on the base of the food pyramid! Base-ic. More than that, disciples are to munch his flesh and drink his blood! How do we ingest this textual Jesus? Eat the paper and drink the ink? No, participation in a Christian community. Institutional church? How about any authentic human community that is striving for peace and justice? Any activity that promotes humane values and contributes to the upbuilding of persons and communities? For me, writing, teaching, meditation, parenting, spousing, conversing deeply with friends. My bread, living bread, which comes down out of heaven. (Look out!) It feels like grace, a gift, not something that I have produced or earned but something given to me. Eucharist.

Thanksgiving meal. My family and I eat off a table my father made many years ago. It was our dinner table when I was growing up. Painful memories attached to that table: my mother rattling on about the washer or dryer, my father reading the paper, and me sitting there thinking and feeling and wanting to speak my thoughts and feelings but not knowing how these people who claimed to be my parents would receive them. That same "hardwood" table sits in our dining room. We generally eat three meals a day off it. Sometimes I struggle to find the eucharist as well here: Ana saying, "I need to go poo-poo," Miranda crying to be picked up, and both Joy and me trying to placate both girls. I too want to say what I think and feel but don't know how it will be received. Sometimes merely eating is thanksgiving enough. Maybe meaningful conversation will happen another time. Maybe it's just enough now to look, to speak, to touch. It is a feast!

"Your Dad's the Devil" / "You Gotta Demon" (John 8:12-59)

Then again Jesus spoke to them, saying,
 "I am the light of the world;
 the one who follows me will never walk around in darkness
 but will have the light of life."
The Pharisees then said to him,
 "You witness concerning yourself;
 your witness is not true."
Jesus answered and said to them,
 "Even if I witness concerning myself, my witness is true,
 because I know where I have come from and where I am going;
 but you do not know where I have come from or where I am going.
 You judge according to the flesh,
 I do not judge anyone.
 But if I do judge, my judgment is true,

because I do not judge alone, but I judge along with the father who
    sent me.
And it is written in your law that the witness of two people is true.
I am the one who witnesses concerning myself
and the father who sent me witnesses concerning me."
Then they said to him,
    "Where is your father?"
Jesus answered,
    "You know neither me nor my father;
    if you knew me, you would know my father also."
He spoke these words in the treasury while teaching in the temple;
and no one tried to seize him,
because his hour had not yet come.

Then he said to them again,
    "I am going away and you'll search for me,
    but you will die in your sin;
    where I am going, you cannot come.
Then the Judeans said,
    "He is not going to kill himself, is he,
    because he says,
        'Where I am going you cannot come'?"
And he said to them,
    "You are from below, I am from above;
    You are from this world, I am not from this world.
    I then said to you that you will die in your sins.
    For if you do not believe that I am,
    you will die in your sins."
They then said to him,
    "Who are you?"
Jesus said to them,
    "What I have said to you from the beginning.
    I have many things to say and to judge concerning you,
    but the one who sent me is true,
    and I say in the world these things that I heard from him."
They did not know that he said to them the father.
Jesus then said to them,
    "When you lift up the son of humanity,
    you will know that I am,
    and I do not do anything from myself,
    but just as the father teaches me, I say these things.
    And the one who sent me is with me;
    he has not left me alone,
    because I always do the things pleasing to him."
When he spoke these things, many believed into him.
Jesus then said to the Judeans who believed in him,

"If you abide in my word, you are truly my disciples.
And you will know the truth, and the truth will free you."
They said to him,
"We are the seed of Abraham
and we've never been enslaved to anyone.
How can you say,
'You will come to be free'?"
Jesus answered them,
"Amen amen I say to you that
everyone who sins is a slave of sin.
But the slave does not abide in the house forever,
the son abides forever.
If the son frees you, you will truly be free.
I know that you are the seed of Abraham;
but you seek to kill me,
because my word does not find room in you.
I speak what I have seen from the father;
you do what you have heard from your father."
They answered and said to him,
"Our father is Abraham."
Jesus says to them,
"If you were the children of Abraham, you would do the works of
Abraham,
but now you seek to kill me,
a person who spoke to you the truth that I heard from God.
Abraham did not do that.
You do the works of your father."
They said to him,
"We were not born of fornication;
we have one father, God."
Jesus said to them,
"If God were your father you would love me,
for I have come from God and am here.
For I have not spoken on my own, but he sent me.
Because of what saying of mine do you not know?
Because you cannot hear my word.
You are from your father the devil
and you want to do the desires of your father.
He was a murderer from the beginning
and he does not stand in the truth,
because there is no truth in him.
When he speaks a lie, he speaks from his own,
because his father is a liar.
But because I speak the truth you do not believe me.
Which one of you convicts me of sin?
If I speak the truth, why don't you believe me?

The one who is from God hears the words of God;
because of this you do not hear,
because you are not from God."

The Judeans answered and said to him,
"Don't we speak right that you're a Samaritan and you have a
demon?"
Jesus answered,
"I do not have a demon,
but I honor my father,
and you dishonor me.
I do not seek my own glory.
There is one who seeks it and judges.
Amen amen I say to you,
Whoever keeps my word will never ever see death."
The Judeans said to him,
"Now we know that you have a demon.
Abraham died, along with the prophets,
but you say,
'Whoever keeps my word will never ever taste death.'
Are you greater than our father Abraham, who died?
And the prophets died.
What do you make of yourself?"
Jesus answered,
"If I glorify myself, my glory is nothing;
my father is the one who glorifies me,
of whom you say,
'He is our God.'
And you do not know him, but I know him.
If I say that I do not know him,
I would be a liar like you;
but I do know him and I keep his word.
Abraham your father was glad to see my day,
and he saw it and rejoiced."
Then the Judeans said to him,
"You are not yet fifty years old and you have seen Abraham?!"
Jesus said to them,
"Amen amen I say to you,
Before Abraham came to be, I am."
Then they picked up stones to throw at him.
But Jesus hid and went away from the temple.

Playing with the Images of the Dispute

Jesus is now again in Jerusalem (7:10–10:21), which is still not the city
of peace for him. When he previously passed-over (and feasted), the

Judeans jumped him (2:13-22; 5:16-47). This time Jesus tabernacle-feasts (tabernacles and reveals his glory, 1:14). He tabernacles and feasts in the temple (7:14), his fathershouse (2:16), where he earlier did some springcleaning (2:15). Here in the temple (not his body but the building; 2:21) Jesus mid-feast teaches. The amazed Judeans tabernacle too—and attempt to feast on Jesus, who says, "You're trying to kill me!" (Are they still mad from the sabbathlamemanwalking and the godfathertalking, 5:2-18?) They say, "You gotta demon!" These people are obviously thirsty, so on the last great day Jesus offers them water—gutsy, flowing, living, enspiriting river-water. The Jerusalemite crowd is divided: "Messiah-prophet!" "No, Galilean." Pharisee-sent temple police try to arrest Jesus, but they too are divided. The Pharisees curse the police and the crowd, but one of them, came-by-night Nicodemus, wants to be a fair Pharisee and give Jesus a law-full hearing. Does he want to hear again about the spirited birth from above (3:1-8)? But the Pharisees curse the Galilean Nicodemus and Jesus.

After non-cursing and non-condemning an adultery-woman (while cursing and condemning the accusing scribes and Pharisees), Jesus speaks to "them" again. (Apparently the crowd that heard him speak about living water has flowed back to him.) Jesus says, I AM the light of the world. I AM. I AM the world's light, the worldly light, the nations' light (Isa 49:6), the shining-in-and-not-overcome-by-darkness light (John 1:5), the coming-into-the-world-enlightening-everyone light (1:9). The fiery-bushy I AM (Exod 3:2, 14) now gives forth light. Light-followers, who are light-children (John 12:36), don't walk around, stumble around, bump around in darkness, not knowing where they're going (11:9), because they have the light of life, living light, light life, enlightened life, the life-light of humanity, which attracts truthdoers but repels evildoers (3:19-21).

The Pharisees (who are not fair, I see) make light of Jesus' self-witness, which they say is not true (but Jesus I AM the truth, 14:6). Jesus, however, who knows where he's coming and going (from the father/to the father, 16:28) has two witnesses: one, himself, and two, his sending father, whom the Pharisees don't know any more than they do Jesus, because know the son, know the father. We know (but the Pharisees don't) that Jesus' light-witnessing words are rich words, spoken from the temple treasury, where Jesus could not be seized because his arresting, glorifying, ascending hour (12:23; 17:1) had come not yet.

Jesus, however, refers to the hour, saying that he's away-going and they come-can't because they're going to sin-die. The Pharisee/Judeans think: Ah, he's going to commit suicide (which, in a way, he is because he's going to of-his-own-accord lay down his life, 10:18). They don't understand because they're from below/this world; Jesus is from above/not from this world. If they don't believe the enlightening I AM, then they're going to sinfully die, because they haven't been born from above through the spirit and eternally have life (3:3-8). The Judeans ask Jesus who he, this from-abover, is, but Jesus has told them from the beginning, when as the word he was with God and was God (1:1). This God, the true sending-Jesus God, is the one from whom Jesus has heard what he in the world says. The Judeans this misunderstand because they know not who Jesus is (I AM), where from he comes (from God), and where from his words he gets (ditto, from God).

They know not now, but they will know: when they lift up the human-son, serpent-like in the wilderness (3:14)—that is, when they kill him—then they will know the enlightening, enlivening I AM, who speaks and does pleasing father-taught things. Ah! ah! This rings a bell with many of the Judeans. Dingdingding! They believe into Jesus the from-above I AM. But like earlier Jerusalemite Judeans, do they merely sign-believe? If so, Jesus knows what's in 'em (2:23-25). Jesus now speaks to these new believers. He says that if they word-abide they will be true, discipled freedpersons. "Freed?!" they say. "We Abrahamseed never been slaves! Whatyamean about being free?!" Never been slaves? Does the word "Egypt" ring a bell? You know, Pharaoh? And after Egypt: Babylon, Greece, and now Rome. Never been slaves?! These folks are not truth-free but ignorance-enslaved. Jesus amenamens that a sinner is a sin-slave who has no abiding place in the father's temple-house; but now the son is a forever abider and can free the slaves so that they can house-abide too. They're Abrahamseed all right, but they seekkill Jesus, because they are not word-abiders, even though they have (supposedly) into Jesus believed. Jesus speaks his father's visions, and they do their father's words. Abraham is our father, they say. Abraham? If they were Abraham's (and Sarah's?) children, they would do Abraham's works, like believe God and have it counted as righteousness (Gen 15:6). But they're kill-seekers (not glory-seekers), seeking to kill God's truth-teller, and Abraham didn't do that. No, uh-huh. They're doing their father's works. They protest that God is their father. But no way. If God father then love Jesus, the come/sent-from-God one. These people are DEAF to Jesus' word (and blind to his light); they're not from God, not from above; they're from below, they're devilchildren not godchildren who have believed into Jesus and been gathered into one (John 1:12; 11:52). The devil was a from-the-beginning murderer and non-truth father-liar; therefore, his children cannot believe the from-the-beginning life-giving truth-teller Jesus. From God, hear God-words; don't hear, not from God: from the devil!

The Judeans then say that Jesus, into whom they believe (?!), is a demonized Samaritan, and they don't have any dealings with Samaritans

(4:9). They then won't receive the lively water that Jesus offers. But no demon has Jesus, who father honors, while they fatherson dishonor. Jesus is not his-own-glory-seeker (because he's not his own word-speaker); God is Jesus' glory-seeker. Amenamen he says, the word-keeper, the non-sin-slave, won't death-see but life-see, because he abides in the fathershouse forever and there sees by the I AM's living light.

The Judeans keep these words all right, which confirm for them that Jesus is demonized, because Abraham and all prophets died, while Jesus says that his word-keepers will not be death-tasters. Is he greater than fatherAbraham (who's really not their father but the devil is) and the prophets, who were all death-tasters? What does he make of himself? Jesus doesn't make anything of himself; he is not a self-made man but a father-made (and father-glorified) son. Though the Judeans say that Jesusfather is their God, they're really lying non-God-knowers (like their true father the devil). Jesus, however, is a non-lying, word-keeping God-knower, and father Abraham rejoiced to see (and saw to rejoice, yippee!) Jesus' day, which is full of light for believers to walk around in (11:9). Abraham rejoiced to see Jesus; what's the problem with his so-called children?

The Judeans are shocked: You've not hit the big 5-0, and you've seen father Abraham?! Jesus amenamens againagain: Before coming-to-be-fatherAbraham (and before baptizingJohn, 1:15, 30, indeed, before allthings, 1:1-3), I AM! IIIIIII AMAMAMAM. I AM: life-giving, lifted-up, before-Abraham light. At the end of this discourse and in the beginning was the word: I AM.

The Abraham-children no more believe into this I AM; indeed, they want to make the I AM "I-was": they lift-up to-throw-at-him stones, thus proving that they are not Abraham-children but really murderous devil-children. Jesus-hour, however, still hasn't come; he hides and leaves the temple, cashing in his chips at the treasury, in order to tabernacle (and reveal his glory and light) elsewhere. I AM not here.

Exploring Likenesses to the Dispute in African-American Poetry

Three images: I AM, slavery/freedom, murderer/life-giver. The I AM makes free, and the I AM is free. Unlike the Judeans, African-Americans remember their time in slavery and pledge never to return to it, as in the spiritual:

> Freedom, O freedom over me
> Before I'd be a slave,
> I'll be buried in my grave
> and go home to my Lord and be free.

And Frances E. W. Harper writes in "Bury Me in a Free Land":

> Make me a grave where'er you will,
> In a lowly plain, or a lofty hill;
> Make it among earth's humblest graves,
> But not in a land where men are slaves.[21]

Slavery, oppression, injustice breed death. And the slaveowners/the oppressors are like the Judeans, murderers who claim to be free. Claude McKay writes in his poem "Tiger":

> The white man is a tiger at my throat,
> Drinking my blood as my life ebbs away,
> And muttering that his terrible striped coat
> Is Freedom's and portends the Light of Day.[22]

No light for the white man/the Judean, only darkness.
Similarly, Henry L. Dumas writes of the white man in "Tis of Thee":

> You are a sinful old man who has no repentance in his heart,
> a lecherous old winebelly vomiting blood.
> You are a murderer of your sons
> and a raper of your daughters.
> You are cold and filled with death.
> Few flowers grow from your gardens
> and the snow and the ice shall be your grave.[23]

Strong words, strong words. Bitter words from a bitter history.

Exploring Likenesses to the Dispute in My Own Soul

As I have noted previously, I have long longed for the confident assertion of I Am, for my own shadowy, lethargic, down-and-out "i am" dances toward Jesus' lively, lifted-up, enlightening I Am. But I stop: Jesus sets forth his I Am against the Judeans' "you are": he says, you are murderous, lying, lowdown, misunderstanding devil-children. Jesus,

[21] Frances E. W. Harper, "Bury Me in a Free Land," in Dudley Randall, ed., *The Black Poets*, 40, from Harper, *The Complete Poems of Frances E. W. Harper* ed. Maryemma Graham (New York: Oxford University Press, 1988).

[22] Claude McKay, "Tiger," in Dudley Randall, ed, *The Black Poets* 62, from McKay, *Selected Poems of Claude McKay* (New York: Harcourt Brace, 1953).

[23] Henry L. Dumas, "Tis of Thee," in Jerry W. Ward, Jr., ed., *Trouble the Water: 250 Years of African-American Poetry* (New York: Mentor, 1997) 304, from Dumas, *Knees of a Natural Man: The Selected Poetry of Henry Dumas,* Eugene B. Redmond, ed. (New York: Thunder's Mouth, 1989).

then, spits living water into the Judeans' faces and shines the light of the world into their eyes. Whether translated "Jews," "Judeans" or "religious leaders," it's all the same: Jesus is here demonizing and de-humanizing those who oppose him. He dances the dance of death, leading not just to Jesus' death but also the death of millions of Native Americans in the European conquest, Africans in the Middle Passage, and Jews in the Holocaust.

And so do I. When rejected, I too dance to this tune: I have the true spirit of light, and those who reject me—whether religious fundamentalists, inept administrators or recalcitrant students—have the lying demon of darkness. Such self-righteousness does enable me to ventilate my rage and pain, but in the long run it does not move me to maturity or build up human community. How can I affirm "i am" without denouncing "you are"?

I am. I-I-I-I-I-I. you are. youyouyouyou. IyouIyouIyou. We are. wewewewe. all the way home.

great question!

4

(More of) My Word against Your Word: Further Disputes with the Judeans (John 9–12)

Jesus continues signing and disputing. Both the first two disputes with the Judeans (chs. 5–6) originated out of a sign. First Jesus healed the paralytic by the pool of Bethzatha and then he disputed with the Judeans about the cooperation of father and son; then Jesus multiplied the loaves and told the Judeans that he was the bread of life. The pattern is reversed, however, with the next two signs and discourses or sayings. First Jesus says that he is light of the world (8:12, discussed in the last chapter), and then he heals a man born blind (ch. 9). Then Jesus says that he is the resurrection and life and raises Lazarus from the dead (11:1-44). Saying / sign; I am / I do.

So we start where we stopped: in Jerusalem with the worldly enlightened, pre-Abraham I Am:

The Blind Leading the Bland (John 9:1-41)

As he was passing by,
he saw a man blind from birth.
And his disciples asked him,
"Rabbi,
who sinned, this man or his parents,
so that he was born blind?"
Jesus answered,
"Neither this man nor his parents sinned,
but he was born blind so that the works of God might be revealed in him.
We must work the works of him who sent me while it is day.
Night is coming when no one can work.
While I am in the world, I am light of the world."

After he said these things, he spat on the ground and made mud from
the spittle and spread the mud on his eyes and said to him,
"Go wash in the pool of Siloam" (which means sent).
And he went away and washed and came back seeing.

Then the neighbors and those who had seen him before as a beggar
began saying,
"Isn't this the man who used to sit and beg?"
Some were saying,
"This man is the one,"
but others were saying,
"No, but he looks like him."
He kept saying,
"I am."
Then they continued asking him,
"How then were your eyes opened?"
He answered,
"The man called Jesus made mud and spread it on my eyes and said
to me,
'Go to Siloam and wash.'
Then after I went and washed I began to see."
They said to him,
"Where is he?"
He says,
"I don't know."

They bring the man who had been blind to the Pharisees.
The day on which Jesus made the mud and opened his eyes was a
sabbath.
Then the Pharisees asked him too how he began to see.
And he said to them,
"He put mud on my eyes and I washed and I now see."
Then some of the Pharisees began saying,
"This man is not from God,
because he does not keep the sabbath."
But others began saying,
"How can a sinner man do such signs?"
And there was a division among them.
Then they say again to the blind man,
"What do you say about him because he opened your eyes?"
He said,
"He is a prophet."

The Judeans, then, did not believe that he had been blind and received
his sight until they called the parents of the man who had received
his sight,

and they asked them,
    "Is this your son, who you say was born blind?"
    How then does he now see?"
Then his parents answered and said,
    "We know that this is our son and that he was born blind;
    but we do not know how it is that he now sees,
    nor do we know who opened his eyes.
    Ask him; he is of age. He will speak for himself."
His parents said these things because they were afraid of the Judeans;
for the Judeans had already decided that
anyone who confesses him as messiah is put out of the synagogue.
Because of this his parents said,
    "He is of age; ask him."

Then they called a second time the man who had been blind,
and they said to him,
    "Give glory to God;
    we know that this man is a sinner."
Then he answered,
    "I don't know if he is a sinner.
    One thing I do know, that though I was blind, I now see."
Then they said to him,
    "What did he do to you?
    How did he open your eyes?"
He answered them,
    "I already said that to you,
    but you didn't hear.
    Why do you want to hear it again?
    You don't want to become his disciples too, do you?"
And they reviled him and said,
    "You are his disciple,
    but we are disciples of Moses.
    We know that God has spoken to Moses,
    but we do not know where this man is from."
The man answered them,
    "For this is an amazing thing,
    that you do not know where he is from,
    yet he opened my eyes.
    We know that God does not hear sinners,
    but he does hear the one who fears God and does his will.
    From the beginning it has not been heard that anyone opened the
        eyes of someone born blind.
    If this man were not from God, he could do nothing."
They answered him,
    "You were born completely in sins,
    and you are trying to teach us?!"
And they threw him out.

Jesus heard that they had thrown him out,
and when he found him, he said,
  "Do you believe into the son of humanity?"
He answered and said,
  "And who is he, master, so that I might believe into him?"
Jesus said to him,
  "You have seen him and he is the one talking with you."
And he said,
  "I believe, master."
And he worshiped him.

And Jesus said,
  "For judgment I have come into the world,
  so that the ones who do not see might see and the ones who see
      might become blind."
Some of the Pharisees who were with him heard these things and said
  to him,
  "We are not blind too, are we?"
Jesus said to them,
  "If you were blind, you would not have sin;
  but since you say,
    'We see,'
  your sin remains."

Playing with the Images of the Dialogue

Unstoned and untempled (8:59), Jesus passes by (but does not by-pass) a man blindly born (from below). (Indeed, aren't all people born from-below born blind? Only the from-above birth enables them to see, 3:3-7.) His disciples, who have not been with him since Simon said that they would never peter out and leave him (6:68-69), ask their rabbi, Nicodemus-like (3:2), if the man or his parents sinned so that he was blindly born. (How do they know that he is in fact born blind? What do they see? The narrator, of course, knows that the man was born blind because the narrator was with the word (and God) in the beginning, 1:1-3.) The disciples see suffering and associate it with sin, for their jealous lordGod, who third and fourth generation punishes (Exod 20:5), has birthed this man blind because either he sinned (in the womb?) or his parents sinned. Is this the God who so loves the world (John 3:16)?

Jesus says that the sinners are neither the man nor his parents, but his bornblindness is so that Godworks might be revealed in him. Let's get this straight: God made this man blind at birth in private so that God might give him sight in public? Is this a showboat God? Maybe the disciples' explanation is preferable. Jesussay that he gotta work his sender's works during the day cuz ain't no work happening at night. The day is illuminated by Jesus, the worldlight (8:12), while he is in the world, and when he leaves to return to the father (16:28), it is night and he can't do any more work.

Having enlightened the disciples (while darkening the reader), Jesus spits living water (4:10-14) on the ground to make mud and anoint (the Christ christens) the man's eyes. Jesus then sends him to wash in the sent pool Siloam. (God sends Jesus, 3:17; 20:21, and Jesus sends the born-blind man to the sent pool. They (and we) are on the s(c)ent!) So he washes, baptizes himself (Does the spirit come to rest on him? 1:33), and he sees. He says nothing, thinks nothing, does nothing, just sees.

The man born-blind-but-now-seeing is then seen by his neighbors, who talk about him. (Everybody first talks about this man and then to him.) They are divided about what they see. Is this the ex-sitter-and-beggar or not? Some yep, some nope. But the man: I am! Jesus' I AM births (from above) this man's I am. They ask him how he now has openeyes, and he tells the story pretty much as it happened (or at least as the narrator tells us). They ask him where Jesus is, and he says that he doesn't know. (We don't know where he is either, for that matter.)

The neighbors then take the ex-blindman to the Pharisees. What good neighbors they are! After all, though, Jesus' mud-making, eye-opening day was a sabbath (just as his paralytic-healing day earlier was a sabbath, 5:2-9), and the Pharisees ought to know. They ask him about his sightgetting, and he tells them about the mudding-washing-seeing. These Pharisees are neighborly, and they too are divided. Some: this mud-maker is not a sabbath-keeper and therefore not from God! Others: a sinner a sign-doer? They then ask the (ex)blindman (again, first speaking about him and then to him; he gets no respect!). He says that this eye-opening-man-called-Jesus is a prophet.

The Pharisees apparently work through their divisions and unite as Judeans—persecuting, murderous, complaining, devilchildren Judeans (5:16-17; 6:41; 8:44) who doubt that this is the formerly-blind-but-now-seeing man, so that they call his parents. Jesus said that they were not sinners (9:3), so will they say that Jesus is a prophet? The Judeans ask them if this seeing man is their born-blind son and if so how he now sees. They say that this is in fact their born-blind son, but they don't know how he sees or who was his eye-opener. They say to ask him, for he is old enough to self-speak. The parents say all this with quivering lips ("Askkkkkk himmmmm") because they are afraid that the Judeans will think that they are messiah-confessors and de-synagogue them.[1]

---

[1] Since the publication of J. Louis Martyn, *History and Theology in the Fourth Gospel* (Nashville: Abingdon, 1968), it has been axiomatic in Johannine scholarship that this reference to being put out of the synagogue, along with those at 12:42 and 16:2, refers to the experience not of the historical Jesus but of the Johannine community, which had been expelled from the synagogue. The gospel, therefore, should be

Ah-ha! This man's parents are in fact sinners ("Who sinned, this man or his parents?" 9:2) because they do not say that their son's eye-opener was messiah, a prophet or even a man-called-Jesus. While their born-blind son now sees, these bornseeing parents are blind!

The sinning, blind parents leave, and the ex-blindman is again summoned. They tell him to give glory to God (which he has to a certain extent by saying that Jesus is a prophet), to tell the truth by agreeing with them that man-called-Jesus is not a prophet but a mud-making, sabbath-breaking sinner! The man says he doesn't know about Jesus but he does know one thing: once blind now see! (He sings "Amazing Grace" right there: "I once was lost but now I'm found. / Was blind but now I see.") They ask him: what? how? He says: "You didn't hear/ listen/heed when I first-time said it; why do you want to again hear it? Hey, maybe you want to become his disciples!" Ooh! He zinged them! This man not only received sight but also speech—bold speech, at that! The word gives words as well as vision.

The Judeans revile the man (and he is The Man); they revile this vile Jesusdisciple who says that his eye-opener is a prophet. There is no profit in that! The man is a disciple of a sabbath-breaking sinner; the Judeans are disciples of Moses. Now Moses is from Sinai, where God spoke to him and where he saw God (Exod 33:17-23), but they don't know where Jesus is from. (From God, you blind bats! Yes, God has spoken to Moses, who testifies to Jesus, John 5:46!) The man is amazed that they don't know where his eye-opener is from. He is from God, obviously. God doesn't hear sinners, only God-fearers and God's-will-doers. Nobody's ever heard of bornblind eyes being opened (it's new creation, in the word), so this prophetic mancalledJesus must be from God or he couldn't do anything!

This really gets the Judeans' blood boiling! As a bornblindman, he is a born sinner, and how dare he try to teach the Judeans, disciples of Godspoken Moses! They toss him out, casting him out demon-like.[2] They de-synagogue, not his parents, but him because he says that this

read on two levels, both as a story of Jesus and as a story of the Johannine community. Cf., however, the thorough critique of this position in Adele Reinhartz, "The Johannine Community and its Jewish Neighbors: A Reappraisal," in Fernando F. Segovia, ed., *"What Is John?" Vol. II. Literary and Social Readings of the Fourth Gospel.* SBL Symposium Series (Atlanta: Scholars, 1998) 111–38. She argues that based on external and internal evidence "the expulsion theory is difficult to maintain" (134). She concludes, "The largely negative portrayal of Jews and Judaism within the Gospel must therefore be grounded not in a specific experience but in the ongoing process of self-definition and the rhetoric which accompanies it" (137).

[2] The verb here is *ekballō,* which is typically used in the synoptic exorcism stories; cf. Mark 1:34.

mancalledJesus is a come-from-God prophet (prophet coming into the world, the messiah, 6:14; 11:27?).

Jesus then returns to the scene. (Where's he been? Debating again with Judeans? Escaping more stonings?) He finds the bornblind-but-now-seeing-and-thrown-out-man and asks him if he believes into the descending/ascending, lifted-up, judging son of humanity (1:51; 3:13-14; 12:23). Addressing Jesus for the first time, calling him master (not rabbi as the disciples do, 9:2), he asks who this son of humanity is so that he can believe into him. Jesus says that he has seen him (with his new eyes) and now hears him (with perhaps new ears too). He says to the master that he believes and worships this prophetic, come-from-god mancalledJesus as son of humanity.

Jesus then says that he has come into the world (as the worldlight, 8:12; 9:5) for judgment, for the father has all judgment given to the son (5:22), who nevertheless says that he judges no one (8:15). His judgment is this: non-seers (like the bornblindman) see, and seers (like the Judeans) are blinded. The Pharisees don't quite get it again and ask Jesus (confronting him for the first time in this episode) if they are the blind. Jesus tells them that if they were like this bornblindman, then they wouldn't be sinners. But because they claim to be seers when they're really blind, then they are sinners. Blind, ignorant sinners. Jesus throws them out of the divine light.

Exploring Likenesses of the Dialogue in African-American Poetry

Jesus, the I AM light, enlightens the man bornblind and transforms him from object to subject. Langston Hughes speaks in much the same way of "Helen Keller":

> She,
> In the dark,
> Found light
> Brighter than many ever see.
> She,
> Within herself,
> Found loveliness,
> Through the soul's own mastery.
> And now the world receives
> From her dower:
> The message of the strength
> Of inner power.[3]

---

[3] Langston Hughes, "Helen Keller," in Hughes, *The Collected Poems of Langston Hughes* (New York: Alfred A. Knopf, 1994) 146.

Like the bornblindman, Keller's darkness too was "lightened up," more brightly than most people were. Her "lightoftheworld," however, did not come from without, from Jesus the worldsavior, but "from within," "through the soul's own mastery" and "inner power." And the world receives her, unlike the wordintheworld, whom the world does not receive (1:10-11). The healed manbornblind, in his dealings with the Pharisaic Judeans, demonstrated his own strength, which was not received by the world either.

Enlightened ones always come into conflict with those still in the dark. The man healed of his blindness is placed on trial by the Judean Pharisees, who maintain that they can see but are blind (9:39-41). Langston Hughes wrote in a similar vein about the House Un-American Activities Committee, whom he called "Un-American Investigators":

> The committee's fat,
> Smug, almost secure
> Co-religionists
> Shiver with delight
> In warm manure
> As those investigated—
> Too brave to name a name—
> Have pseudonyms revealed
> In Gentile game
>> Of who,
>> Born Jew,
>> Is who?
> Is not your name Lipshitz?
>> Yes.
> Did you not change it
> For subversive purposes?
>> No.
> For nefarious gain?
>> Not so.
> Are you sure?
> The committee shivers
> With delight in
> Its manure.[4]

---

[4] Langston Hughes, "Un-American Investigators," in Dudley Randall, ed., *The Black Poets: A New Anthology* (New York: Bantam, 1971) 79–80, from Hughes, *The Collected Poems*, 560. This poem may refer to Hughes' appearance in 1953 before Joseph McCarthy and his Senate Sub-Committee on Un-American Affairs. Cf. *The Collected Poems*, 691 n. 560. Cf. also Arnold Rampersad, *The Life of Langston Hughes* (New York: Oxford University Press, 1988) II.211–22.

The Judeans who brought to trial the man formerly blind are depicted as "smug, almost secure co-religionists." ("We are disciples of Moses." . . . "Surely we are not blind, are we?" John 9:28, 40.) It is interesting that the Un-American Activities Committee was attempting to uncover secret Jews, while the Pharisees are trying to find secret Christians.

The trial results in the Judeans expelling the man from the synagogue (9:34). He is separated, alienated from his community. African-Americans know what it is to be separate (but equal?) and alien in society at large. Claude McKay writes in "Outcast,"

> Something in me is lost, forever lost.
> Some vital thing has gone out of my heart,
> And I must walk the way of life a ghost
> Among the sons of earth, a thing apart.
>
> For I was born, far from my native clime,
> Under the white man's menace, out of time.[5]

Langston Hughes in his poem "I, Too" says, "They send me to eat in the kitchen / When company comes," but tomorrow he will be at the table and no one will tell him to eat in the kitchen.[6] Alice Walker, however, does not rue her alienation but celebrates it and tells others to "Be Nobody's Darling" and "Be an outcast." She says, "Take the contradictions / Of your life / And wrap around / You like a shawl, / To parry stones / To keep you warm." She invites the outcasts to the river bank "Where thousands perished / For brave hurt words / They said." As an outcast, one is "Qualified to live / Among your dead."[7] Yes, be cast out—of white society, by the white male establishment. Wrap life's contradictions (light/darkness, life/death, above/below) around you. Warm yourself by a charcoal fire (John 18:18), or better, gather with other outcasts along the banks of the river of living waters (4:4-14; 7:38), where many have perished (not received eternal life) because they have rejected the word. Be an outcast, who has heard a voice and lives among the dead (5:25, 29).

[5] Claude McKay, "Outcast," in idem, *Selected Poems of Claude McKay* (New York: Harcourt Brace, 1953) 41.

[6] Langston Hughes, "I, Too," in Deirdre Mullane, ed., *Crossing the Danger Water: Three Hundred Years of African-American Writing* (New York: Doubleday Anchor, 1993) 501, from Hughes, *The Collected Poems*, 46.

[7] Alice Walker, "Be Nobody's Darling," in Jerry W. Ward, Jr., ed., *Trouble the Water: 250 Years of African-American Poetry* (New York: Mentor, 1997) 425–26, from Walker, *Revolutionary Petunias & Other Poems* (New York: Harcourt Brace, 1972).

Exploring Likenesses to the Dialogue in My Own Soul

I know what it is to be an outcast, to be alien, to be "not of this world." Indeed, as I noted in the introduction,[8] that is why I identify so much with the Johannine Jesus; he is an alien, from above and not of this world. I have felt myself an alien throughout my life, and this gospel legitimates my lifestyle, helps me feel good about myself and my pilgrimage. I am an academic, an intellectual, a scholar, and therefore I am somewhat different because I earn my daily bread thinking and leading others to think. I supposedly have more learning than others, and I allegedly bring a more objective perspective to events. Yet even within academia I feel like an alien: I am concerned not only with thinking but feeling, not only with mind but also body, not only with the cognitive but also with the creative. (Perhaps some of those concerns are reflected in this book.) And I feel like an alien at my institution, Howard University School of Divinity, where I am a white (European American) among blacks (African Americans).

Being an alien (or different), being alienated, and being cast out are three different things, yet I have experienced all three. And it is in being an outcast that I identify most with this man healed of his bornblindness. He had been blind, but Jesus healed him and emboldened him to discourse with the Pharisees about Jesus as God's representative. They expelled him from the synagogue, but he found meaning through the worship of Jesus. I was blindly (blandly?) ignorant until I was enlightened by critical biblical studies in college, seminary, and graduate school. (Perhaps I was also blind to how these studies had "darkened" me as well.) I became a Southern Baptist missionary, commissioned to teach in the Venezuela Baptist Seminary. While I was in language training in Costa Rica, I discussed theology one evening with a fellow Southern Baptist missionary who was considerably more conservative theologically than I was. He then wrote a secret letter to a pastor friend in the U.S. telling him to contact trustees of the mission board about me. (Like good neighbors, they brought me to the Pharisees.) The letter found its way to the board president, who sent my supervisor to investigate me. I was subjected to a two-hour interrogation with the supervisor in Costa Rica and another with the board president and vice-president in Atlanta. They asked me to resign, which I did initially, but I later withdrew my resignation because administrators had distorted my theological positions. The full board dismissed (terminated!) me a few weeks later. (And they threw me out.) For the next year I was unemployed, living with my mother. During that year I devoted much time

---

[8] Cf. above, xxvii–xxviii.

to prayer, journaling, and drawing. My basement study was my tomb(womb)! (I worshiped this master, this son of humanity.)

Perhaps I understand just a little bit of the marginalization that my African-American colleagues and students have experienced. I say "just a little bit" because my one experience can be matched and surpassed many times over by many incidents of discrimination, injustice, and racism. I also realize that "my people" have been the ones who have denied people of color their rights, and I have benefited from this. Perhaps my firing makes me more sensitive to their oppression. God is on the side of the oppressed—my side!—against the oppressors. Their (missionary, pastor, trustees, administrators) side! My guilt and shame is ameliorated through identifying with the man born blind. My outcastness, my alienation is legitimated. I stand in the light with Jesus and his followers and gaze on those in the darkness who fired me! Does the light, though, blind me to my own darkness and to the light in my antagonists?

Lazy Lazarus Rises (John 11:1-44)

> Now there was a certain man who was ill, Lazarus from Bethany, from
>> the village of Mary and Martha her sister.
> Now Mary was the one who anointed the master with myrrh and
>> wiped his feet with her hair, whose brother Lazarus was ill.
> The sisters therefore sent word to him saying,
>> "Master, the one whom you love is ill."
> When Jesus heard this, he said,
>> "This illness is not to death but for the glory of God,
>> so that the son of God might be glorified through it."
> Now Jesus loved Martha and her sister and Lazarus.
> When he heard that he was ill,
> he nevertheless stayed in the place where he was two days.
>
> Then after this he says to his disciples,
>> "Let's go again into Jerusalem."
> The disciples say to him,
>> "Rabbi, the Judeans were just now seeking to stone you,
>> and you want to go there again!?"
> Jesus answered,
>> "Aren't there twelve hours in a day?
>> One who walks around in the day doesn't stumble,
>> because he sees the light of this world.
>> But one who walks around in the night stumbles,
>> because he doesn't have the light in him."
> He said these things, and after this he says to them,
>> "Our beloved Lazarus has fallen asleep;

but let's go wake him up."
The disciples then said to him,
   "Master, if he has fallen asleep, he'll be saved."
Now Jesus was speaking about his death,
but they thought that he was speaking about sleep.
Then Jesus said to them plainly,
   "Lazarus has died.
   And I rejoice for you that I was not there, so that you might believe.
   Now let's go to him."
Then Thomas, who is called the Twin, said to his fellow disciples,
   "Let's go too so that we can die with him."

Then when Jesus came, he found Lazarus already in the tomb for four
   days.
Bethany was near Jerusalem about fifteen stadia [about two miles].
And many of the Judeans had come to Martha and Mary to console
   them concerning their brother.
Therefore, when Martha heard that Jesus had come, she went out to
   meet him,
but Mary sat in the house.
Martha said to Jesus,
   "Master, if you had been here, my brother would not have died;
   but I know now that whatever you ask God, God will give you."
Jesus says to her,
   "Your brother will rise."
Martha says to him,
   "I know that he will rise in the resurrection in the last day."
Jesus said to her,
   "I am the resurrection and the life.
   The one who believes into me, even though that one dies, will live,
   and everyone who lives and believes into me will never die;
   do you believe this?"
She says to him,
   "Yes, master, I believe that you are the messiah,
   the son of God who is coming into the world."

And when she said this, she went away and called Mary her sister,
   saying privately,
   "The teacher is here and calls you."
And when she heard, she rose up quickly and went to him.
Now Jesus had not yet come into the village,
but he was still in the place where Martha met him.
Then the Judeans who were with her in the house and were
   consoling her,
seeing that Mary rose up quickly and went out,
followed her, thinking that she was going to the tomb to weep there.

When Mary came where Jesus was and saw him, she fell at his feet
and said to him,
"Lord, if you had been here, my brother would not have died."
Then when Jesus saw her weeping and the Judeans who came with
her also weeping,
he was troubled in spirit and deeply moved.
And he said,
"Where have you laid him?"
They say to him,
"Lord, come and see."
Jesus wept.
Then the Judeans were saying,
"See how he loved him."
But others of them said,
"Was this one who opened the eyes of the blind not able to do
something in order that this one would not have died?"

Then Jesus, again deeply moved, comes to the tomb.
Now it was a cave and a stone was placed on it.
Jesus says,
"Take away the stone."
Martha, the sister of the one who had died, says,
"He smells bad,
for it is the fourth day [since he died]."
Jesus says to her,
"Did I not say to you that if you believe you will see the glory of
God?"
Then they took away the stone.
And Jesus raised his eyes and said,
"Father, I give thanks to you because you have heard me.
But I know that you always hear me,
but I spoke because of the crowd standing around
in order that they might believe that you sent me."
And when he said these things, he cried out with a loud voice,
"Lazarus, come out."
The dead man came out,
his feet and hands bound with bandages and his face wrapped with
a handkerchief.
Jesus says to them,
"Loose him and let him go."

Playing with the Images of the Sign

Jesus, now across the Jordan after once again escaping Jerusalem
Judean stoning and arresting (10:31, 39-40), goes to the Johnbaptizing

place, where many people, remembering Johnwitness, believe into him (10:41-42). There he hears that his beloved Lazarus, who lives in Bethany with his sisters Mary (the master-anointer and feet-hair-wiper, though that story hasn't been told yet, 12:1-8) and Martha, has gotten sick. (What do the sisters want from Jesus, for him to come and heal him? If so, why don't they say so plainly, like the Capernaum royal official, 4:47?) Jesus says that this sickness is not deadly but Godglorious (thus lively?) and thus godsonglorious (like the manbornblindsighting, 9:3, and the waterwining, the latter of which led to disciple-belief, 2:11). Jesus' beloved disciples are Martha, her sister Mary, and her brother Lazarus, and because he loves them so much . . . he stays there, abides there, dwells there (with the spirit, 1:32) where he is across the Jordan TWO DAYS. What a friend they have in Jesus! But no one tells Jesus what to do, not his mother (2:3-4), not his brothers (7:3-9), not even his beloved friends . . . only the father (5:19-20), who apparently has not told or shown him that he is to go to Lazarus.

But after the two days are up, Jesus announces, "Go to Jerusalem again!" Disciples: "Rabbiteacher, we have something to teach you: the Judeans gave you a rocky time there before (when you said I AM before-Abraham and one-with-the-father, 8:59; 10:31). Go there again!?" Jesus: "Twelve hours in a day (and non-working night coming, 9:4). A day-walker a non-stumbler because light-of-this-world seer. Night-walker stumbler because no inner light. (Don't have the worldly light/lively light, which is with you a little while, to walk around in and show you where you're going, 8:12; 12:35.)" What does this have to do with going to Jerusalem? The disciples, and the reader, are in the dark and are stumbling! Jesus attempts to enlighten them: "Our beloved Lazarus is sacked out and we need to wake him up." The disciples, still stumbling, are trying to "master" this situation. If he's sleeping, then he'll be saved. In other words, we don't need to go and wake him up. But Jesus was death-talking not sleep-talking. So he shines the light of this world on his words: "Bulletin: Lazarus dead STOP. And I'm glad that I wasn't there, so that you can believe, because you obviously don't believe now. So let's go, so that Lazarus can be a liver, and you all can be believers—and see my glory!" Thomas, always appearing when death and resurrection come up (20:24-29), says, "Hey, guys, let's go so that we can die with him—with Jesus and with Lazarus."

When Jesus Bethany-arrives (two miles from Jerusalem), Lazarus entombed four days. (He's not barely dead; he's very dead! Waking him up will require new creation!) A Judean lot had come to mourn with MarthaMary. (They don't have stones behind their backs, do they?) Jesus comes, however, Martha hears, goes out to meet him, Mary still in house (with the Judeans). Martha to Jesus: You'd been here, you coulda mastered his sickness and he wouldna died. (So why didn't you come earlier?! We told you that he was sick. Why'd you tarry?) But hey God'll give ya whatever ya ask (if of course you ask in your own name, 14:13-14; 15:7, 16; 16:23-24). (Maybe you can ask him to raise my brother, huh?)" God has (lovingly) given Jesus everything all-things (3:35). What is she asking here? Whatever she asks of Jesus, he will give her? What does she want Jesus to ask God? to raise her brother? Jesus tells her that her brother's gonna rise. That's what he's going to ask God, but he doesn't need to, because God has already given him the power to raise the dead (5:25-29). Jesus will shepherd goodly Lazarus right out of the tomb; he will call him by name and lead him out (10:3). Beloved of Jesus, he is a dogooder, who will rise into the resurrection of life (5:28-29). Samaritan-like, Martha says she knows that (4:25-26). She knows that Lazarus will rise, but not now but on the last day, the *eschaton*, that great gittin' up morning, when Jesus raises the into-him believer, whom the father has given him (6:44). Oh no, another Msunder-standing! Hey, Martha, what you don't know is that the coming hour is NOW! (4:23; 5:25). Jesus says: I AM I AM i am resurrection and life, resurrected life, living resurrection, living breaded enlightened shep-herded resurrection (8:12; 10:11). The into-I AM believer is a dier but liver because this believing liver is a never-dier. (So, does the "beliver" die or not? What kind of death/life is this?) Jesus asks Martha if she be-lives it, all this believing, dying, living, resurrecting stuff. Martha says that she does, she has mastered it, be-living that he is the messianic, godson world-comer. Ah-ha! The confession that the gospel is looking for: read these signs (deadraising etc.), believe that Jesus is messiah-son-of-God and have in-his-name LIFE (20:31). Martha model believer/ reader.

Conversation over. (What more is there to say?) Martha maryly goes to get her sister. The teacher (why doesn't she say messiahgodson?) is calling for you. (But Jesus hasn't said that, has he?) Mary doesn't ques-tion. Perhaps he needs his head anointed again (or for the first time). So she rises up (like Martha knows their brother will do) and goes to Jesus, who's still in the Martha-met place. (Jesus is the stillpoint, the center of this story, whom people come to.) Mary doesn't come alone, though; she comes with her "comforters" (not the holy spirit, 14:16), who come alongside her 'cause they think that she's going to tomb-weep. Mary falls at Jesus' feet (a familiar place for anointing Mary) and says the same (initial) thing that Martha said. Jesus, perhaps rolling his eyes, sees all this weeping—Mary weeping, Judeans weeping—he's spiritually troubtroubtroubled . . . and moved in himself (12:27; 13:21). What's going on for Jesus? Mad at unbelieving weeping? Sad at Lazarus' death? Upset at his own coming death? Whatever he's feeling, he asks where they've laid him these four days ago. Philip-like they say, "Comesee!" (Can anything good come out of the tomb? Come and see—ascending-descending angels on the humanson! 1:46, 51.) Now it's Jesus'weeping time. (Again why?) Judeans think that tears show how much of a beloved disciple Lazarus is. But they ain't seen nothing yet. Others say, Hey couldn't this blindeyeopener, who's said to be a from-God prophet (9:1-7, 17, 33), have done something—anything—to keep his buddy from being a dier? (Jesus still dividin' the people, 7:12, 40-44.) Yeah, Jesus will do something all right, because he's the world-coming messiah-son-of-God, and this illness ain't deathly but glorious.

Jesus moves deeply toward the tomb. (He not only comes and sees but comes and feels.) The tomb is caved and stoned, and Jesus says to unstone it. (The Judeans know about "stones," 8:59; 10:31, so they should be able to do it.) Sister Martha says, in her best King James English, "He stinketh." It is after all the fourth day since he died. Hey, what's wrong with Martha, the I AM-resurrection-and-life believer? Is she going to let a little stench get in the way of eternal life for her bro? Jesus: Hey, didn't I say (to you or to the disciples or someone) that you're going to (come-and)see God's(waterwining/blindeyeopening)glory and believe into the glorified son of God (whom you say you believe into)? So they (the Judeans?) unstone the tomb.

Before raising Lazarus, Jesus first raises his eyes and thanks his hearing godfather who always hears him (just as he always sees the father doing things, which the son automatically does, 5:19). Jesus spoke (when? just now, thanking God or earlier?) for the standing-room-only crowd so that they stand in belief that he's (truly and lovingly) God-sent (17:8, 21, 23). (This time God doesn't thunder back in response, 12:28-29). He's spoken to God, to the Judeans, and to Martha; now—finally—he speaks to Lazarus. He LOUDLY CRIES OUT (after all, he's got to wake him up): LAZARUS, COME OUT! Hey, you sheep, this is the goodshepherd speaking, and I'm calling you by name and leading you out into eternal life (10:3). The coming hour now is. Do you hear my son-of-God voice? COME OUT, and live! (5:25-29)."

And he does. The dead man, who is not dead anymore, comes out . . . and lives, though he's a bit restricted now: he's feet-and-hand-bandaged and face-kerchiefed (clothes that Jesus will know well very soon, 20:6-7). Now Jesus speaks again to "them," presumably the same ones who removed the stone, saying to unbandage and unkerchief him and let him go. Go where? Home, of course, where in a few days he's going to sit at table with Jesus (and be in his bosom, where a beloved disciple belongs, 13:23) at a prepassover dinner, where Mary will anoint his feet (12:1-8). Before that, though, many Judeans come-see(his glory), believe into Jesus, but others go to the Pharisees, who chiefly plot with the priests to kill Jesus (so that the nation—and all gathered godchildren—might live, 11:45-53). The Judeans never quit, do they? Life for Lazarus, death for Jesus . . . but life for the world!

Exploring Likenesses to the Sign in African-American Poetry

The related characters of the story—Mary, Martha, and Lazarus—as well as the themes of life and rising from the dead appear in African-American poetry. The spiritual "Mary, Don You Weep" says,

> Mary, don you weep an Marthie don you moan,
> Mary, don you weep an Marthie don you moan;
> Pharoah's army got drown-ded,
> Oh Mary don you weep.[9]

It is interesting how the exodus theme is interspersed with the resurrection theme. The reason for Mary and Martha not to grieve is not that their brother Lazarus will be raised but that Pharoah's army (of death?) has been drowned, perhaps by Jesus' own tears (John 11:35). This water meant death for the Egyptians but life for the Israelites, who apparently include Mary, Martha, and Lazarus. "Lazarus, come out!" Jesus says, and the dead man makes his exodus out of the tomb (11:43). Mary weeps when she sees Jesus (11:32), and Martha moans: "If you had been here, my brother would not have died" (11:21) and "He smells bad, for it is the fourth day [since he died]" (11:39). But no more weeping, no more moaning, only believingly see God's glory.

Lazarus does come out in Frank Horne's "Walk," in which he is "trying to learn to walk again." He says that it is like "a timorous Lazarus / commanded / to take up the bed / on which he died. . . ." (Lazarus is in fact given no such command. Horne seems to have confused the dead man with the paralytic at the pool of Bethzatha, who is told to "take up his bed and walk," 5:8.) The poet says that he will walk again "in answer / to your tender command."[10] Jesus does command Lazarus, though not so softly and tenderly, but crying out with a loud voice (11:43). And Lazarus does walk again, though we do not know if he is "timorous" or not. The poet's disability has been like a death to him, so that he identifies not with the paralytic but with Lazarus. He too wants to be beloved (11:3, 5) and made alive.

---

[9] Anonymous, "Mary, Don You Weep," in Jerry W. Ward, Jr., ed., *Trouble the Water: 250 Years of African-American Poetry* (New York: Mentor, 1997) 5.

[10] Frank Horne, "Walk," in Randall, ed., *The Black Poets* 75, from Horne, *In Haverstraw* (London: Paul Bremen, 1963).

Loved Lazarus lives . . . though dead. Jesus loves him and enlivens him. Jolene Smith, a middle school student in East Capitol Dwellings, a crime-ridden neighborhood in Washington, D.C., says what "Poetry Is":

> Poetry can make a dead man come alive;
> It is the pain when you walk through a beehive.[11]

Poetry is the word that brings her life in her deadly community. Part of that coming alive, however, is feeling the pain of a bee sting. Coming back from the dead means coming back to joy and suffering, pleasure and pain.

Similarly, Gerald Barrax writes "For a Black Poet": "Men make revolutions / Poems will brings us to resurrection." He continues, "dress to kill / shoot to kill / love to kill / if you will / but write to bring back the dead."[12] Jesus is that poetic word; he is resurrection and life. And the fourth gospel is written "so that you might have life in the name of Jesus-son-of-God-messiah" (John 20:31). Melvin Tolson writes in "Do" (the musical note on which the Liberian national anthem begins) as part of his "Libretto":

> You are
> Black Lazarus risen from the White Man's grave,
>   Without a road to Downing Street,
> Without a hemidemisemiquaver in an Oxford stave![13]

Exploring Likenesses to the Sign in My Own Soul

I was terminated as a Southern Baptist missionary—not just cast out but killed. So I was buried in the tomb of my mother's house. But the tomb became a womb. Daily in my basement study I wrote, drew, and meditated. One day I focused my meditation on this story of the raising of Lazarus. After reading the story and spending some time in silence, I decided that I would become Lazarus, for I felt dead professionally and emotionally. I lay on the cold tile floor, closed my eyes, and imagined what it would be like to be dead. I felt scared, angry. But then I

---

[11] Colbert I. King, "Speak, Children," *The Washington Post* (July 17, 1999) A19.

[12] Gerald Barrax, "For a Black Poet," in Ward, ed., *Trouble the Water,* 276; from Barrax, *Leaning Against the Sun* (Fayetteville: University of Arkansas Press, 1992). Similarly, Langston Hughes wrote near the end of his life, "Politics can be the graveyard of the poet. And only poetry can be his resurrection" (*The Collected Poems,* 4).

[13] Melvin Tolson, "Do," *Libretto for the Republic of Liberia* (New York: Twayne, 1953) lines 37–40.

realized that if I were dead I wouldn't feel anything! So I lay on the floor and felt nothing. (How relaxing—sort of!)

In my feeling-nothingness I heard a distant voice (a male voice, not my mother's!) calling me by name (Michael! Michael!) and leading me out of the tomb. I felt something! What was it? Not sure, but I call it life. Slowly I got up off the floor. How hard it seemed! I stood up, walked through a door and opened up another to see a set of stairs leading upward and light streaming in from an outside door. I ascended the stairs and opened the door. I adjusted my eyes to the bright sunshine; I breathed deeply, I looked around at the familiar yet strangely new sights: the trees, the grass, the flowers. I then saw a man standing before me. His was the voice that called me. He was bearded and white robed, as if he had just stepped out of a Sunday School picture. He smiled tenderly and embraced me. "Welcome back," he said. Yes, welcome back . . . to life.

Yes, welcome back. Professional life came back over the next two or three years. I took a visiting teaching position at Saint Paul (Methodist) School of Theology a year after returning from the foreign mission field. The next year I taught as an adjunct at Central Baptist Seminary and Nazarene Theological Seminary, and the following year I began full-time teaching at Howard. Personal life also returned as I moved into my own apartment and began dating the woman who became my wife. (Single I died, and married I rose, with a newheart.)

Dying: being fired as a Southern Baptist missionary. Being raised: being hired as a Howard University professor. Other dyings/risings: single dies, husband rises; childless dies, father rises. But dying and rising intermingled: no clear demarcation between the two. Anxiety and depression are a death in which I struggle to live. Each day is a rising. The death of writer's block, the raising of a manuscript. Dying/rising. Newbirth, new heart. New new new. Loud voice: "Michael, COME OUT!"

5

ByeWord:
The Farewell Discourses (John 14–17)

Jesus' Judean-jousting now comes to an end, as he gets his feet washed (the Christ is christened), enters Jerusalem, hears that the (geeky) Greeks have come, and hides himself, saying, "Hour come!" (12:1-36). Judean-jousting over; disciple-discussion begins. Wash 'em up (christ-en them), talk about his glorification and their betrayal, denial, and love (13:1-38). Spend the rest of the time explaining (elaborating, confusing) what you just said. So begin the farewell discourses.[1] I will focus on the first discourse (14:1-31) and the prayer for the disciples (17:1-26).

Going and Coming (John 14:1-31)

> "Don't let your hearts be stirred up.
> You believe into God; believe also into me.
> In my father's house are many dwelling places.
> If it weren't so, would I have told you that I go to prepare
>   a place for you?
> And if I go and prepare a place for you,
> I'll come again and take you to myself,
> so that where I am you might be too.
> And you know the way where I am going."

> Thomas says to him,
>> "Master, we don't know where you are going.
>> How can we know the way?"

---

[1] It is difficult to know where the farewell discourse formally begins. Most see it beginning at 13:31: e.g., Fernando F. Segovia, *The Farewell of the Word: The Johannine Call to Abide* (Minneapolis: Fortress, 1991) 64. Francis J. Moloney, *Glory not Dishonor: Reading John 13–21* (Minneapolis: Fortress, 1998) 29, however, takes 13:1-38 as a "coherent, self-contained narrative" and notes that there is "a new development in the narrative strategy of the author in 14:1." I therefore begin the discourse proper at

Jesus says to him,
>"I am the way and the truth and the life.
>No one comes to the father except through me.
>If you know me, you will know my father too.
>And from now on you do know him and have seen him."

Philip says to him,
>"Master, show us the father, and we will be satisfied."

Jesus says to him,
>"Haven't I been with you all this time, and still you don't know me,
>   Philip?
>The one who has seen me has seen the father.
>How can you say,
>   'Show us the father'?
>Don't you believe that I am in the father and the father is in me?
>The words that I speak to you I don't speak from myself,
>but the father dwelling in me does his works.
>Believe me that I'm in the father and the father is in me;
>but if not, believe because of the works themselves.

>Amen amen I say to you,
>the one who believes into me will do the works that I do
>and will do greater works than these because I go to the father.
>And whatever you ask in my name I will do it,
>so that the father might be glorified in the son.
>If you ask me anything in my name, I will do it.

>If you love me you will keep my commandments.
>And I will ask the father and he will give you another paraclete,
>who will be with you forever:
>the spirit of truth, which the world cannot receive,
>because it does not see it or know it.
>You know it, because it dwells with you and will be in you.
>I will not leave you orphans; I will come to you.
>Yet a little while and the world will no longer see me,
>but you will see me.
>Because I live you will live too.
>In that day you will know that I am in my father and you are in me
>   and I am in you.
>The one who has my commandments and keeps them is the one
>   who loves me,
>and the one who loves me will be loved by my father,
>and I will love that one and will reveal myself to that one."

14:1. Verses 31-38 function as "hinge verses" between the narrative of 13:1-30 and the discourse of 14:1-31.

Judas, not Iscariot, says to him,
    "Master, how will you reveal yourself to us and not to the world?"
Jesus answered and said to him,
    "The one who loves me will keep my word,
    and my father will love that one,
    and we will come and make our dwelling place with that one.
    The one who does not love me does not keep my words;
    and the word that you hear is not mine but the father's who sent me.
    "I have spoken these things to you while I remain with you;
    but the paraclete, the holy spirit, whom the father will send in my
        name,
    will teach you all things and will remind you of all that I have said
        to you.

    "Peace I leave with you,
    my peace I give to you;
    I do not give to you as the world gives.
    Don't let your hearts be stirred up
    nor let them shrink back.
    You heard that I said to you,
        'I am going away,
        and I am coming to you.'
    If you loved me,
    you would have rejoiced that I go to the father,
    because the father is greater than I.
    And now I have spoken to you before it comes to be,
    so that when it comes to be,
    you will believe.
    I will no longer speak much to you,
    for the ruler of the world is coming;
    and he does not have anything in me,
    but so that the world might know that I love the father,
    and just as the father has commanded me, so I do.
    Rise, let's go forward!"

Playing with the Images of the Discourse

It is now night—Nicodemus-coming, Judas-going night (3:2; 13:30). (Satan-entered Judas goes on washed feet, though he's not clean, 13:5, 10.) It is night . . . but it is light night because it is son-of-humanity and God-glorified night, in which Jesus goes where his lil-chillun no-come (13:31-33). Before going, Jesus new-commands them lovingly (13:34-35) and then tells Simon that he will peter out. He will neither follow Jesus nor for him life-lay-down but pre-cock-crowing he will crow his own denial thricely (13:38). (Simon contrasts with the Lazarus-like disciple whom Jesus loves, who is in his bosom and asks for Peter who the betrayer is, 13:23-25. What a group of disciples: a denier, a betrayer, and a bosom buddy!)

Jesus now begins his farewell discourse to the disciples, his "bye-word." (Bye, word. Bye-bye, fleshy word.) As he goes dis course, will the disciples fare well? Well, well. (This well is deep, and we don't have a bucket! 4:11.) Jesus tells his disciples that they will fare well if they don't let their hearts get stirred up. (They'll have Jesus' peace, 14:27. But who's going to stir up their hearts? Judas-entering Satan? Jesus-glorifying God?) They already into-God believe; they need also to into-Jesus believe (because after all, God sent Jesus, 12:44).

Jesusfathershouse, which is not the temple but Jesus' body (2:16, 21), is a many-dwellinged place. Lots of room for father and son and children to gather into one (11:52). Jesus goes there (why does he need to go to his fathershouse if he is it?) for the disciples place-prepare one of those many dwellings. After going, Jesus gonna come again to the disciples to receive them into his prepared bodyhouse so that they, his servant-followers, his father-given-ones, can be with him where he is and see his loving glory (12:26; 17:24). And hey, the disciples know where Jesus is going. (Peter has just asked that very question, and Jesus didn't give him a straight answer, 13:36. Nevertheless, Jesus continues to be confident that they do know, 16:5.)

Thomas, then, who was ready to die with Jesus in Jerusalem (11:16), says, "Uh, master, uh, we don't know where you're goin', so we, huh, certainly don't know the way!" Alas and alack, the disciples are not faring well in this farewell discourse. They are still mismisMISunder-standing. Thomas (like Philip later) calls Jesus MASTER, but he has not yet MASTERED the disciples' MISunderstanding! Jesus says (as he so often does when faced with misunderstanding, 6:35; 8:12; 11:25) I AM AM I I AM. I AM the waytruthlife. True living way. Lively truthful way. Way true and alive! Way—enlightened, shepherded way to pasture (8:12; 10:9, 11). And the way is truly true truth—freeing truth, sanctifying Godsworded truth, belonging testified truth (8:32; 17:17; 18:37). And this truthful way is living, lively, alive life. Life—worded, illuminated, eternal, believing, resurrected (raised up out of the tomb) life (1:4-5; 3:15-16; 5:25-28; 6:63, 67; 11:25; 20:31). Through this living truthful way which Jesus the I AM is, people come to the father. (Only no exceptions! Jesus is the father's only broker.) Knowing Jesus means knowing the father. (Know Jesus, know father; no Jesus, no father; and the Judeans certainly don't know either Jesus or his father, 7:28-29; 8:19; 15:21; 16:3.) And knowing the father means seeing him, even though no one has seen the father (1:18; 5:37; 6:46). The disciples do, through the son.

Philip, go-between of Jesus to Nathanael and Greeks (1:45-47; 12:20-22), wants to "come and see" (1:46) and asks Jesus to father-show them so that they can come and see (the father) and be satisfied (their hearts no longer stirred up). But Jesus been with 'em all this time ALL THIS TIME and still *still* they don't know him (if they did they would know the father). Know Jesus, know father; see Jesus, see father (12:45). Father-show? I've been treating you to that show all the time! 'Cuz Jesus in father and father in Jesus (and Jesus in disciples and disciples in Jesus, 10:38; 14:20; 17:21, 23). Jesus' words (and his works) are not his own, but they are produced by the father dwelling in his house Jesus (5:19, 30; 8:28). Believing into him, knowing him, means believing that he's in father and father in him, abiding together, loving together in the fathershouse. Don't believe the words; believe the works: waterwining, breadmaking, eyeopening, deadraising. But believe!

Amenamen say: Into-Jesus' believers gonna do Jesus' works and even greaterworks (greaterthings you gonna see, 1:50, and greaterworks you gonna do, like the father shows the son greaterworks, 5:20) because Jesus father-goes. (That's where he's going, to be glorified, 13:31. Come from God, go to God, 13:3; 16:28.) Greaterworks gonna get worked because asking in Jesus' name (believe into his name, have life in his name, ask in his name, 1:12; 20:31), he (and/or father) gonna do it gonnadoit GONNADOIT (15:7-8, 16; 16:23, 26) so that father in-son might be glorified (and disciples might be completely joy-full, 16:24). Glory, glory, glory! Glory in Jesus' works, glory in Jesus' hour, glory in disciplesworks. Ask Jesus (or father) anything—ANY THING—Jesus (or father) will do it.

Jesus' lovers are also Jesus' commandmentskeepers (just as Jesus is fathercommendmentkeeper, 15:10). Jesuscommandment new: love-one-another-as-I-have-loved-you commandment (13:34-35; 15:12, 17). Love Jesus / love one another / abide in Jesus' love, branching off from the true vine and bearing lovely, loving fruit (15:4-8). For his lovers, his commandmentkeepers, Jesus gonna ask (in his own name?) the father to give (or Jesus gonna send on his own, 14:26; 15:26; 16:7) them another (because Jesus is the first) paraclete/advocate/helper/comforter/one-called-alongside. (This is the paraclete, not parakeet, though it does dove-like descend, 1:32.) (Greek *parakletos*, literally, one called along-side, called-alongside as the comforter to dry the beloved believer's tears, and/or called-alongside as the advocate to defend the believed belover's case in a casting-out-of-the-synagogue trial, 16:2). This called-alongside paraclete will be a disciple-forever-with-er. Eternal life, eternal paraclete. With you for-ever—teach/guide/testify/speak/glorify-ing (14:26; 15:26; 16:7, 13). This is the spirit of truth (after all,

Jesus I AM the truth, 14:6), the truthful spirit, spiritual truth, truly spirited, through whom true worshipers fatherworship (4:23-24).

World can't receive this spirit (or this truth, or, for that matter, the word, 1:11-12) because being from below and not born from above it doesn't see the spirit (or the father in Jesus, 14:9) or know it (or the son or the father, 7:28; 8:19; 16:3). Know Jesus, know father, know paraclete. (Trinity of knowledge?!) But the Jesus-loving commandmentkeeping disciples, having been born from above, know it (because they know Jesus and the father) (but do they see paraclete?) cuz it abides/dwells/stays/remains (makes its dwelling—Jesus has prepared that place too) with the disciples, just as it abides etc. with/on/in Jesus (1:32). With you it now dwells, and in you it will be. Paraclete abiding in disciples, Jesus in disciples, disciples in Jesus, Jesus in father (17:21, 23). Through paraclete-dwelling, the disciples will not orphaned be (They're children of God, 1:12; how can they be orphans?!) when Jesus fathergoes and placeprepares, but he will come to them (to take them to himself and to breathe on them holy spirit of peace, 14:3; 20:19, 22, 26). Lil-while world (including temple police, 7:33) no-see Jesus (disciples won't see him either for a lilwhile, and they will suffer laborpains, 16:10, 16, 20-21), but disciples will see Jesus (and rejoice, 16:22), and because he is living (and resurrecting) they will be living (and resurrecting) too. On that day (that Easter hour) the disciples gonna know (and be satisfied, 14:8) that Jesus in father, disciples in Jesus, and Jesus in disciples—all through the paraclete, being perfectly one (17:21, 23).

Judas (not the Iscariot, because he has already night-gone-out to Jesus-betray, 13:30) asks the master how he's gonna reveal himself to them and not to the world. (Oh-oh, another unmastered misunderstanding!) Jesus says again that his lover will be a his-word(s)-keeper/his-commandments-keeper (14:15). Furthermore, Jesusfather will be a Jesuslover-lover, and Jesusandhisfather will come to their lover (blown in by the wind of the spirit, the paraclete) and will make their dwelling-place, their preparedplace (vv. 2-3) with their lover, so that where Jesus the I AM is, his lover also is (v. 4). New home, new family, dwelling/abiding together in love, in the spirit.

Non-Jesuslovers, however, are non-Jesusword(s)-keepers. (They're also presumably non-abiders in the Jesusandfatherhome.) But Jesus'-word(s) is(are) really fathersending Jesus' words, spoken by the lifted-up son of humanity, the I AM (8:28; cf. also 3:34; 12:49; 15:15; 17:7-8).

Jesus now speaks these things in the lil-while he's still making his dwellingplace with the disciples (13:33). But the paraclete, the holy spirit (spirit-of-truth, 14:17), who will be father-sent-in-Jesus-name (father sent Jesus, father sends paraclete in Jesus' name), will be an allthings-teacher and an allthings-Jesus-said-reminder, helping them to understand the strange things Jesus said and did (2:22; 12:16; 20:9).

One of the all-things the paraclete teaches is peace—courageous-amidst-persecution peace (16:33), breathy, resurrected, holy-spirited peace (20:21-22). This Jesus-giving peace is different from the Jesus-rejecting-world peace. (Is there any peace with that? The world hates Jesus and his disciples, 15:18-20.) This peace, this believing-in-God-and-Jesus/place-prepared peace pacifies the stirred-up/shrunk-back heart. Jesus reminds the disciples of what he has already said to them: he's away-going but to them coming (going to placeprepare and coming to take them to that place, 14:3). If they love him, they would rejoice that he is father-going (but the rejoicing will only really come when the resurrection baby is born, 16:21; 20:20), because the father, with whom he is one (10:30) and in whom he is (14:10), is greater than he. (After all, the father gives him his words and his works!) But he has before-told them these things, so that when they happen (during the hour) they will believe (I Am, 13:19) . . . and love and rejoice . . . and remember, through the spirit (16:1, 4). Jesus won't many-things-speak to them, for the worldruler comes. (Indeed, he has already entered into night-going, betraying Judas, 13:27, 30.) But because Jesus is not of this world, this worldruling Satan, the accuser as opposed to the advocating paraclete, doesn't have anything (nor does the Judearuling Pilate, 19:10-11) in him or over him or on him. Hey, in the lifting-up hour, the worldruler is exorcised, and his world is judged (12:31; 16:11)! But Jesus submits himself to the worldruling Satan (and his minions such as Judas and Pilate and the Judeans), so that the Satan-ruled world might know that Jesus fatherloves (and fathergoes and discipleloves). Father commands the good shepherd to lay down his life (and take it up again, 10:18), and Jesus does it (to the end, 13:1). So, Jesus says to the spirit-indwelled disciples, let's do it; let's go forward, from here, from this conquered world (16:33)—to the father!

Exploring Likenesses to the Discourse in African-American Poetry

I am particularly moved by three images in this discourse: house, spirit, and love. First, the house. The father's house. The son taking the believer to that house. The father and son homing in on the believer. House/home. Longing for a place to be family, to have property, to set one's boundaries, to be a person. In African-American poetry we see this theme, as folks yearn for a place to call their own. Nayo Barbara Malcolm Watkins writes about such a feeling in "Black Woman Throws a Tantrum." She cries out that she wants a home, a land that's hers. She has lost her home through the fault of a "nigger" who has let "that cracker take my home." She wants a home so that she "can set a spell / and breathe fresh air / and ease my mind / live— / and love— / and be buried / in a land that's mine."[2] The poem is reminiscent of Frances Ellen Watkins Harper's "Bury Me in a Free Land,"[3] but Harper's quiet supplication to God is now turned into ranting against an "ass-sitting nigger." Yet after ventilation of her anger at losing her home, her space, her flesh, she fictively resides in that house-yet-to-be-built, where she breathes fresh air (the holy spirit that the risen Jesus breathes on her, John 20:22), eases her mind (and her heart is not stirred up and she experiences unworldly peace, 14:1, 27), lives the resurrected life after the death of homelessness ("I AM resurrection, way, truth, and life," 11:25; 14:6), loves her one-anothers ("This is my commandment," 15:12, which makes a house a home united in love, 14:23), and dies . . . though she continues to live through the land. This house is paradise, Eden, entered only through the garden tomb (19:41).

Such a place is "Where the Heart Is" for Ntozake Shange. She longs for a seaside mansion or castle, which has a single door through which she alone can enter, to shelter her from the ferocious world and from her own fearful and self-hating mind. Here, "I can love myself in an empty space / & maybe fill it with kisses."[4] There is, then, her house, "where her heart is," her unstirred-up heart (John 14:27), and there is "the world," which is "ferocious" and leads to misunderstanding, fear, and self-hatred. ("In me you may have peace. In the world you have tribulation," 16:33.) Her needed house, however, which she enters through her one and only door ("I Am the Door/Way," 10:7, 9; 14:6), is a place empty of fears and misunderstanding but filled with self-love. In her house she has peace; in the world she has persecution. But she takes courage, for she has conquered the world—through building her longed-for house in her imagination, where she drinks of the living water.

Similarly, Naomi Long Madgett goes through many "Exits and Entrances":

> Through random doors we wandered
>   into passages disguised as paradise
>   and out again, discarding,

[2] Nayo Barbara Malcolm Watkins, "Black Woman Throws a Tantrum," in Jerry W. Ward, Jr., ed., *Trouble the Water: 250 Years of African-American Poetry* (New York: Mentor, 1997) 369.

[3] See above, chapter 3, 70.

[4] Ntozake Shange, "Where the Heart Is," in Clarence Major, ed., *The Garden Thrives: Twentieth-Century African-American Poetry* (New York: Harper Perennial, 1996) 318–19, from Shange, *Ridin' the Texas Moon* (New York: St. Martin's, 1987).

embracing hope anew, discarding again:
exits and entrances to many houses

Without joy we sang,
without grace we danced.
our hump-back rhythms colliding
with our sanity,
our beauty blanching in a hostile sun.

How should we, could we
sing our song in a strange land?

Through random doors we have come
home to our kingdom, our own battleground,
not with harps, not with trumpets even,
but armed with the invincible sword and shield
of our own names and faces.[5]

The poet and her folk first "wandered" in many joyless, hopeless, grace-less houses. But after quoting Ps 137:4 they "come home" to their own kingdom ("Unless you are born from above/again, you will never see the kingdom of God," John 3:3), where they take up the armor of their own names and faces. Perhaps they hear the good shepherd's voice at the door calling them by name and leading them out (10:3).

This house is the home of the paraclete, the spirit, which abides in and with the disciples. George Barlow entitled the third stanza of his epic poem *Gabriel* "Spirit in the Dark." The refrain tells the reader, "Here is the spirit in the dark," and later says to hear, see, touch, feel, and get "the spirit in the dark." This spirit was experienced as one heart, voice, purpose, people, dream, and collective beauty as they sang and played the spirituals, soul, blues, and jazz.

Under an old roof that leaks
& an old system
that won't let them breathe
they blow their urgency,
rebirth & survival, sweetly
like wind through reeds & treetops.

The old system (which is not born anew because it is from below) leaves them breathless. Nevertheless, they blow their rebirth—from above, from the wind/spirit (3:5-8), which provides a Re(e)dSea exodus through the deadly tree. In the spirit they experience heart, soul,

[5] Naomi Long Madgett, "Exits and Entrances," Ward, ed., *Trouble the Water,* 184–85, from Madgett, *Exits and Entrances* (Detroit: Lotus, 1978).

love, and freedom (untroubled heart and soul, love for one another, and truthful freedom): all this through "the spirit in the dark."[6] The "dark" here has a double meaning, as it does in many poems by African-Americans. It refers both to the skin color of African-Americans and to the "horror of the times" of slavery, segregation, and discrimination. The spirit shines in the midst of the dark through the dark.

Julius E. Thompson says that he sees "In My Mind's Eye" the spirit moving him "Back and forth between / Two worlds" (much as the spirit moves the disciples from the world below to the world above). The spirit also moves him to see "500 million / Walking home free!"[7] Again, the spirit frees folks (through the truth, John 8:33) and brings them home.

At home the spirit engenders love—love for God and Jesus demonstrated in love for one another. S.I.M.B.A. (Safe In My Brothers Arms), a group of young African-American males at the Sojourners Neighborhood Center in Washington, D.C., collectively wrote "Brotherhood":

> I love my brothers
> for whatever they do.
>
> We help each other
> and we're special too . . .
>
> We all should have peace
> in the 'hood.
>
> If everybody would
> just do what they should!
>
> We sing with praises
> because we're proud.
>
> That's why we
> always speak up loud.
>
> We teach our brothers
> each and every way.
>
> Because violence happens
> every single day.
>
> We are strong
> because we are kings

---

[6] George Barlow, *Gabriel*, in Ward, ed., *Trouble the Water*, 455–56, from Barlow, *Gabriel* (Detroit: Broadside Press, 1974).

[7] Julius E. Thompson, "In My Mind's Eye," in Ward, ed., *Trouble the Water*, 496.

Black
experience
more like
John's community
more communal

We are the finest
of all human beings

We are the Brothers
of SIMBA yes we are

We fight for our rights
and we are going far![8]

Surely this is the "beloved community" that Jesus envisioned when he commanded his disciples to love one another (John 13:34). Such love results in peace (Jesus-given peace, 14:27). Folks teach one another (under the guidance of the fathersent holyspirit-paraclete, who teaches the disciples everything, 14:26) because the beloved community is subject to violence, hatred, persecution, expulsion, even death (15:18, 20; 16:2). But they are sustained by their pride (encouraged by the conquering of the world, 16:33) and strength of kings (so they have been born from above into the kingdom, 3:3). And they are going far—all the way to a spiritual house where family lives and loves in peace. ("Rise, let's go forward," 14:31.)

Loving, living and loving. Living lovingly. Sterling D. Plumpp writes about such a love-life in "Black ethics," which makes "man strong, / ready to die for his / woman / child / and country /" No greater love than this: laying down one's life, dying . . . for others, for the sheep (John 15:12; 10:11, 15). The love-life is love-death, yet it is the "excavated gem," the "priceless dynamo" that fulfills one's humanity and moves one from self-separation (stirred-up heart) to self-pride (peace).[9]

Exploring Likenesses to the Discourse in My Own Soul

Yes, I too want a house, a house wherein dwells the spirit of love. In my house growing up there was no such spirit, or I should say that I did not find the spirit of love blowing there envigorating me, but a breath of control stifling and constricting me. It was my father's house, where he ruled. He was the unquestioned boss, but we all observed that more than he exerted it. My father's house became dominated by my father's body. He became diabetic, and my mother observed a very strict diet in which everything was weighed and every meal was served exactly at the appointed hour. If we could control the diet, then perhaps we could control the disease. But we couldn't. The disease

---

[8] S.I.M.B.A., "Brotherhood," in Geoff Zylstra and Reba Mathern, eds., *The Voices of Children: Stories From Our Future* (Washington, D.C.: Sojourners Neighborhood Center, 1996) 27.

[9] Sterling D. Plumpp, "Black ethics," in Jerry W. Ward, ed., *Trouble the Water*, 374.

went out of control, and so did our house. My father, like Jesus, went away, but unlike Jesus he did not come again or send a paraclete.

I long to dwell in a loving house, where there is peace, where my anxiety is quelled. I find that house in reading the gospel, writing about it, teaching it. There a house is constructed for me where Jesus, the father, and the paraclete come to live with me. They love me and breathe into me the breath of life. Yet I am not perfectly at peace in this house. "I am the way . . . no one to the father but through me"?!? Of course no one comes to the Christian God except through the Christ. Makes sense. But that's not the way it's usually interpreted. Usually: no authentic religion apart from Christianity. None. Not Buddhism, not Hinduism, not Islam, not "secular humanism," and certainly not Judaism, for the Jews rejected Jesus, according to the gospel. Only Christ, that is, Christianity, that is, the church, that is, the institutional church, has THE TRUTH, and everyone else has at best a pale reflection of the truth. (Okay, now's the time to get on my soapbox, be prosaic.) This kind of rhetoric simply legitimates the authority of the institution and those who hold power in it. Such talk strengthens the boundaries between the church and the world and sets up an "us vs. them" mentality. We have the truth, but you do not. Such rhetoric may draw church members together, but it also alienates them from others, leading perhaps to oppression and violence. (Okay. Down off soapbox now. Go over to the parkbench and resume doodling.)

The father's house—yes, yes, that's what we're talking about—is also a patriarchal house. (Oh, oh, am I stepping back up on the box again? When I say those big words—"rhetoric," "patriarchal"—I feel my body stiffen and rise to the platform. A kind of resurrection? If so, let's go forward, 14:31!) In the father's house the father and son dwell there with believers in the spirit, but what about the mother and the daughter? Is this house built on sexist foundations and therefore cannot stand?

The father. I am the father now, with a wife and two daughters. I pray that my house—our house (on 57th Avenue, Berwyn Heights, Maryland, you can't miss it: it has the Japanese maple out front)—is spirited by love. Love that recognizes all people—male or female, parent or child—as worthy and gifted. Love that does not exclude but includes. Love that empowers and strengthens. Love, love, love. Love, peace, joy.

Father and Son Won / One (John 17:1-26)

> After Jesus said these things, he lifted his eyes up to heaven and said,
> "Father, the hour has come.
> Glorify your son,

so that the son might glorify you,
just as you have given him power over all flesh,
so that to everything that you have given him he might give eternal life.
And this is eternal life:
that they might know the only true God and the one whom you have
   sent,
Jesus Christ.
I have glorified you upon the earth by completing the work that you
   gave me to do.
Now glorify me, father, with the glory which I had with you before the
   world was.

I have made known your name to the ones that you've given me from
   the world.
They were yours,
and you gave them to me,
and they have kept your word.
I know that all that you have given me is from you,
for I have given to them the words that you have given to me.
They have received them and known truly that I have come from you,
and they have believed that you sent me.

I pray for them.
I do not pray for the world, but for the ones you have given me,
because they're yours,
All that is mine is yours, and I have been glorified in them.
I am no longer in the world,
but they are in the world,
and I am coming to you.
Holy father, keep them in your name that you have given me,
so that they might be one just as we are one.
When I was with them, I kept them in your name that you have given
   me.
I guarded them,
and none of them was lost, except the son of lostness,
so that the scripture might be fulfilled.
But now I am coming to you.
I am speaking these things in the world
so that my joy might be fulfilled in them.
I have given them your word,
and the world has hated them,
because they are not of the world,
just as I am not of the world.
I don't pray that you should take them out of the world,
but that you might keep them from the evil one.
They are not of the world, just as I am not of the world.
Sanctify them in truth;

your word is truth.
Just as you have sent me into the world,
I also send them into the world;
and I sanctify myself for them,
so that they might be sanctified in truth.

I don't pray only for them,
but also for the ones who believe into me through their word,
that they all might be one,
just as you, father, are in me and I in you,
that they also might be in us,
so that the world might believe that you sent me.
I have given to them the glory that you gave to me,
in order that they might be one just as we are one,
I in them and you in me,
so that they might be completed as one,
so that the world might know that you sent me,
and you have loved them just as you loved me.

Father, I want the ones that you have given me to be with me
     where I am,
so that they might behold my glory,
which you have given to me because you loved me from the
     foundation of the world.
Righteous Father, the world does not even know you,
but I know you,
and they know that you have sent me.
I have made your name known,
and I will make it known,
so that your love for me might be in them and I in them."

Playing with the Images in the Prayer

Jesus the world-conquerer (16:33) said these things—these paraclete-promising (14:26;15:26), love-one-another-commanding (13:34-35; 15:12), father-going (14:28; 16:10, 28) things, and then he heaven-lifts his eyes (as he did at Lazarus' tomb when he prayed so that the crowd might believe [11:41-42]. Is he now praying so that the disciples might believe?). Jesus addresses "father," the one to whom he goes, the one who is in him and the one in whom he is (14:10). He says, Hour come. Hour coming now is (4:23; 5:25). Hour not yet at Cana (2:4), at stoning (7:30), but coming and ising NOW—hour for dead-raising (5:25), true-spirit-worshiping (4:23), disciple-scattering (16:32). It's come—with the festi-val-worshiping Greeks, the hour to fall into the earth and die and, as the true vine, bear much fruit (12:20-24). The hour has come, the hour to pray to father for glorification, son(ofhumanity)-glorification and father-glorification (cf. also 13:31-32). GLORY, glory, GLO(w)ry, as of an only son, fully gracious and true (1:14). Father glorifies son, son glorifies father. (Glorify, glory-fly—to heaven, to father, to above!)

Father's given son over-all-flesh power: power to childrenofGod make (1:12), power to judge (5:22), and power to lifegive (5:21)—eternally, for God solovesthe world (3:16). Lifeternal means knowing the only true God (who has sent the true light, 1:9, and the true bread, 6:32) and his sent one JesusChrist, through whom gracious truth came to be (1:17). Through the signs (water-wining, dead-raising, etc.) Jesus has fatherglorified and fathersworkcompleted (for that's his food, 4:34), so now he's asking father to Jesus-glorify with before-world glory, in-the-beginning-word-with-God-glory (1:1-2). Glory in the beginning (creation), glory in the middle (signs, discourses), and glory at the end (death, resurrection, ascension).[10] From glory to glory! (Yet the final glory is gory glory! Deathly glory, glorified death. How oedipally complex! The father kills the son, or better said, he commands the son to kill himself, 10:17-18. But the father bathes the son's dark death in glorious light, so that he not only dies but rises, ascends, gives the spirit, and reunites with the father. It's still death, but what a way to go![11])

Jesus has fatherglorified by makingknown the fathersname (I AM?) to the father-given-from-the-world-to-the-son-ones. (Through the signs they have believed in Jesus'Godgivenglory, 2:11.) They were the father's, given to the son, so securely that the son couldn't drive them away or lose them (6:37, 39; 18:9) and no one could snatch them out of the son's hand (10:29). These father-given-to-the-son-ones have kept the father's word (given to them through the son's word, 14:24), because they love the son (and therefore love one another, 13:34-35), and the father loves them, and the father/son home in on them (14:23). The son knows that the father loves him too (because he has kept the fathersword to lay down his life, 10:17), and therefore he has given him all things (cf. 3:35), including words for the word to speak, given in turn to the father-givenones, who have received (kept) the fathersonwords (and have become children of God, 1:12) and have known/believed that Jesus has from-God-come/been-sent (though it has taken them a while to come to that belief/knowledge, 16:29-30, for throughout their time with Jesus they have received his words with misunderstanding, cf. 14:9-10).

[10] As Ernst Käsemann said in *The Testament of Jesus: According to John 17,* translated by Gerhard Krodel (Philadelphia: Fortress, 1966) 21, protology is placed beside eschatology.

[11] For a clear, concise summary of Sigmund Freud's Oedipus theory and Paul Ricoeur's restatement of it see Robert Hamerton-Kelly, *God the Father: Theology and Patriarchy in the Teaching of Jesus.* Overtures to Biblical Theology (Philadelphia: Fortress, 1979) 7–18.

For these believing knowers (these gnostics) Jesus prays, not for the disciple-hating, word-rejecting world (15:18, i.e., the Judeans, who were trying to kill Jesus, 5:18; 7:1) but for father-given-to-the-son-ones, who are the father's but the son's too because everything that's the father's is also the son's (16:15), given from father to son (3:35; 13:3). In these father-given-ones the son has been glorified (as they ask in Jesus' name and do greaterworks, 14:12-13). (Glorified even in/through their misunderstanding?!) But Jesus not in the world anymore. Left his fathergivenones behind, still in-the-world. Jesus not intheworld, going to the father. (Going, going, GONE!) Come from godfather/going to godfather, who's greater than Jesusson (13:3; 14:28). Jesus is suspended between heaven and earth, between above and below; he's already on his glorious way! From his going-to-the-father position, son prays that holy father, sanctified father, will in his name keep fathertotheson-givenones, so that in I AM they are, they are one, father-in-son one, made possible by the paraclete (14:16-17, 21). While with them, Jesus kept/guarded them in the father-to-the-son-givenname, I AM, so that none might be lost except son-of-lostness (that satan-entered, gone-out-into-the night Judas Iscariot, 13:2, 27, 30, who is a devil, 6:70), who is lost so as to scripture-fulfill. (Exactly what scripture is that? Presumably father knows because son is not telling.) The scripture, like Jesus, is thirsty and must be filled full (19:28).

Son's a'comin' to father, these-things speaking in the world (So do his words remain in the world even though he does not?), so as to full-fill not just the scriptures but also the disciples' joy—abiding, birthing (from-above), asking/receiving joy (15:11; 16:20-24). (YIPPEE!) Jesus has given the fathergivenones the fathersword (and they have kept it). For that the world hates them (even though they love one another), but world hated son (and father, 15:23) before it hated them because neither son nor fathergivenones are of the world (not-of-the-word / not-of-the-world); they're aliens, from above. Son has chosen the fathergivenones from the world, and the world hates them (15:18-19). But son doesn't pray that father should take them out of the world (as he is doing with son, who seems to have an easier job than they do because he is returning to the loving father and they are staying in the hating world). Son prays that father would keep them from the evil one, the satan (the accuser, over against the advocate), who is not only of the world but rules the world (14:30) and is father of the murderous Judeans (8:44). He has no power over son or fathergivenones because they are not-of-the-world. The non-worldly son prays that holy, sancti-fied father might sanctify, holy-fy, the fathergivenones in truth, fathers-word truth (fathers-fleshly-word gracious truth, 1:14, 18; 14:6), spirit truth (that is in them / with them, 14:16-17). Just as father has sent son into world not to judge it but save it (3:17), son sends the father-givenones into world, breathing on them holy resurrection spirit (20:22). Son holies himself (though father has already holied him in sending him into world, 10:36), thus, holy father, holy son, so that the father-given-ones might be holied in the whole, sanctified, spirited, living truth.

Son doesn't just pray for the father-given-ones but also for all into-him, through-their-word believers, who, not Thomas-like, believe without seeing (20:29). If the father-given-ones keep fathersword and receive sonswords, then people will believe through their word. Word-wordword! Believers are of word not world, born from above. Son (word from above) prays that all these word-not-world believers might one be (dispersed children-of-God gathered into one flock by one laying-down-his-life shepherd, 10:16; 11:52), just as father in son and son in father and believers in father and son. Youinme and Iinyou and theyinus. I AM/we are/we all are (cf. 10:38; 14:10, 20). So that, so that the world, that disciple-hating, word-rejecting world, might believe that father sent son. Sent son's given the wordbelievers glory, glorious words, worded glory, enfleshed worded glory (1:14), signed glory (2:11), father-given glory, so that they one (through loving one another) as fatherson (we) one. Son in wordbelievers and father in son. Iinthem and youinme. So that completed/fulfilled (filled full, joyfully and scripturally) as one ONE one (won: conquered world, 16:33). So that world might know (the world might become gnostic) /believe that father is a son-sender and a believer-lover (coming to beloved believer along with son to make a home, 14:23) as well as a son-lover (and son-all-things-giver and son-all-his-doings-shower, 3:35; 5:20).

Beloved son calls loving father: he wants/desires/longs that his father-given-ones (his servant/friends, 12:26; 15:15) be with him where he is. He has after all prepared a place in the fathershouse, and he plans to take them there to be in the father with him and be one and be loved (14:1-3). Here all are family: disciples are Jesus' brothers (not sisters?) and God is their father (20:17). (But does this happen in the world or not? How can believers be where son is if they are in the world and he is not?) In the fathershouse the father-given-ones will see the sonsglory, father-given-to-the-son in love before worldfoundation (and before worldrejection of the word, 1:10). Righteous and just (and holy) father is not known by the world (though the world was founded by father through the word, 1:3), but son knows father, and father-given-ones know that he is father-sent. (He has father's scent.) Son known-made fathersname (I AM, through signs, through discourses) and will known-make it (through going to the father), so that fathersonlove might be in father-given-ones and therefore son might be in them, abiding in love through the truthful, fruitful, vining spirit (15:1-11). In the beginning was glory; in the end love.[12]

Exploring Likenesses to the Prayer in African-American Poetry

Here in his final discourse to the disciples, Jesus returns to the theme of the first public discourse (5:19-47): the oneness of the father and the son. The oneness here, however, is a oneness in death. Generally, fathers die in the presence of their sons. Cornelius Eady opens his book of prose poems about his father's illness and death with "I Know (I'm Losing You)":

> Have you ever touched your father's back? No, my fingers tell me, as
>   they try to pull up a similar memory.
> There are none. This is a place we have never traveled to, as I try to lift
>   his weary body onto the bedpan.
> I recall a photo of him standing in front of our house. He is large,
>   healthy, a stocky body in a dark blue suit.
> And now his bowels panic, feed his mind phony information, and as I
>   try to position him, my hands shift, and the news shocks me more
>   than the sight of his balls.
> O, bag of bones, this is all I'll know of his body, the sharp ridge of spine,
>   the bedsores, the ribs rising in place like new islands.
> I feel him strain as he pushes, for nothing, feel his fingers grip my
>   shoulders. He is slipping to dust, my hands inform me, you'd
>   better remember this.[13]

Eady remembers his father's "weary body . . . slipping to dust." He is not only into the father's bosom (John 1:18) but into his bones, back, bowels, and balls. This is not the living father but the dying father.

Dying, dying. Fathers die, and they live a ghostly, ghastly existence in the lives of their sons. D.J. Renegade writes of an unholy trinity, "Father, Son and the Wholly Ghost."

> We meet only
> in the alleys of memory.
> Our broken smiles
> litter the ground.
> Although we wear the same name,
> identical scars,

---

[12] See Stephen Moore's eloquent Lacanian meditation on God's desire in John in his *Poststructuralism and the New Testament: Derrida and Foucault at the Foot of the Cross* (Minneapolis: Fortress, 1994) 62–64. As I noted in the introduction (n. 18), Jacques Lacan's method, is somewhat similar to my own.

[13] Cornelius Eady, "I Know (I'm Losing You)," in idem, *You Don't Miss Your Water: Poems* (New York: Henry Holt, 1995) 1.

you can't remember what day I was born.
Anger spills
down the side
of my face.
This is what you have taught me:
needles are hollower
than lies,
leave bigger holes in families,
than arms.
Now a prisoner in death's camp,
you grow thinner every day
until I can count your T-cells
on one hand.
The phone rings
Mama pleads
Please buy a dark suit to wear.
I tell her
I wear black every day,
all day,
anyway.[14]

The ghost that haunts Renegade, like Jesus' paraclete, does remind him
of his father's words and all that he has taught him (cf. John 14:26-27).
These words, however, do not bring joy or peace but anger. (His heart
is stirred up!) His father has taught him lies, not the truth, holes and
nothing holy.

The father dies, and sometimes the son dies . . . at the hands of the
father. Ralph Dickey's "Father" beats the poet's mother to death, and
says to him, "I want you to kill a man for me . . . / I'll give you a hundred dollars . . . / here's a piece of paper / with the man's name / kill
him I'll give you / a hundred dollars / I opened the paper my name /
was on it . . . / what is this I said / some kind of . . . / joke I never
joke / about money / he said."[15] The word from the father has the son's
name on it; he is to kill him. His payment is love and union with the
father. It is no joke; the father doesn't joke about resurrection.

Exploring Likenesses to the Prayer in My Own Soul

My father died, as I have said a number of times in this book, after a
two-year illness. My father and I were not one at that time. I was a

---

[14] D. J. Renegade, "Father, Son and the Wholly Ghost," in E. Ethelbert Miller, ed.
Beyond the Frontier (Baltimore: Black Classic Press, 2001).

[15] Ralph Dickey, "Father," in Michael S. Harper and Anthony Walton, eds., *Every
Shut Eye Ain't Asleep: An Anthology of Poetry by African Americans Since 1945* (Boston:
Little, Brown, 1994) 222–23.

teenager who liked long hair, tight pants and thrice-weekly church-going. (The youth group was my new family, since my old one was falling apart.) He was a middle-aged man who liked short hair, baggy pants and twice-yearly (Christmas and Easter) churchgoing. We were not one, as Jesus and his father were. Indeed, we became "two-er" as he became weaker (and I became stronger). One memory that is seared into my brain is from the time when I was fifteen and my father was in the hospital, as he often was those two years before he died. A friend of mine, David Barker, was also in that hospital, not far from my father's room. Dad was sitting in a chair throwing up into a bedpan. He looked at me, with my longish hair, and said through his vomit, "Barber, barber, go to barber." In my typical adolescent (read "smart-aleck") way back then, I said, "Barker? Oh yes, David Barker is down the hall, and I'm going to go see him after I leave here." I knew exactly what my father meant, but I refused to let him control me. He tried to do that all of my life and I was not going to let him do it at the end of his life.

We were not one, either in life or in death. When I start complaining about Dad, my mother often says (usually angrily), "You're just like him." I suppose she's right. For all of our differences we were just alike: two thin, dark-haired, handsome (!?), witty, angry, perfectionistic con-trol freaks.

Are all fathers—parents, pastors, priests, professors, and project managers—control freaks? So our "children" (parishioners, students, employees) must be one with us, and they are rewarded with love, grades, money, and the assurance of life beyond death. So the sheep die for the shepherd, and they are "good sheep" of the "good shepherd," who calls them by name and leads them out of their will, their desires, their gifts . . . their spirit.

But what about love as letting go rather than controlling, as releasing rather than holding fast, as being two rather than being one? What about . . . ?

Hmm. Does Ana need a haircut?

6

UpWord:
Jesus' Return to the Father (John 18–21)

Jesus goes to the father through death and resurrection. Upward! Up, word! He goes up, to the world above, where he comes from. So we read about "the main event," "the hour," which has finally come after "not-yet-coming" throughout the gospel. I focus on two moments in the hour: the trial before Pilate and the appearances to Mary Magdalene and the disciples.

Jesus is on his way to the father. Let's put it in high gear!

On Automatic Pilate (John 18:28–19:16a)

Then they take Jesus from Caiaphas into the praetorium.
Now it was early,
and they did not enter into the praetorium,
so that they might not defile themselves for eating the passover.
Then Pilate came out to them and said,
　　"What charge do you bring against this man?"
They answered and said to him,
　　"If he were not an evildoer, we would not have handed him over to
　　　you."
Pilate then said to them,
　　"Take him yourselves, and judge him according to your law."
The Judeans said to him,
　　"It is not right for us to kill anyone."
This happened so that the word of Jesus might be fulfilled which he
　　said indicating by what death he was about to die.

Then Pilate went into the praetorium again and called Jesus and said
　　to him,
　　"Are you the king of the Judeans?"
Jesus answered,
　　"Do you say this on your own, or did others say it to you about me?"

Pilate answered,
>"I'm not a Judean, am I?
>Your nation and chief priests handed you over to me.
>What have you done?"

Jesus answered,
>"My kingdom is not of this world.
>If my kingdom were of this world, my helpers would have fought
>so that I might not be handed over to the Judeans.
>But my kingdom is not from here."

Then Pilate said to him,
>"Then you are a king, aren't you?"

Jesus answered,
>"You say that I am a king.
>I have been born and come into the world for this,
>that I might witness to the truth.
>Everyone who is of the truth hears my voice."

Pilate says to him,
>"What is truth?"

And after saying this Pilate again went out to the Judeans and said to
them,
>"I find no crime in him.
>It is your custom that I release someone to you at the festival.
>Do you want me to release to you the king of the Judeans?"

Then they cried out again saying,
>"Not him but Barabbas."

Now Barabbas was a bandit.

Then Pilate took Jesus and had him flogged.
And the soldiers plaited a crown of thorns and put it on his head and
dressed him in a purple cloak.
And they kept coming up to him and saying,
>"Hail, King of the Judeans!"

And they were slapping him.

And Pilate went out again and says to them,
>"See, I am bringing him out to you,
>so that you might know that I find no crime in him."

Then Jesus came out, wearing the crown of thorns and the purple cloak,
and Pilate says to them,
>"See the man."

Then when the chief priests and the helpers saw him, they cried out
saying,
>"Crucify him! Crucify him!"

Pilate says to them,
>"Take him yourselves and crucify him,
>for I find no crime in him."

The Judeans answered him,
> "We have a law, and according to that law he ought to die,
> because he has made himself son of God."

When Pilate heard this word, he became all the more afraid.
And he went into the praetorium again and says to Jesus,
> "Where are you from?"
But Jesus did not give him an answer.
Then Pilate says to him,
> "Do you speak to me?
> Don't you know that I have power to release you
> and I have power to crucify you?"
Jesus answered,
> "You have no power over me except that which was given to you
>> from above.
> Because of this the one who handed me over to you has greater sin."
From this time on Pilate was seeking to release him,
but the Judeans cried out saying,
> "If you release him, you are not a friend of Caesar.
> Everyone who makes himself a king speaks against Caesar."

Then when Pilate heard these words he brought Jesus out and sat on
> the tribunal on the place called the Stone Pavement, in Hebrew
> *Gabbatha.*
And it was the sixth hour of the day of preparation of the Passover.
And he says to the Judeans,
> "See your king."
Then they cried out,
> "Away with him! Away with him! Crucify him!"
Pilate says to them,
> "Crucify your king?"
The chief priests answered,
> "We have no king but Caesar."
Then he handed him over to them to be crucified.

Playing with the Images of the Trial

After finishing his fatherglorifyme-and-make-them-one prayer (17:1-
26), Jesus decides to garden, and this is an arresting moment, for Judas
comes by night, along with the Judean police, who fall for I AM and
then take him disciple-less (at his request) to Annas, annual high
priest's pop-in-law (18:1-14). Simon Peter-out, along with the 'nother
known-to-the-high-priest disciple, follows Jesus coldly and thus needs
a this-worldly-light, fired charcoal, says I AM NOT. Cockadoodledoo!
Jesus, however, is doing his own crowing to the high priest, thus earn-
ing a faceslap (police brutality!), to which Jesus does not turn the other

cheek. (This is John, not Matthew.) Annas binds him up (Lazarus-like) and sends him to Caiaphas.

Jesus goes from Annas to Caiaphas (the better-one-man-die-for-the-people person, 11:50) to Peter's I AM NOT (cockadoodledoo!) to the praetorium, where the Judeans "prae" (prey, certainly not "pray") on Jesus. It was early, still night. The Judeans don't actually go into the praetorium because they would then be defiled with Gentile stain and would have to pass-over the feast. But they certainly don't want to pass over getting Jesus killed. Praetorium prefect Pilate comes out and asks them what charge (card?) they're using. Judeans: "Evildoer, so hand over to you." (Evildoer? Jesus only does the fatherswill, 5:19.) Pilate: judge him according to yourlaw, law of Moses (who witnesses to Jesus, 5:45-46). Judeans: Hey, ain't right for us to kill nobody. (Thou shalt not kill, ya know. But no problem gettin' you to kill somebody, that is, crucify him.) They said this not of their own accord (Nobody does anything of his or her own accord in this gospel), but said it (God had them say it?) so that Jesusword (which of course he's received from the father, 14:10) that he would be up-lifted (and all people draw) might be full-filled (for Jesus' word is now scripture, 2:22) in which he said how he was going to die (12:32-33). Up-lifted, crucified. Roman (not Judean) penalty. But demanded by Judeans.

Pilate goes back into the praetorium. Pilate always in and out, inandout. Or really out and in, outandin. Out to talk to Judeans, in to talk to Jesus.[1] Pilate asks if he's the Judean king. (After all, he's got to write the charge on his cross, 19:19. Maybe he heard the crowd earlier "palm him off" as Israelite king, 12:13.) If so, then he's up-setting himself against the real Judean king: Caesar. And this supposed Judean king will need to be done away with. King? Yeah. King of Israel, broker of the king-dom of God (1:49; 3:3, 5). And yeah, king of the Judeans in a way, in that he is the one through whom the world (and the Judeans) was made (1:10), he judges them (though he says that he judges no one, 5:30; 8:15). But not a king to be taken by force (as the loafing crowd wanted to do, 6:15) but one believed into, so that one can enter the king-dom of God. Jesus asks Pilate if this is his own conclusion or that of others. (Why does Jesus need to ask? He knows what's in a person, 2:24-25.) Pilate protests that he's not a Judean, is he? Of course not, he's a Roman, a Gentile. But if he sides against Jesus, he puts himself with the Judeans

---

[1] It has often been pointed out that the story of the appearance before Pilate is structured in seven scenes, in which #1, 3, 5, and 7 take place outside the praetorium, and #2, 4, and 6 take place inside. Cf. Raymond Brown, *The Gospel According to John, XIII–XXI,* AB 29A (Garden City, N.Y.: Doubleday 1970) 858–59; idem, *The Death of the Messiah: From Gethsemane to Grave* (New York: Doubleday, 1994) 757–59.

and therefore becomes an honorary Judean. So Pilate, are you a Judean or not? Pilate continues that Jesus' nation, for which he is about to die (11:51-52), and chief priests (hey, they're not Jesus' chief priests, but they are priests in that they're getting ready to sacrifice him on the altar!) handed him over to Pilate. So what's he done? (God's will, that's what.)

Jesus, never giving a straight answer, says that his king-dom is of this world NOT. His kingdom is the kingdom of God; it is from-above (3:3, 7; 8:23). If Jesus' kingdom were this-world-of, then his helpers, servants, disciples, assistants would have been fighting so that he wouldn't be handed over (by God?) to the Judeans. And they wouldn't have done puny stuff like slicing off a highpriestly slave-ear (18:10)! But hey, Jesus' kingdom isn't from here; it's from above.

Pilate: If you've got a king-dom, then you must be a king. Right? Jesus: That's what you say. People always wanting to call me king, but I've been born (from above) and come into the world (as the messiah-godson, 11:27) for this one thing: to not king-ruling but truth-witness-ing (John-like, 5:33)! Truth-belonging sheep hear my goodshepherding voice (10:3-5, 16, 27). Rolling his eyes and shaking his head, Pilate says, "What's TRUTH?" . . . Hello! Truth is Godsword, spoken by this one, who is the truth and gives the spiritoftruth (14:6, 17; 17:17). Pilate is really a Judean because he doesn't know the truth, doesn't hear Jesus' voice.

Out of praetorium he goes again to tell the Judeans that he's found no grime of crime in Jesus. (Perhaps he does know something of the truth.) "But you've got a festive custom that I pass-over and release someone. This year want me to set into exodus the Judean king? (Perhaps he can lead you out into the wilderness.)" But the Judeans cry out BARABBAS! Barabbas (*bar*, "son," *abba*, "father"). They want this bandit son of the father rather than the truth-witnessing son of the father God. (So, does Pilate release Barabbas, or not? One assumes so, but doesn't say.)

Pilate takes Jesus (inside) and flogs/whips/scourges him (to satisfy the Judeans?). Then the soldiers thorn together a crown and cloak him in purple. Hail! they say. Hail (save?), Judean king! Unconsciously they worship him. He is king. And they slap him: Slap, slap, slap, O king! Slap, you sap. But they are the slapping saps. Like the gardening soldiers, they too fall down and worship I Am (18:6).

Pilate goes out again to the Judeans to say No in-him crime. And thorny-crowned and purple-robed, Jesus comes out. Behold/see/look at the man/human/person. See him (see his glory? see the father? 1:14; 14:9). But the priestly chiefs and assistants only see one who needs to be crucified. So they shout: CRUCIFYCRUCIFY!! Pilate says, You crucify him yourselves and leave me out of it! No crime, remember? The Judeans persist that they've gotta law (that came through Moses but gracious truth through Jesus Christ, 1:17), and legally he should die because he's made himself godson and equal to God (5:18). DIEDIEDIE!!!

Pilate hears this lawful dying word and becomes even more afraid. (Has he been afraid up 'til now?[2] What's he afraid of? He's got the whole power of the empire on his side. What's so big and bad 'bout this Judean law?) So he and Jesus go back into the praetorium and he asks Jesus where he's from. (Since he's really a Judean, he doesn't know where Jesus is from, 7:27-29; 8:14; 9:29.) But for Jesus mum's the word. No word from the word. Pilate doesn't know what the truth is anyway. Why bother? Pilate says, "You ain't talkin', huh? I've got power, releasing-you power and crucifying-you power. Now that's the truth!" (Pilate thinks that he is the son of humanity to whom the father has given all judgment, 5:27!) But Jesus says: No power o'er me 'cept what's been given you from above, from God, who has given all things, all judgment to the son, but has given this power over the son so that he can be lifted up and draw all people to himself (12:32). He continues: My hand-over-er is the greater sinner. (Who 'dat? Judas? Caiaphas? . . . God? Who is the blind sinner who thinks that he can see? 9:41)

So now Pilate was release-seeking him. (Jesus says to Pilate, What are you seeking, 1:38? Pilate says, trying hard to keep a straight face, To release you! That's the truth! Hahaha.) (He has that releasing power, right? It of course was above-given to him.) But why does he want to? Is he still afraid—of Jesus? of the Judeans (like the disciples, 20:19)? of power-given-to-him God? Or is Pilate set up here (by God? by the narrator?) to make the Judeans the fall guy?[3] Pilate wants release-him but Judeans say that he's not a Caesar-friend if he does it. (Don't be a Jesus friend and do what he commands, love-one-another, 15:14-15.) All self-made kings are agin' Caesar the emperor. (But what difference does that make to Pilate? Why does he even listen to the Judeans? He has from-above-given power to release Jesus. So why doesn't he just do it? Does he really have the power to release Jesus? Or is his role in this divine play—comedy? tragedy?—simply to crucify Jesus, at the request of the Judeans?)

---

[2] David K. Rensberger, *Johannine Faith and Liberating Community* (Philadelphia: Westminster, 1988) 94, prefers the translation, "he became fearful indeed" or "exceedingly."

[3] Rensberger (ibid. 95) challenges the consensus that Pilate is a weak character. "He is callous and relentless, indifferent to Jesus and to truth, and contemptuous of the hope of Israel that Jesus both fulfills and transcends. . . . Pilate is thus in fact a hostile figure second only to 'the Jews' themselves."

Pilate, who wants to be Caesarfriend, brings Jesus out and sits (him?) down on the tribunal, or *bēma* (where he beams), the place Hebrew- (or really Aramaic) called *Gabbatha*, Greek-called *Lithostrōtos,* English-called "Stone Pavement." Simon the Rock has petered out, so this is his new foundation stone, from which he will go to God. It's now noon (hour six) of passover-preparation (time when passover-lambs being killed, lamb of God being killed too?) So at high noon Pilate prepares the lamb by presenting to the Judeans their king. But they acclaim him by saying away-crucify him! Kill the passover lamb! Pilate says, You want me to crucify your king? Chief priests: No king, no king, NO-KING but . . . but . . . God, right? No, they don't say that. They say No king but Caesar, Pilate's friend. No king but . . . Caesar. The pass-over hymn is being sung: We have no king but God.[4] Not for these chiefpriests. Caesar's their king not God. Ultimate apostasy! They are still in captivity in Egypt and in Rome! No passover, no exodus for them. They have now defiled themselves from eating the passover. So to these Caesarservants Pilate hands Jesus (and God) over to be cruci-fied. Pilate is in fact a Judean; he rejects the enfleshed word. And that's the truth!

Exploring Likenesses to the Trial in African-American Poetry

Eugene B. Redmond, in his classic study of African-American poetry, writes that a traditional theme is that of equating black suffering and Jesus' crucifixion. For example, George Leonard Allen's "Pilate in Modern America" pleads with God for redemption, claiming that "one man's voice" (of dissent) could not be heard in the din of the lynch mob. But God's voice (the white man's conscience) tells "Pilate" that his guilt is as great as the crowd's.[5]

In one of his most controversial poems Langston Hughes depicts "Christ in Alabama":

> Christ is a nigger,
> Beaten and black:
> Oh, bear your back!
>
> Mary is His mother:
> Mammy of the South,
> Silence your mouth.

---

[4] As Brown notes, a Passover hymn of later Judaism proclaimed, "Beside You, we have no King," (*Death of the Messiah* 1:849). Cf. also Paul Duke, *Irony in the Fourth Gospel* (Atlanta: John Knox, 1985) 135.

[5] Eugene B. Redmond, *Drumvoices: The Mission of Afro-American Poetry* (Garden City, N.Y.: Doubleday Anchor, 1976) 204.

> God is His father:
> White Master above
> Grant Him your love.
>
> Most holy bastard
> Of the bleeding mouth,
> Nigger Christ
> On the cross
> Of the South.[6]

At the cross the holy family is gathered: father, mother, son. It is not a happy reunion, though. Christ is black and God is the "White Master above," who is implored to grant his love to his son. It does not sound as if this father spontaneously loves the son (3:35; 5:20).

Haki R. Madhubuti writes in "The Black Christ": "without a doubt / rome did the whi / te thing when it / killed / christ." He continues, "history repeats / itself ask / st. malcolm / all because j. c. / was a nigger / the only things that didn't change were his words."[7] Malcolm X's assassination, then, is often compared to Jesus' crucifixion. Similarly, Ethridge Knight, in his poem "It Was a Funky Deal," writes,

> In the beginning was the word,
> And in the end the deed.
> Judas did it to Jesus
> For the same Herd. Same reason.
> You made them mad, Malcolm. Same reason.[8]

Redmond also notes, "Practically every black poet since the end of the Civil War has written a poem about lynching."[9] And lynching is often described in terms of Jesus' crucifixion. Toi Derricotte's second stanza of "A Note" is representative:

> II. A picture in a book,
> a lynching
> The bland faces of men
> who watch Christ go up in flames, smiling,

[6] Langston Hughes, "Christ in Alabama," in Arnold Rampersad, ed., *The Collected Poems of Langston Hughes* (New York: Alfred A. Knopf, 1994) 143.

[7] Haki R. Madhubuti, "The Black Christ," in Jerry W. Ward, Jr., ed., *Trouble the Water: 250 Years of African-American Poetry* (New York: Mentor, 1997) 393, 395.

[8] Ethridge Knight, "It Was a Funky Deal," in Dudley Randall, ed., *The Black Poets* (New York: Bantam, 1971) 207, from Knight, *Poems from Prison* (Detroit: Broadside Press, 1968).

[9] Redmond, *Drumvoices*, 8.

as if he were a hooked
fish, a felled antelope, some
wild thing tied to boards and burned.
His charring body
gives light—a halo
burns out of him.
His face scorched featureless;
the hair matted to the scalp
like feathers.
His head flops back, looking up,
as if his last words were a blessing.
One man stands with his hand on his hip,
another with his arm
slung around the shoulder of a friend,
as if this moment were large enough
to hold affection.[10]

Jesus' body (which is the temple, his father's house) gives light (light of the world, John 8:12) as it dies, drawing all people (12:32). Among his last words is a kind of blessing to those standing near: the disciple whom he loves, and his mother. He tells her to sling her arm around the shoulder of his friend (19:26). This moment is large enough to hold affection, the affection that Jesus has for his own to the end (13:1).

One of the most famous poems in this genre is Claude McKay's "The Lynching,"[11] which uses Johannine imagery. In the poem the father bids the lynching victim, like Jesus, to his bosom through death, "the cruelest way of pain." It is at his father's "wild whim," for perhaps like Jesus he has received this command from the father (10:18). And also like Jesus, this victim dies in the company of women, who "thronged to look" (cf. 19:25). In his death his spirit "in smoke ascends," while Jesus himself ascends and his spirit is given up (19:30).

Exploring the Likenesses to the Trial in My Own Soul

The trial. The closest thing that I ever had to a trial was the series of meetings, interrogations, one in San Jose, Costa Rica, and one in Atlanta, Georgia, which resulted in my being fired as a Southern Baptist missionary. It was my passion, comparable in many ways to that of Jesus.

---

[10] Toi Derricotte, "A Note," in E. Ethelbert Miller, ed., *In Search of Color Everywhere: A Collection of African-American Poetry* (New York: Stewart, Tabori & Chang, 1994) 75, from *Callaloo,* 10:4.

[11] Claude McKay, "The Lynching," in Clarence Major, ed., *The Garden Thrives: Twentieth-Century African-American Poetry* (San Francisco: HarperPerennial, 1996) 16, from McKay, *Selected Poems of Claude McKay* (New York: Harcourt Brace, 1953).

I was betrayed by a friend, a fellow missionary, and I was tried twice before leaders who were interested not in justice but in being a Caesar-friend and keeping their jobs and empire intact. Not long after my firing, I remember walking the Stations of the Cross at a Catholic retreat center, where I was taking spiritual direction. I connected Jesus' Via Dolorosa with my own.

The Pilates in my story were the administrators, who were not interested in truth but in having one man die for the people rather than having the whole missionary enterprise be destroyed. The critical methods that I practiced, they said, were appropriate for seminary education in the U.S. but not overseas because of the "sensitivity of the situation." What is truth? Truth is power, used here to eliminate, terminate, those who had less power than they. The hierarchy was protected: administrators over missionaries over nationals. If a missionary taught something to the nationals that encouraged them to think, they might question the power of the missionaries and administrators, and that could not be tolerated!

I hesitate to associate my firing too closely with Jesus' crucifixion, for such rhetoric sanctifies my own victimhood and leads to self-righteousness. I am aware that in contemporary America there are those who are imprisoned or even executed as a result of unjust trials. It seems that this happens disproportionately to African Americans. Jesus, then, continues to be tried and executed. Pilate continues to be uninterested in truth but not in power. Crucifixions continue.

Appearing Mary-ly and Undoubtedly (John 20:1-31)

> Now on the first day of the week
> Mary Magdalene comes to the tomb early while it is still dark
> and sees the stone taken away from the tomb.
> And then quickly she goes to Simon Peter and the other disciple, whom
>   Jesus loved, and says to them,
>   "They've taken the master from the tomb,
>   and we don't know where they've laid him."
> Then Peter and the other disciple went out and were going to the tomb.
> And the two were running together,
> but the other disciple ran ahead of Peter,
> and came to the tomb first.
> And bending down, he sees the bandages lying there,
> but he did not go in.
> And then Simon Peter comes following him
> and he went into the tomb,
> and he sees the bandages lying there along with the handkerchief that
>   was on his head,

but it is not lying with the bandages but rolled up, lying in one place
    by itself.
Then the other disciple, who had come first to the tomb,
came in and saw and believed;
for they did not yet know the scripture that he must rise from the dead.
Then the disciples went away to their homes.

But Mary stood outside the tomb weeping.
Then as she was weeping, she bent over into the tomb.
And she sees two angels in white seated where the body of Jesus had
    been lying.
And they say to her,
    "Woman, why are you weeping?"
She says to them,
    "They have taken my master,
    and I don't know where they have laid him."
When she had said these things, she turned around and sees Jesus
    standing there,
but she didn't know that it was Jesus.
Jesus says to her,
    "Woman, why are you weeping?
    Whom are you seeking?"
Thinking that he is the gardener, she says,
    "Master, if you have carried him away,
    tell me where you have laid him,
    and I will take him."
Jesus says to her,
    "Mary."
She turns and says to him in Hebrew,
    "Rabbouni!" (which means teacher).
Jesus says to her,
    "Stop holding on to me,
    for I have not yet ascended to the father.
    But go to my brothers and say to them,
        'I am ascending to my father and your father,
        to my God and your God.'"
Mary Magdalene goes announcing to the disciples,
    "I have seen the master."
And she told them these things that he had told her.

Then when it was evening of that day, the first day of the week,
and when the doors were locked where the disciples were
because of fear of the Judeans,
Jesus came and stood in their midst and says to them,
    "Peace to you."
And after he said this, he showed them his hands and side.
Then the disciples rejoiced when they saw the master.

Then Jesus said to them again,
    "Peace to you.
    Just as the father sent me,
    I send you too."
And after he said this, he breathed on them and says to them,
    "Receive holy spirit;
    If you forgive anyone's sins, they are forgiven them.
    If you retain them, they are retained."

Now Thomas, one of the twelve, who is called Twin, was not with
    them when Jesus came.
The other disciples then said to him,
    "We saw the master."
But he said to them,
    "Unless I see the place of the nails in his hands
    and put my finger in the place of the nails
    and put my hand into his side,
    I will never believe."

And after eight days the disciples were again inside,
and Thomas was with them.
Although the doors were locked,
Jesus comes and stands in their midst and says,
    "Peace to you."
Then he said to Thomas,
    "Take your finger here and see my hands
    and take your hand and put it into my side,
    and do not be unbelieving but believing."
Thomas answered and said to him,
    "My master and my God."
Jesus says to him,
    "Is it because you have seen me that you have believed?
    Blessed are the ones who have not seen yet have believed."

Now Jesus did many other signs in the presence of his disciples,
which are not written in this book;
but these are written
in order that you might believe that
the messiah, the son of God is Jesus,
and that by believing in his name you might have life.

Playing with the Images of the Appearance Stories

It was the first week-day: a Sunday/son-day, a day in which the son shines brightly. But the first day weakly begins in the dark, when Mary Magdalene, a cross-bystander (along with Mary Clopas and the motherofJesus and sister and the beloveddisciple, 19:25-26), tomb-goes. (Is she going to the tomb to weep there? It seems like that's what Marys in this gospel do, 11:31.) There she finds the tomb unstoned, and she runrunruns to Simon Peter (last seen denying Jesus, cockadoodledoo! 18:27) and the disciple other, the beloved (last seen taking Jesus' mother into his home at Jesus' command, 19:26-27). She says to them that "they" (Romans? Judeans?) have taken the master out of the tomb, and she's agnostic about where they've laid him. (People always in the dark about where Jesus is and where he's going, 7:33-36; 13:36; 14:5). So Peter-and-beloved (It seems that they're always paired) go to the tomb, running (huff-puffing; this situation is quite energizing for folks!) together. The "other" gets there first, not because he's younger but because Jesus loves him. (This I know, for the gospel tells me so.) Bending down into the tomb, he sees the lying linen wrappings, but he doesn't go in. Seeing is enough for him. But not for Peter, who's following ("Follow me," 21:19) and goes into the tomb. He too sees the wrapping linen lyings but also Jesus' rolled-up headcloth in its own place away from the linens lying wrapping. (Laz still had this cloth on when he got up from his tomb, 11:44.) The other, the tomb-first-reacher, goes in too now. (He's prepared the way for Peter, and now Peter prepares the way for him.) He sees too, and he believes. (After all, seeing is believing.) But what does he believe? That Jesus has risen? (Maybe Jesus' love for him has opened his eyes; maybe it's the sight of the headcloth that did it. "Y'know, Laz's head was clothed when he came out of the tomb. Has Jesus too come out?!") If so, he doesn't say anything. Indeed, neither he nor Peter understand the scripture about Jesus rising from the dead. (Exactly what scripture is that anyway? Or are we talking about Jesus' word, which is now essentially the same as scripture, 2:22?) The other believes and misunderstands. (Presumably Peter doesn't believe or understand. Again, the other is one up on Peter, but since Jesus loves the other, how can he misunderstand?) The seeming contradiction doesn't seem to bother him, for the two silently return home. Apparently they go to lock the doors for Judean fear. What do they believe? What do they (mis)understand?

Mary stands outside the tomb of the unknown Jesus and weeps. She bends over into the tomb and through her tears she sees two whitened angels. (Has it now become light or does the angel's apparel allow Mary to see them?) They sit at the place where Jesus' body (the father's house, 2:21) has been. They ask Mary (together?), "Woman (so much like the motherofJesus and Sam), why are you weeping?" (Isn't it obvious? Is this a set-up?) She essentially says the same that she said to Peter and the other, but this time she says "my (not "the") master" and "I (not "we") don't know." Mary doesn't wait for an answer. (They are angels, and maybe they know what you—singular and plural—do not.) She turns around and sees Jesus himself! But she's still an agnostic (a not-knower) because she not only doesn't know where "they've" taken him but also doesn't know that he's standing right in front of her. (Maybe it's still dark, and he is not whitened.)

Jesus says to her the same thing the angels said, but he also asks her whom she is seeking, much as he had asked his first two disciples (Andrew and the other?) what they were seeking (1:38). Mary thinks that he is the gardener of this garden where this new tomb is located (19:41). Mary misunderstands too—though not completely, for Jesus does tend this garden, transforming it into Eden by raising himself (10:17-18) and by cleaning and pruning the branches of the true vine (15:1-3). She unwittingly calls him "master" (or "sir") and asks him to tell her where he's taken Jesus so she could take him. (Nobody takes Jesus anywhere; he goes very much of his own accord.) Jesus calls her by name, not "Woman" but "Mary." (Mary makes out better than Jesus' own mother, 19:26). The good shepherding gardener calls his own sheep by name (Cephas, Lazarus, 1:42; 10:3; 11:43) and leads them out of the darkness of unknowing. Mary turns (she's already turned toward him once. Has she turned away from him when she thought that he was the gardener?) and speaks in Hebrew, or better, Aramaic, the language typically spoken by first-century Palestinians: *"Rabbouni"* (teacher). When Jesus asked the two seeking disciples, they called him, "Rabbi" (teacher, 1:38). Jesus tells her to stop holding on to him. (Apparently that's what she's doing, holding on to the rabbi-teacher, rather than letting the risen lord go where he will, like the wind-spirit (3:8). He hasn't yet father-ascended. Jesus is still in mid-hour, ascending through death and resurrection. But he says to go to his brothers (not servants or even friends, but brothers because with the son they are children of God that have been gathered into one by Jesus' death, 11:51). (But what about Jesus' sisters . . . and mother!? Shouldn't they know too?!) Mary is to tell them that Jesus is ascending (goin' up) to his father and their father, his/their God. (Mary's father-God too?) So she goes and announces: BULLETIN: I HAVE SEEN THE MASTER (stop). She has seen and, like the other, believed, but not like the other, understood that the master (not teacher) Jesus is risen. Then she tells them what he told her, about ascending to his/their godfather.

And they were silent, or at least the episode ends there. Did they now believe and understand? Perhaps not, for at evening the doors were locked(click)/shut (and their hearts were shut too), because they Judeans-feared—feared that the Judeans would toss them outta the synagogue and even kill them as they killed Jesus (16:2). Didn't their love for the risen Jesus (particularly that of the other-beloved) cast out all fear?

But just then poof! Jesus comes to them. He said in the farewell discourse that he would come to them (cf. 14:3, 18), and now, even though dead (but now alive), even though the doors are locked shut (but he is the door), he comes to them and in their midst standing says, "Peace to you." Again farewelldiscoursing, promised peace (14:27); now they gottit. And when Jesus handed and sided them (nailed hand/wounded side—apparently these didn't heal at the resurrection), the seeing-the-master disciples rejoiced (Yeah!). They went through the birthpangs of Jesus' death and had sorrow, but now that he is (re)born in resurrection, they have joy, just as Jesus said (16:16-22).

Jesus peaces them again and then says, "Justas fathersentme, Isendyou too." While discoursingfarewell Jesus has told the father that he has into the world sent the disciples (17:18), and now he really does. Father sends Jesus sends the disciples. And he breathes on them (huh!) and says, "Receive holy spirit," the paraclete, the spiritoftruth, sent in Jesus' name to be with the disciples forever (cf. 15:26; 16:7). Jesus breathes into them the breathoflife, and now they are living souls (Gen 2:7). Thus enspirited, thus ensouled, the disciples will sin-forgive some (who will be sin-forgiven by God and Jesus), and they will sin-retain (hold fast) others (who will be sin-retained by God and Jesus). Disciples now agents of Jesus, just as Jesus agent of God. The agent forgives/ holds fast.

Thomas, however, a Twin-called-disciple, who was willing to die with Jesus (but apparently not to rise with him), who didn't know the way where Jesus was going (and still doesn't, John 11:16; 14:5), isn't there when Jesus comes. (Where was he? Did he go out to buy food? 4:8) When he returns, the disciples say (in unison, in their best mary magdalene voice), "WE SAW THE MASTER!" Tom-Tom (after all he is a twin) says that he will never ever believe until he sees the hand nailprints (a reasonable enough request, the disciples got to see) AND he puts his fingerhand into the nailprints and sidewound (an *un*reasonable enough request: he wants more than the disciples got; he wants not only to see but also TOUCH!).

So eight days later (the next week's first day, another sonday) the disciples are insiders, and Tom-Tom is there too, about to be changed from an outsider to an insider. Again Jesus poofs through the lockedclickshut doors and peaces them. He says to Tom-Tom, "Finger-see my hands and hand-cast my side. Don't disbelieve but believe: believe that you must die in order to rise, that you must follow my way, that they have master-seen." For Tom-Tom seeing is believing; eye is sufficient not hand and finger. He say: "My master—risen master—and my God —word-in-the-beginning, only-begotten, revealing the father God!" Jesus says, "Seeing is believing for you? Blessed are the non-seeing believers, who are believers in the disciplesword (17:20)," that is, those who are this gospel readers.

How does Tom-Tom respond to all this? Dontno. The narrator jumps in: Jesus signs lots more before his disciples (the resurrection a sign then? death/resurrection/ascension?) than what's written here, but these water-wining, distance-healing, paralytic-raising, bread-making, sight-giving, dead-enlivening signs are written so that you readers might blessedly believe that the messianic godson is Jesus, and in his name believing (and becoming godchildren, 1:12) you might have life, the lightoflife, the waytruthandlife, resurrectionandlife (8:12; 11:25; 14:6). LIFE!!!!!!!!!!!!!!

Exploring the Likenesses to the Appearance Stories in African-American Poetry

I now rise up early (while still dark) to look for poetic resurrections. Joseph Henderson Brooks speaks of "The Resurrection" of Jesus as beginning in this way: "A muffled whiff of sudden breath / Ruffled the passive air of death." He goes on to say that Jesus "woke and raised Himself in bed" and "coolly put His grave-clothes by." The poem ends with this stanza:

> The early winds took up the words,
> And bore them to the lilting birds,
> The leafing trees, and everything
> That breathed the living breath of spring.[12]

Yes, the wind takes the word, and the word takes the wind and breathes spring (of living water? John 4:14) into everything, including the disciples, to whom he says, "Receive holy spirit" (20:22).

African Americans have often spoken of great leaders of the past as continuing to live in their message. Langston Hughes, for example, says that Frederick Douglass was bold in sounding the call to freedom, and though he died in 1895, "He is not dead."[13] So the dead-but-not-dead Jesus continues to sound the call to freedom, truth, and life. Sonia Sanchez writes in the wake of the death of "Malcolm": "when the cold air cracks / with frost, I'll breathe / his breath."[14] In the frosty, locked-

---

[12] Joseph Henderson Brooks, "The Resurrection," in Jerry W. Ward, Jr., ed., *Trouble the Water,* 136–37.

[13] Langston Hughes, "Frederick Douglass: 1817–1895," in idem, *The Collected Poems,* 549.

[14] Sonia Sanchez, "Malcolm," in idem, in *Shake Loose My Skin: New and Selected Poems* (Boston: Beacon, 1999) 6.

door air, the disciples breathe Jesus' breath (John 20:22) and are inspir(it)ed.

Jazz musicians are also said to live on after death. After alto saxophonist Charlie "Bird" Parker died in March 1955, his fans used the phrase "Bird Lives" as something of a motto. Charles Mingus, bassist and Parker's sometime bandmate, spoke about Parker's death in such a way that George Barlow turned his comments into "Mingus Speaks: Found Poems":

> 1.
> the soloists
> at Birdland
>
> had to wait for
> Parker's next record
>
> to find out
> what to play
>
> what
> will they do now
>
> 2.
> hey dig
> Bird ain't dead
> he's hiding out
> somewhere
>
> & he'll be back
> with some new shit
>
> that will scare
> everyone to death[15]

The first stanza of this poem captures the feeling of the weeping-outside-the-tomb Mary Magdalene and the locked-inside-the-house disciples (John 20:11, 19). Indeed, what will they do now? Who will they go to? Jesus has the eternal-life words (6:68). In the second stanza, however, Bird-disciples' pain is turned into joy at the prediction that he will return (16:20, 22). They are to "dig" (into the garden tomb?) that Bird's not dead but hiding, soon to return with material "that will scare everyone to death." The disciples are now scared—by the Judeans

---

[15] George Barlow, "Mingus Speaks: Found Poems," in E. Ethelbert Miller, ed., *In Search of Color Everywhere*, 210, from Barlow, *Gabriel* (Detroit: Broadside, 1974). For more on Bird's life, death, and "resurrection," see Ted Gioia, *The History of Jazz* (New York: Oxford University Press, 1997) 205–9, 216–33.

(20:19), but soon everyone will be scared—by the non-dead living one, so scared that the living ones will be dead! The hour is coming and now is (5:25)!

Mingus wrote a tribute to another jazz great who died in the 1950s, Lester Young (also an alto saxophonist from Kansas City) in his 1959 "Goodbye Pork Pie Hat." Almost a decade later Larry Neal poetically responded, "Don't Say Goodbye to the Pork-Pie Hat." He writes:

> Shape to shape, horn to horn
> the Porkpie Hat resurrected himself
> night to night, from note to note
> skimming the horizons, flashing bluegreenyellow lights
> and blowing black stars
> and weird looneymoon changes; chords coiled about him
> and he was flying
> fast
> zipping
> past
> sound
> into cosmic silences.
> . . .
>
> No, don't say goodbye to the Porkpie Hat—
> he lives, oh yes.
>
> Lester lives and leaps
> Bird lives
> Lady lives
> . . .
> we live
> live
> spirit lives and sound lives
> . . .
> spirit lives
> SPIRIT ! ! !
>
> SWHEEEEEEEEEEEEEEEET ! ! !
>
> take it again
> this time from the top[16]

Resurrection and spirit. Lester lives . . . and blows, breathing new life into his disciples. Yes, spirit lives. (The risen Jesus breathes on the dis-

---

[16] Larry Neal, "Don't Say Goodbye to the Pork-Pie Hat," in Jerry W. Ward, Jr., ed., *Trouble the Water*, 334–37, from Neal, *Hoodoo Hollerin' Bebop Giants* (Washington, D.C.: Howard University Press, 1968).

ciples: "Receive holy spirit," John 20:22.) He resurrects himself "night to night," much as Jesus appears while it is still dark, in the evening of the first day of the week, and just after daybreak (20:1, 19; 21:4). It is swheeeeeeeeeeeeeet, giving joy and peace to the disciples (20:19-20). And they take it again, from the top. ("Just as the father sent me, I send you," 20:21.)

Dead but still living: Bird, Lester, and Trane. Coltrane. John Coltrane. A. B. Spellman's "Did John's Music Kill Him?" "o john death will not contain you."[17] Kimberly W. Benston says that this is an example of a genre of modern African-American poetry she calls the "Coltrane poem." She writes, "The death of Coltrane becomes, in modern black poetry, a central topos of renewal and is accepted ultimately as beginning—as a question: How long how long has that Trane been gone?"[18]

Relatives also continue to live even after death. Gwendolyn Brooks gives us "Rites for Cousin Vit,"[19] in which her dead cousin, like Jesus leaves her grave cloths ("stuff and satin") behind (cf. John 20:2-7). She "rises in the sunshine" (like the risen Jesus, who was recognized at daybreak, 21:4) in order to return to the bars and brothels she frequented. Yes, she is "too vital" (Jesus said, "I am the life," 11:25; 14:6); she must emerge (as Jesus does from his tomb). She "is," just as Jesus I Am.

These poets also speak of their own survival through pain in terms of resurrection. In his "Index to a Black Catharsis," Richard W. Thomas uses imagery from the passion and resurrection narratives to express both rage and relief. He calls for no more "white Christ" or "gray folks / Playing cool with new nickels under our crosses between black thieves." After he vents his anger, he says, "(I'm feeling good now)," and then, "After the third day I woke / Banged on the rock / Got out. / Saw Mary and Mamma crying. / Took them home."[20] The poet emerges from his tomb of pent-up emotion and sees the weeping Mary. (Does

---

[17] A. B. Spellman, "Did John's Music Kill Him?" in Stephen Henderson, ed. *Understanding the New Black Poetry* (New York: William Morrow, 1973) 262.

[18] Kimberly W. Benston, "Performing Blackness: Re/Placing Afro-American Poetry," in Houston A. Baker, Jr., and Patricia Redmond, eds., *Afro-American Literary Study in the 1990s* (Chicago: University of Chicago Press, 1989) 176. She is alluding to another example of the Coltrane poem, Jane Cortez's "How Long Has Trane Been Gone," in eadem, *Pisstained Stairs and the Monkey Man's Wares* (New York: Phrase Text, 1969).

[19] Gwendolyn Brooks, *Selected Poems*. Griot Editions: Voices of the African Diaspora (New York: Quality Paperback Book Club, 1995) 58.

[20] Richard W. Thomas, "Index to a Black Catharsis," in LeRoi Jones and Larry Neal, eds., *Black Fire: An Anthology of Afro-American Writing* (New York: William Morrow, 1968) 194–95.

she recognize him? Does he call her by name? John 20:15-16.) He takes his mother home, for there is no beloved disciple there to do it (19:26-27).

Maya Angelou says triumphantly, "Still I Rise" after she looks at a personal and collective history of death. First the poet considers how she has overcome personal affronts. She writes in one representative stanza:

> You may shoot me with your words,
> You may cut me with your eyes,
> You may kill me with your hatefulness,
> But still, like air, I'll rise.

Like air, like wind, like the spirit. So it is with everyone born from above/anew (John 3:8).

Her concluding stanza proclaims her resurrection from the collective death of her people, in which she goes from the night into daybreak. (Judas went out into the night of betrayal, and Jesus spoke to the disciples at the daybreak of resurrection, 13:30; 21:4.) She writes:

> Out of the huts of history's shame
> I rise
> Up from a past that's rooted in pain
> I rise
> I'm a black ocean, leaping and wide,
> Welling and swelling I bear in the tide.
> Leaving behind nights of terror and fear
> I rise
> Into a daybreak that's wondrously clear
> I rise
> Bringing the gifts that my ancestors gave,
> I am the dream and the hope of the slave.
> I rise
> I rise
> I rise.[21]

Exploring the Likenesses to the Appearance Stories in My Own Soul

And I rise too. Rise out of firing ("terminated!") and unemployment, out of the lies and deceit of a fellow missionary and administrators. Yes, you may (and did!) shoot me, stab me (in the back), betray me, crucify me! But still . . . still I riSE! Into tenure, into family, into writing!

[21] Maya Angelou, "Still I Rise," in E. Ethelbert Miller, ed., *In Search of Color Everywhere* 68, from Angelou, *And Still I Rise* (New York: Random House, 1978).

But my history is with the crucifiers, white rich males, who have killed, enslaved, imprisoned, segregated and despised African-Americans, people of color, anyone who is different. Do I rise from that? I like to think so. But how much more do I need to rise? Perhaps I need to sink, to fall, to understand how I still carry that attitude, those violent tendencies, and that power. My first daughter is named Anastasia, which means "resurrection." My second daughter is Miranda, "wondrous." My last name is Newheart, a name my wife Joy and I both took when we married. Resurrection wonder, new heart. Rising wonderful new heart. Heartfelt, wondering rising anew. Oh joy!

I rise. I rise. i RISE!

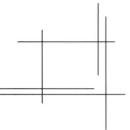

Conclusion

I have come to the end of this soul-journey, journey into the soul of the Fourth Gospel and into my own soul. I hope that you have journeyed into your soul as well. I encourage you to play with the passages as well, to find poetry, to draw, to dance, to write your own poetry. The "scholar" in me thinks that I should include in this conclusion a summary of the book, in which I say what I said (The old debate style: Tell what you're going to tell 'em, tell 'em, and tell 'em what you told 'em.), and a discussion of the "contemporary significance of the gospel." Yawn! How ponderous and pretentious that sounds! I remember several years back at a scholarly meeting in which I presented a paper a colleague asked me, "What's your point, Michael?" I was somewhat taken aback because I thought my point was quite clear. I think that he was saying that he disagreed with my point (and my perspective), but in typical academic fashion he posed his disagreement in terms of a question. I have since learned to anticipate such "questions," especially as I have in the last few years pursued my "soul hermeneutic." In some ways, there is no point to this project; it is point-less, if having a point means that the content of the book can be boiled down to one or two sentences. My previous book (my wisdom book)[1] was certainly that way, but this one (my foolish book) is not. The proof is in the putting, or with this book, the point is in the playing; that is, if this book says anything, it is said in the wordplay. Style is content, and content is style. This is truly a postmodern project, one with poetry and indeterminacy and ambiguity.

In this conclusion I would like to tie up some loose ends (or at least state clearly that I am leaving them dangling). I will first discuss something of the story behind this book; then I will address the opportunities and challenges of Johannine rhetoric; finally, I will conclude with a poem.

---

[1] Michael E. Willett, *Wisdom Christology in the Fourth Gospel* (San Francisco: Mellen Research University Press, 1992).

The Story Behind the Book

This book was first conceived (but never born—either from above or below) as an orthodox Jungian interpretation of the gospel entitled "Word and Psyche: A Psycho-Literary Reading of the Fourth Gospel."[2] Indeed, I even submitted a book proposal to a publisher. Of course, the editor wanted to see a chapter. However, I was not approved for promotion and tenure because my colleagues contended that I had yet to show the relevance of the Jungian interpretation of the New Testament to the African-American community, which the university serves. Not long after that, I began participating in a discussion group on the writings of James Hillman, the post-Jungian psychologist. I was impressed with his approach to the psyche as soul, use of image and likeness, and his wordplay. "Soul" is often associated with African-American culture; biblical images often have their likenesses in African-American poetry, in which I read widely before coming to Howard. And the wordplay was similar to that done by African-American poets. So I had an idea, which became another book proposal (with the present title), which became a paper for the 1996 regional meeting of the Society of Biblical Literature, which became the first chapter of the book.

While I was working on this book, important events took place in my life. When I first began in earnest in 1996, my wife Joy was pregnant with Anastasia, and she was born the week after I finished revising the paper into chapter 1. At the same time I was also working on my application for promotion and tenure, which was approved in 1997. So we bought our first house, in suburban Washington, that summer. The following summer Joy was pregnant again, with Miranda, and in the fall I fell into a depression (due in part to anxiety about the book). I recovered soon enough for Miranda's birth in spring 1999, and I completed the book during her infancy (and sometimes when she was on my back in the pack!)

This has been a deeply personal book, as I have attempted to reflect theologically, biblically, johannine-ly on my journey, especially my relationship with my father, my firing as a Southern Baptist foreign missionary, and my teaching at Howard Divinity School. I have tried to understand my nearly lifelong fascination with the gospel. This way has been hard; it has led to some difficult truth, but it has also meant life. The truth has made me (both odd[3] and) free, free to realize how

---

[2] See my essays noted above in the Introduction, n. 35.

[3] David K. Rensberger, "Sectarianism and Theological Interpretation in John," *What Is John? Vol. II. Literary and Social Readings of the Fourth Gospel*, ed. Fernando F. Segovia, SBL Symposium Series (Atlanta: Scholars, 1998) 140, quotes (without citation) Flannery O'Connor: "You shall know the truth, and the truth will make you odd."

bound I am. I am not sure that I have been successful in processing my own story. The material has been too much, sometimes overwhelming. I am not sure that I have a handle on what has been going on for me with the gospel; I have only guessed. At least it has put me on a journey, not from Galilee to Jerusalem, not from above to below to above, but from a little less light to a little more, from a little more darkness to a little less. Or maybe there is more darkness now. But I feel that there is more light.

Opportunities and Challenges of Johannine Rhetoric

I will turn my gaze from my own story to the world's story, especially as it has been informed (deformed? transformed? certainly formed) by John's story. Since I am a preacher teaching preachers, I am particularly concerned with how the rhetoric of this gospel is used today in the church and world. In what ways has the Johannine rhetoric been used for oppression, dehumanization, disempowerment, fragmentation? In what ways has it been (can it be) used for liberation, humanization, empowerment, community?

The following comments are no more than "Johannine journal jottings," my comments on subjects that have pricked my conscience and imagination as I have written this book (and have studied and taught this gospel lo these many years). Perhaps they will spur reflection and discussion.

I've organized my ramblings under four rubrics: community and alienation, exclusivism, anti-Judaism, and patriarchialism.

COMMUNITY AND ALIENATION

In our contemporary world it seems that everyone feels like an alien. Perhaps that is due in part to the presence of "aliens" (both legal and illegal) among us, that is, the large numbers of people coming from other countries to live in the United States. But people who have lived in this country for several generations also feel like aliens in this postmodern, technological world. They feel adrift in the sea of moral relativity, from which they cannot taste the living water. These people perceive that they have no power in society; they cannot sing their Lord's song in this foreign land. In particular African-Americans feel that they are powerless and that the small gains they have made are being rolled back.

In the Gospel of John, Jesus offers community. He commands believers to love one another. He offers them a spirit that comforts and convicts. He offers a home in the father and the son. The anger and sadness in alienation is now replaced by the joy and peace in community. John is the "spiritual gospel," yes, but the spirit that enlivens it is the spirit of community.

EXCLUSIVISM

But a community of the alienated can often legitimize their aliena-tion through a world-view that sanctifies their behavior and demonizes society at large, which they believe has alienated them. Their anger and frustration are projected upon God, who damns this world to hell. We are the chosen ones only. We are of God, born from above, born of the spirit; those who have rejected us are of the devil, born from below, born of the spirit of falsehood. Often this dualism is imaged, as it is in the gospel, as light and darkness. I am in the light; you are in darkness. Such a perspective fails to see the good in others and evil in ourselves. Furthermore, it often leads to violence, whether rhetorical violence or physical violence. And it certainly leads to self-righteousness, which in turn leads to more alienation from society at large.

The rhetoric of the gospel has led to denigration of persons who are not professing Christians or even members of a particular institution, based on passages in the gospel such as: "I am the way, the truth, and the life; no one comes to the father except through me" (John 14:6). Per-sons who do not use specifically Christian language, or even Johannine language, are said not to have meaningful existence, even though these persons might say they do. As a result, the boundary is drawn, and there is no appreciation for other value systems. No attempt is made at dialogue, and no collaborative work is done for justice. Justice is only found in using the right language and having the right relationships, not in right action.

But the gospel does say, "The light enlightens all humanity" (1:9). "When the spirit comes, it will lead you into all truth" (16:13). Perhaps we will find truth in what we considered evil, light in what we con-sidered darkness. Jesus says to love one another, that is, one's fellow community member. He implies that one is to hate one who is not a community member, who is part of "the world." All humanity, how-ever, is part of our "community." What practical steps can we take? You might bring to mind someone whom you know who dwells in dark-ness. Where is the light in that person? You might also think of groups that experience discrimination from the church or the larger society because they do not use in-group language. How can the group in which you participate reach out to those groups? In what ways do they have truth? Truth and light are found in the outcast, in the marginal-ized. If we are going to see "more truth and light," then we must go back to those whom we have ostracized.[4]

---

[4] Rensberger, ibid. 145 writes, "To make appropriate theological sense of John will mean to look for John's God in unexpected places and among those without any expectation."

ANTI-JUDAISM

One group that the gospel marginalizes is called in Greek the *Ioudaioi*, which I translate as "Judeans" but is usually translated "Jews." Characters identified with this term are cast out of the divine light. They debate with Jesus, accuse him of having a demon, attempt to stone him, and convince Pilate to crucify him. They are the villains in this gospel. They replace the Pharisees in the synoptics. They are "shadow figures" in more ways than one. They are in the darkness, from below, children of the devil, servants of Caesar. This rhetoric has led to discrimination, slander, pogroms, and the holocaust. And I am not so naïve as to believe that merely changing the translation to "Judeans" is going to solve the problem.

As I write this my former denomination, the Southern Baptist Convention, has urged its members to evangelize Jews during the Jewish holy days of Rosh Hashanah and Yom Kippur. When a denominational leader was asked about this, he said that Southern Baptists were not the ones who said, "I am the way, the truth, and the life." In other words, the Gospel of John provides their support and motivation. Are they not following Jesus' command, not only in this gospel but others as well, to evangelize Jews and all non-Christians? Non-Christians, then, are asked to repudiate their community and participate in the Christian community. Such a practice especially becomes strange in the case of Judaism since the Gospel of John is meaningless without Jewish Scripture. The gospel, like most if not all the New Testament documents, was written when Christians were still a Jewish (Judean) sect. Indeed, the acceptance of the gospel as Scripture is reflective of and contributed to the "parting of ways" between Jews and Christians.

The answer is in dialogue, not monologue. Yes, Christians have a word, but Jews have one too, and that word has created for them meaning and community. Christians can appreciate the rich Jewish heritage, which is part of their own. Christians must acknowledge the Jews' word in the decalogue, just as they acknowledge the Christians' word in Jesus. Christians must present a witness but not a witless witness, rather a witness of meaningful existence in the Christian community, listening to others' witness as well. The Christian legacy of anti-Semitism (or anti-Judaism) is long, deep, and wide, and Christians simply must repent.

Here I hesitate because of the tense relations between Jews and African-American Christians. To spotlight Christian mistreatment of the Jews and expose it as evil is not to condone Jewish (or Christian) mistreatment of African Americans. Both are evil; both stem from prejudice and racism and result in the diminution of life, not only for the victims but for the perpetrators as well.

PATRIARCHIALISM

In the gospel the power in the universe is imaged as male: the father and the son. Thus power in the human community is also imaged as male. Women are marginalized. Like the mother of Jesus, they are first distanced and then given under the control of male power (John 19:26-27). The male language is used to legitimate male leadership and suppress women. One alternative is to supplement language, that is, speak about God in masculine terms at times and feminine terms at other times. Another possibility, however, is to use divine language sparsely and instead to use human language primarily to speak about human action. Then the language, whether human or divine, could be analyzed and evaluated. What does this language say about human behavior? Does it promote community or tear it down? Does it ennoble persons or denigrate them? Does it further justice or hinder it? All language, whether it speaks of God or persons, must serve the human community.

Conclusion to the Conclusion and to the Book

I have been on my soapbox the last several paragraphs. I have been serious and not so playful. So I will conclude with a poem:

> What can I say? What?
> watt indeed?
>   light   word
>   spirit
>   life
> above
>   sent   glory   son
>   father
>
> in the beginning   middle   and   end
> word/s
>
> but no more
>   now time for flesh

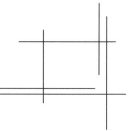

Bibliography

Aland, Kurt. "Eine Untersuchung zu John 1.3-4: über die Bedeutung eines Punktes," *ZNW* 59 (1968) 174–209.

Anderson, Janice Capel, and Jeffrey L. Staley, eds. *Taking it Personally: Autobiographical Biblical Criticism. Semeia* 72. Atlanta: Scholars Press, 1995.

Anderson, Paul N. *The Christology of the Fourth Gospel: Its Unity and Disunity in Light of John 6.* Valley Forge, Pa.: Trinity Press International, 1997.

Ashton, John, ed. *The Interpretation of John.* Issues in Religion and Theology 9. Philadelphia: Fortress, 1986.

Ausejo, Serafin de. "¿Es un himno a Cristo el prólogo de San Juan?" *EstBíb* 15 (1956) 223–77, 381–427.

Baker, Houston A. Jr., and Patricia Redmond, eds. *Afro-American Literary Study in the 1990s.* Chicago: The University of Chicago Press, 1989.

Ball, David Mark. *'I Am' in John's Gospel: Literary Function, Background and Theological Implications.* JSNTS 124. Sheffield: Sheffield Academic Press, 1996.

Baraka, Amiri. *The LeRoi Jones/Amiri Baraka Reader.* Ed. William J. Harris. New York: Thunder's Mouth, 1991.

Barrett, C. K. *The Prologue of St John's Gospel .* London: Athlone Press, 1971.

_____. *The Gospel According to St John: An Introduction with Commentary and Notes on the Greek Text.* 2nd ed. Philadelphia: Westminster, 1978.

Barrett, Leonard E. *SOUL-FORCE: African Heritage in Afro-American Religion.* C. Eric Lincoln Series on Black Religion. Garden City, N.Y.: Doubleday Anchor, 1974.

Bassler, Jouette M. "Mixed Signals: Nicodemus in the Fourth Gospel," *JBL* 108 (1989) 635–46.

Bennett, Lerone. *The Negro Mood.* New York: Ballantine, 1965.

Bible and Culture Collective, The. *The Postmodern Bible.* New Haven: Yale University Press, 1995.

Boers, Hendrickus. *Neither on This Mountain nor in Jerusalem: A Study of John 4.* SBLMS 35. Atlanta: Scholars, 1988.

Boismard, Marie-Emile. *Moses or Jesus: An Essay in Johannine Christology.* Minneapolis: Fortress, 1993.

Borgen, Peder. "Logos was the True Light: Contributions to the Interpretation of the Prologue of John," *NovT* 14 (1972) 115–30.

Brodie, Thomas L. *The Gospel According to John: A Literary and Theological Commentary*. New York: Oxford University Press, 1993.

Brooks, Gwendolyn. *Selected Poems*. Griot Editions: Voices of the African Diaspora. New York: Quality Paperback Book Club, 1995.

Brown, Raymond E. *An Introduction to New Testament Christology*. New York: Paulist, 1994.

_____. *The Gospel According to John*. AB 29, 29A. Garden City, N.Y.: Doubleday, 1966, 1970.

_____. *The Community of the Beloved Disciple*. New York: Paulist, 1979.

_____. *The Death of the Messiah. From Gethsemane to Grave. A Commentary on the Passion Narratives in the Four Gospels*. 2 vols. ABRL. New York: Doubleday, 1994.

Bultmann, Rudolf. *The Gospel of John: A Commentary*. Translated by G. R. Beasley-Murray. Philadelphia: Westminster, 1971.

Burge, Gary M. *The Anointed Community: The Holy Spirit in the Johannine Tradition*. Grand Rapids: Eerdmans, 1987.

Burns, David D. *The Feeling Good Handbook*. New York: William Morrow and Company, 1989, 73–96.

Cooper-Lewter, Nicholas C., and Henry H. Mitchell. *Soul Theology: The Heart of American Black Culture*. San Francisco: Harper & Row, 1986; Nashville: Abingdon, 1991.

Cousineau, Phil, ed. *Soul: An Archaeology*. San Francisco: HarperSanFrancisco, 1994.

Culpepper, R. Alan. *Anatomy of the Fourth Gospel: A Study in Literary Design*. Foundations and Facets. Philadelphia: Fortress, 1983.

_____. *The Johannine School: An Evaluation of the Johannine-School Hypothesis Based on an Investigation of the Nature of Ancient Schools*. SBLDS 26. Missoula: Scholars, 1975.

_____. "The Pivot of John's Prologue," *NTS* 27 (1981) 1–31.

Culpepper, R. Alan, and Fernando F. Segovia, eds. *The Fourth Gospel from a Literary Perspective*. Semeia 53. Atlanta: Scholars, 1991.

Dahms, J. V. "The Johannine Use of Monogenēs Reconsidered." *NTS* 27 (1983) 1–31.

Dodd, C. H. *The Interpretation of the Fourth Gospel*. Cambridge: Cambridge University Press, 1953.

_____. "A Hidden Parable in the Fourth Gospel." In idem. *More New Testament Studies*. Grand Rapids: Eerdmans, 1967, 30–40.

Dols, William L. *Awakening the Fire Within: A Primer on Issue-Centered Education*. St. Louis: The Educational Center, 1994.

Duke, Paul D. *Irony in the Fourth Gospel*. Atlanta: John Knox, 1985.

Dunbar, Paul Lawrence. *The Complete Poems of Paul Lawrence Dunbar*. New York: Dodd, Mead, 1905.

Dunn, James D. G. "Let John be John: A Gospel for Its Time." In Peter Stuhlmacher, ed., *Das Evangelium und die Evangelien: Vorträge vom Tübinger Symposium 1982*. Tübingen: J.C.B. Mohr [Paul Siebeck], 1983.

Eady, Cornelius. *You Don't Miss Your Water: Poems*. New York: Henry Holt, 1995.

Eltester, Walther. "Der Logos und sein Prophet." *Apophoreta. Festschrift für Ernst Haenchen zu seinem 70. Geburtstag am 10. Dezember 1964.* BZNW 30. Berlin: Töpelmann, 1964, 109–34.

Fehribach, Adeline. *The Women in the Life of the Bridegroom: A Feminist Historical-Literary Analysis of the Female Characters in the Fourth Gospel.* Collegeville: The Liturgical Press, 1998.

Fortna, Robert T. *The Fourth Gospel and Its Predecessor: From Narrative Source to Present Gospel.* Philadelphia: Fortress, 1988.

Giblin, Charles H. "Two Complementary Literary Structures in John 1:1-18." *JBL* 104 (1985) 87–103.

Gioia, Ted. *The History of Jazz.* New York: Oxford University Press, 1997.

Goldenberg, Naomi. *Returning Words to Flesh: Feminism, Psychoanalysis, and the Resurrection of the Body.* Boston: Beacon, 1990.

Hamerton-Kelly, Robert. *God the Father: Theology and Patriarchy in the Teaching of Jesus.* Overtures to Biblical Theology. Philadelphia: Fortress, 1979.

Harris, Elizabeth. *Prologue and Gospel: The Theology of the Fourth Evangelist.* JSNT 107. Sheffield: Sheffield Academic Press, 1994.

Harper, Michael S., and Anthony Walton, eds. *Every Shut Eye Ain't Asleep: An Anthology of Poetry by African Americans Since 1945.* Boston: Little, Brown, 1994.

Harvey, Anthony E. *Jesus on Trial: A Study in the Fourth Gospel.* London: SCM, 1972.

Henderson, Stephen. *Understanding the New Black Poetry.* New York: William Morrow, 1973.

Hillman, James. *Blue Fire: Selected Writings by James Hillman.* Ed. Thomas Moore. New York: HarperCollins, 1989.

_____. "Further Notes on Images." *Spring* 40 (1978) 152–82.

_____. "Image-Sense." *Spring* 41 (1979) 130–43.

_____. "An Inquiry into Image." *Spring* 39 (1977) 62–68.

_____. *Insearch: Psychology and Religion.* New York: Charles Scribner's Sons, 1967.

_____. *Re-Visioning Psychology.* New York: Harper & Row: 1975.

_____. *Suicide and the Soul.* New York: Harper & Row, 1964.

Hirsch, Edward. *How to Read a Poem: And Fall in Love with Poetry.* New York: Harcourt Brace and Company, 1999.

Howard-Brook, Wes. *Becoming Children of God: John's Gospel and Radical Discipleship.* Maryknoll, N.Y.: Orbis, 1994.

Hughes, Langston. *The Collected Poems of Langston Hughes.* Ed. Arnold Rampersad. New York: Knopf, 1994.

Jasper, Alison. *The Shining Garment of the Text: Gendered Readings of John's Prologue.* Sheffield: Sheffield Academic Press, 1998.

Jones, Leroi, and Larry Neal, eds., *Black Fire: An Anthology of Afro-American Writing.* New York: William Morrow & Company, 1968.

Jung, Carl Gustav. *The Collected Works of C. G. Jung.* Herbert Read, Michael Fordham, and Gerhard Adler, eds. 20 vols. in 21. Bollingen Series 20. Princeton: Princeton University Press, 1966–1979.

Käsemann, Ernst. "The Structure and Purpose of the Prologue to John's Gospel." *New Testament Questions of Today.* London: SCM, 1969.

_____. *The Testament of Jesus: According to John 17.* Trans. Gerhard Krodel. Philadelphia: Fortress, 1968.

Kelber, Werner. "The Birth of a Beginning: John 1:1-18." *Semeia* 52 (1990) 121–44.

Kennedy, X. J., and Dana Gioia. *An Introduction to Poetry.* 9th ed. New York: Longman, 1997.

Kgositsile, Keorapetse. *My Name Is Afrika.* Garden City, N.Y.: Doubleday, 1971.

King, Colbert I. "Speak, Children," *The Washington Post,* July 17, 1999.

Koch, Kenneth. *Making Your Own Days: The Pleasures of Reading and Writing Poetry.* New York: Scribner, 1998.

Koester, Craig R. "'Savior of the World' (John 4:42)." *JBL* 109 (1990) 665–80.

_____. *Symbolism in the Fourth Gospel: Meaning, Mystery, Community.* Minneapolis: Fortress, 1995.

Lacan, Jacques. *Écrits: A Selection.* Trans. Alan Sheridan. New York: Norton, 1977.

Major, Clarence, ed. *The Garden Thrives: Twentieth-Century African-American Poetry.* San Francisco: Harper Perennial, 1996.

Malina, Bruce J. *The Gospel of John in Sociolinguistic Perspective.* Protocol of the 48th Colloquy, March 1984. Berkeley: Center for Hermeneutical Studies, 1985.

_____. "John's: The Maverick Christian Group: The Evidence of Sociolinguistics," *BTB* 24 (1994) 167–82.

Martyn, J. Louis. *History and Theology in the Fourth Gospel.* Rev. ed. Nashville: Abingdon, 1979.

Maud, Ralph. "Archetypal Depth Criticism and Melville," in Richard P. Sugg, ed., *Jungian Literary Criticism.* Evanston: Northwestern University Press, 1992.

McGann, Diarmuid. *Journeying Within Transcendence: The Gospel of John Through a Jungian Perspective.* New York: Paulist, 1988.

McKay, Claude. *Selected Poems.* New York: Harcourt Brace, 1953.

McKnight, Edgar V., and Elizabeth Struthers Malbon, eds. *The New Literary Criticism and the New Testament.* Valley Forge, Pa.: Trinity Press International, 1994.

Metzger, Bruce M. *A Textual Commentary on the Greek New Testament: A Companion Volume to the United Bible Societies' Greek New Testament.* London: United Bible Societies, 1971.

Miller, David L. *Christs: Meditations on Archetypal Images in Christian Theology.* New York: Seabury, 1981.

_____. *The Three Faces of God: Traces of the Trinity in Literature and Life.* Philadelphia: Fortress, 1986.

_____. *Hells and Holy Ghosts: A Theopoetics of Christian Belief.* Nashville: Abingdon, 1989.

Miller, E. Ethelbert. *Whispers Secrets & Promises.* Baltimore: Black Classic Press, 1998.

_____, ed. *Beyond the Frontier*. Baltimore: Black Classic Press, 2001.

_____, ed. *In Search of Color Everywhere: A Collection of African-American Poetry*. New York: Stewart, Tabori & Chang, 1994.

Miller, Ed L. "The Logic of the Logos Hymn." *NTS* 29 (1983) 552–61.

Miranda, José. *Being and the Messiah: The Message of St. John*. Trans. John Eagleson. Maryknoll, N.Y.: Orbis, 1977.

Moloney, Francis J. *Belief in the Word: Reading John 1–4*. Minneapolis: Fortress, 1993.

_____. *Glory not Dishonor: Reading John 13–21*. Minneapolis: Fortress, 1998.

_____. *Signs and Shadows: Reading John 5–12*. Minneapolis: Fortress, 1996.

_____. *The Gospel of John*. Sacra Pagina 4. A Michael Glazier Book. Collegeville: The Liturgical Press, 1998.

Moore, Stephen D. *Literary Criticism and the Gospels: The Theoretical Challenge*. New Haven: Yale University Press, 1989.

_____. *Poststructuralism and the New Testament: Derrida and Foucault at the Foot of the Cross*. Minneapolis: Fortress, 1994.

Moore, Thomas, ed. *Blue Fire: Selected Writings by James Hillman*. New York: HarperCollins, 1989.

Moyers, Bill. *The Language of Life: A Festival of Poets*. New York: Doubleday, 1995.

Mullane, Deirdre, ed. *Crossing the Danger Water: Three Hundred Years of African-American Writing*. New York: Anchor Books, 1993.

Neyrey, Jerome H. *An Ideology of Revolt: John's Christology in Social Science Perspective*. Philadelphia: Fortress, 1988.

O'Day, Gail R. *Revelation in the Fourth Gospel: Narrative Mode and Theological Claim*. Philadelphia: Fortress, 1986.

_____. "John," *The New Interpreter's Bible*. Vol. 9. Nashville: Abingdon, 1995.

Okure, Teresa. *The Johannine Approach to Mission: A Contextual Study of John 4:1-42*. Tubingen: J.C.B. Mohr, 1988.

Packard, William. *The Poet's Dictionary: A Handbook of Prosody and Poetic Devices*. New York: HarperCollins, 1989.

Painter, John. "Christology and the History of the Johannine Community in the Prologue of the Fourth Gospel." *NTS* 30 (1984) 460–74.

Paris, Peter J. "The Soul of Black Religion: A Lesson for the Academy (Basic African American Values)," unpublished paper presented at the annual meeting of the American Academy of Religion, November 1996.

Pasteur, Alfred B., and Ivory L. Toldson. *Roots of Soul: The Psychology of Black Expressiveness*. Garden City, N.Y.: Doubleday Anchor, 1982.

Petersen, Norman R. *The Gospel of John and the Sociology of Light: Language and Characterization in the Fourth Gospel*. Valley Forge, Pa.: Trinity Press International, 1993.

Pippin, Tina. "'For Fear of the Jews': Lying and Truth-Telling in Translating the Gospel of John." *Semeia* 76 (1996) 81–97.

Potterie, Ignace de la. "Structure du Prologue de Saint Jean." *NTS* 30 (1984) 354–81.

Randall, Dudley, ed. *The Black Poets*. New York: Bantam, 1971.

Redmond, Eugene B. *Drumvoices: The Mission of Afro-American Poetry*. Garden City, N.Y.: Doubleday Anchor, 1976.

Reinhartz, Adele, ed. *"God the Father" in the Gospel of John. Semeia* 85. Atlanta: Scholars Press. Forthcoming.

Rensberger, David. *Johannine Faith and Liberating Community*. Philadelphia: Westminster, 1988.

Ringe, Sharon H. *Wisdom's Friends*. Louisville: Westminster/John Knox, 1999.

Rochais, G. "La formation du prologue (Jn 1, 1-18)." *Science et Esprit* 37 (1985) 5–44, 161–87.

Rohrbaugh, Richard L. "The Gospel of John in the Twenty-First Century," in Fernando F. Segovia, ed., *What is John? Readers and Readings of the Fourth Gospel*. SBL Symposium Series. Atlanta: Scholars, 1998.

Rollins, Wayne G. *Jung and the Bible*. Atlanta: John Knox, 1983.

Sanchez, Sonia. *Shake Loose My Skin: New and Selected Poems*. Boston: Beacon, 1999.

Schaer, Hans. *Religion and the Cure of Souls in Jung's Psychology*. Trans. R.F.C. Hull. Bollingen Series XXI. New York: Pantheon, 1950.

Schlatter, Friedrich W. "The Problem of Jn 1:3b-4a." *CBQ* 34 (1972) 54–58.

Schnackenburg, Rudolf. "Logos-Hymnus und johanneischer Prologue." *BZ* 1 (1957) 69–109.

_____. *The Gospel According to John*. 3 vols. Trans. Kevin Smyth, et al. New York: Crossroad, 1968–82.

Segovia, Fernando F. *The Farewell of the Word: The Johannine Call to Abide*. Minneapolis: Fortress, 1991.

_____, ed. *"What Is John?" Readers and Readings of the Fourth Gospel*. 2 vols. SBL Symposium Series 3, 7. Atlanta: Scholars, 1996, 1998.

_____, and Mary Ann Tolbert, eds. *Reading from this Place*. 2 vols. Minneapolis: Fortress, 1995.

Sithole, Elkin T. "Black Folk Music." In Thomas Kochman, ed., *Rappin' and Stylin' Out: Communication in Urban Black America*. Urbana: University of Illinois Press, 1972.

Staley, Jeffrey L. "The Structure of John's Prologue: Its Implications for the Gospel's Narrative Structure." *CBQ* 48 (1986) 241–64.

_____. *The Print's First Kiss: A Rhetorical Investigation of the Implied Reader in the Fourth Gospel*. SBLDS 82. Atlanta: Scholars, 1988.

_____. *Reading with a Passion: Rhetoric, Autobiography, and the American West in the Gospel of John*. New York: Continuum, 1995.

Steptoe, Javaka, illust. *In Daddy's Arms I Am Tall: African Americans Celebrating Fathers*. New York: Lee & Low, 1997.

Tolmie, D. François. *Jesus' Farewell to the Disciples: John 13:1–17:26 in Narratological Perspective*. Biblical Interpretation Series 12. Leiden and New York: E. J. Brill, 1995.

Tompkins, Jane P., ed. *Reader-Response Criticism: From Formalism to Post-Structuralism*. Baltimore: Johns Hopkins University Press, 1980.

Vawter, Bruce. "What Came to Be in Him Was Life, Jn 1,3b-4a." *CBQ* 25 (1963) 401–6.

Wade-Gayles, Gloria, ed. *Father Songs: Testimonies by African-American Sons and Daughters.* Boston: Beacon, 1997.

Ward, Jerry W., Jr., ed. *Trouble the Water: 250 Years of African-American Poetry.* New York: Mentor, 1997.

Willett, Michael E. *Wisdom Christology in the Fourth Gospel.* San Francisco: Mellen Research University Press, 1992.

_____. "Opposition to Women Ministers Is Unforgivable Sin" *SBC Today,* April 1988.

Willett Newheart, Michael. "Johannine Symbolism." In David L. Miller, ed., *Jung and the Interpretation of the Bible.* New York: Continuum, 1995.

_____. "Lent 4: John 9:1-41." *The Bible Workbench* 6:3 (Lent 1 to Easter Sunday 1999) 53–68.

_____. "Toward a Psycho-Literary Reading of the Fourth Gospel." *"What Is John?" Readers and Readings of the Fourth Gospel,* ed. Fernando F. Segovia, SBL Symposium Series 3. Atlanta: Scholars, 1995.

Witherington, Ben III. *John's Wisdom: A Commentary on the Fourth Gospel.* Louisville: Westminster/John Knox, 1995.

Wright, N. T. *The New Testament and the People of God. Vol. 1. Christian Origins and the Question of God.* Minneapolis: Fortress, 1992.

Zylstra, Geoff, and Reba Mathern, eds. *The Voices of Children: Stories From Our Future.* Washington, D.C.: Sojourners Neighborhood Center, 1996.

Appendix

Amiri Baraka

The Invention of Comics

I am a soul in the world: in
the world of my soul the whirled
light / from the day
the sacked land
of my father.

In the world, the sad
nature of myself. In myself
nature is sad. Small
prints of the day. Its
small dull fires. Its
sun, like a greyness
smeared on the dark.

The day of my soul, is
the nature of that
place. It is a landscape. Seen
from the top of a hill. A
grey expanse; dull fires
throbbing on its seas.

The man's soul, the complexion
of his life. The menace
of its greyness. The
fires, throbs, the sea
moves. Birds shoot
from the dark. The edge
of the waters lit
darkly for the moon.

And the moon, from the soul. Is
the world, of the man. The man
and his sea, and its moon, and
the soft fire throbbing. Kind
death. O,
my dark and sultry
love. [1]

State/meant

The Black Artist's role in America is to aid in the destruction of America as he knows it. His role is to report and reflect so precisely the nature of the society, and of himself in that society, that other men will be moved by the exactness of his rendering and, if they are black men, grow strong through this moving, having seen their own strength, and weakness; and if they are white men, tremble, curse, and go mad, because they will be drenched with the filth of their evil.

The Black Artist must draw out of his soul the correct image of the world. He must use this image to band his brothers and sisters together in common understanding of the nature of the world (and the nature of America) and the nature of the human soul.

The Black Artist must demonstrate sweet life, how it differs from the deathly grip of the White Eyes. The Black Artist must teach the White Eyes their deaths, and teach the black man how to bring these deaths about.

We are unfair, and unfair.
We are black magicians, black art
s we make in black labs of the heart.

The fair are
fair, and death
ly white.

The day will not save them
and we own
the night.[2]

---

[1] Amiri Baraka, "The Invention of Comics," in Clarence Major, ed., *The Garden Thrives: Twentieth-Century African-American Poetry* (San Francisco: Harper Perennial, 1996) 133, from Baraka, *The Dead Lecturer* (New York: Sterling Lord Literistic, 1964). Stanza 1 of this poem is quoted in chapter 3, 60.

[2] Amiri Baraka, "State/meant," *The LeRoi Jones/Amiri Baraka Reader*, ed. William J. Harris (New York: Thunder's Mouth, 1991) 170; from *Home: Social Essays* (New York: William Morrow and Co., 1966). A portion of the "prose section" of this poem is quoted in chapter 1, 11; the "poetic" section is quoted in chapter 2, 27.

Gwendolyn Brooks

Primer for Blacks

Blackness
is a title,
is a preoccupation
is a commitment Blacks
are to comprehend—
and in which you are
to perceive your glory

The conscious shout
of all that is white is
"It's Great to be white."
The conscious shout
of the slack in Black is
"It's Great to be white."
Thus all that is white
has white strength and yours.

The word Black
has geographic power,
pulls everybody in:
Blacks here—
Blacks there—
Blacks wherever they may be.
And remember, you Blacks, what they told you—
remember your Education:
    "one Drop – one Drop
maketh a brand new Black."
    Oh mighty Drop.
_____ And because they have given us kindly
so many more of our people

Blackness
stretches over the land.
Blackness—
the Black of it,
the rust-red of it,
the milk and cream of it,
the deep-brown middle-brown high-brown of it,
the "olive' and ochre of it—
Blackness
marches on.

The huge, the pungent object of our prime out-ride
is to Comprehend,

to salute and to Love the fact that we are Black.
which *is* our "ultimate Reality,"
which is the lone ground
from which our meaningful metamorphosis,
from which our prosperous staccato,
group or individual, can rise.

Self-shriveled Blacks.
Begun with gaunt and marvelous concession:
YOU are our costume and our fundamental bone.

All of you—
you COLORED ones,
you NEGRO ones,
those of you who proudly cry
"I'm half INDian"—
those of you who proudly screech
"I'VE got the blood of George WASHington in
MY veins—"

ALL of you—
you proper Blacks,
you half-Blacks,
you wish-I-weren't Blacks,
Niggeroes and Niggerenes.

You.[3]

LANGSTON HUGHES

American Heartbreak

I am the American heartbreak
Rock on which Freedom
Stumps its toe—
The great mistake
That Jamestown
Made long ago.[4]

---

[3] Gwendolyn Brooks, "Primer for Blacks," in E. Ethelbert Miller, ed., *In Search of Color Everywhere: A Collection of African-American Poetry* (New York: Stewart, Tabori & Chang, 1994) 85–86; from Brooks, *Primer for Blacks* (Chicago: Third World Press, 1991). Stanzas 1 and 4 of this poem are quoted in chapter 1, 16.

[4] Langston Hughes, "American Heartbreak," in idem., *The Collected Poems of Langston Hughes,* Arnold Rampersad, ed. (New York: Alfred A. Knopf, 1994) 348. Lines 1–3 of this poem are quoted in chapter 1, 13.

The Black Man Speaks

I swear to the Lord
I still can't see
Why Democracy means
Everybody but me.

I swear to my soul
I can't understand
Why Freedom don't apply
To the black man.

I swear, by gum,
I really don't know
Why in the name of Liberty
You treat me so.

Down South you make me ride
In a Jim Crow car.
From Los Angeles to London
You spread your color bar.

Jim Crow Army,
And Navy, too—
Is Jim Crow Freedom the best
I can expect from you?

I simply raise these questions
Cause I want you to state
What kind of a world
We're fighting to create.

If we're fighting to create
A free world tomorrow,
Why not end *right now*
Old Jim Crow's sorrow?[5]

Me and My Song

Black
As the gentle night
Black
As the kind and quiet night

---

[5] Langston Hughes, "The Black Man Speaks," in idem., *The Collected Poems*, 288–89. Stanzas 2, 4 and 5 of this poem are quoted in chapter 1, 13.

Black
As the deep productive earth
Body
Out of Africa
Strong and black
As iron
First smelted in
Africa
Song
Out of Africa
Deep and mellow song
Rich
As the black earth
Strong
As black iron
Kind
As the black night
My song
From the dark lips
Of Africa
Deep
As the rich earth
Beautiful
As the black night
Strong
As the first iron
Black
Out of Africa
Me and my
Song.[6]

The Negro

I am a Negro:
    Black as the night is black,
    Black like the depths of my Africa.

I've been a slave:
    Caesar told me to keep his door-steps clean.
    I brushed the boots of Washington.

[6] Langston Hughes, "Me and My Song," in idem., *The Collected Poems*, 296–97.
Lines 1–4, 20–21, and 27–28 of this poem are quoted in chapter 2, 27.

I've been a worker:
>   Under my hand the pyramids arose.
>   I made mortar for the Woolworth Building.

I've been a singer:
>   All the way from Africa to Georgia
>   I carried my sorrow songs.
>   I made ragtime.

I've been a victim:
>   The Belgians cut off my hands in the Congo.
>   They lynch me now in Texas.

I am a Negro:
>   Black as the night is black,
>   Black like the depths of my Africa.[7]

Bob Kaufman

I, Too, Know What I Am Not

No, I am not death wishes of sacred rapists, swinging on candy gallows.

No, I am not spoor of Creole murderers hiding in crepe-paper bayous.

No, I am not yells of some assassinated inventor, locked in his burning machine.

No, I am not forced breathing of Cairo's senile burglar, in lead shoes.

No, I am not Indian-summer fruit of Negro piano tuners, with muslin gloves.

No, I am not noise of two-gun senators, in hallowed peppermint hall.

No, I am not pipe-smoke hopes of cynical chiropractors, traffickers in illegal bone.

No, I am not pitchblende curse of Indian suicides, in bonnets of flaming water.

No, I am not soap-powder sighs of impotent window washers in pants of air.

No, I am not kisses of tubercular sun addicts, smiling through rayon lips.

No, I am not chipped philosopher's tattered ideas sunk in his granite brain.

No, I am not cry of amethyst heron, winged stone in flight of cambric bullets.

---

[7] Langston Hughes, "The Negro," in idem., *The Collected Poems*, 72. Lines 1–3 of this poem are quoted in chapter 2, 27.

No, I am not sting of the neurotic bee, frustrated in cheesecloth gardens.
No, I am not peal of muted bell, clapperless in the faded glory.
No, I am not report of silenced guns, helpless in pacifist hands.
No, I am not call of wounded hunter, alone in the forest of bone.
No, I am not eyes of the infant owls hatching the roofless night.
No, I am not the whistle of Havana whores with cribs of Cuban death.
No, I am not shriek of Bantu children, bent under pennywhistle whips.
No, I am not whisper of the African trees, leafy Congo telephones.
No, I am not Leadbelly of blues, escaped from guitar jails.
No, I am not anything that is anything I am not.[8]

---

[8] Bob Kaufman, "I, Too, Know What I Am Not," in Clarence Major, ed., *The Garden Thrives*, 79, from Kaufman, *Solitudes Crowded with Loneliness* (New York: New Directions, 1965). Lines 1–3 and 23 (the last line) of this poem are quoted in chapter 3, 60.

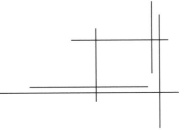

Scripture Index

New Testament

Hebrew Bible and Apocryphal/Deutero-Canonical Books